THE DRIVEN ORGANIZATION

AND

WHAT WE NEED TO BE HAPPY AND PRODUCTIVE AT WORK

OMAR GARCIA

LIBRARY OF CONGRESS CONTROL NUMBER: 2013947608

FUTURE APPROVED WORKS
1079 E 9 MILE RD # 28A
HAZEL PARK, MI 48030
INFO@FUTUREAPPROVED.ORG

CONTENT ADVISERS: PAULINA GAWELDA, TINA LAFORTEZA
DEVELOPMENTAL EDITOR ADVISER: MARY ELLEN WALSH
COPY EDITOR: NANCY SIXSMITH
COVER DESIGN: JACEK KITA, PAULINA GAWELDA

FIRST EDITION
ISBN: 978-0-9896096-0-9

PRINTED IN THE UNITED STATES OF AMERICA

10 9 8 7 6 5 4 3 2 1

To the biggest gift the universe has given me: my wife.

Contents

Chapter 1:

The Big Idea.

"Without work, all life goes rotten. But when work is soulless, life stifles and dies." Albert Camus, French journalist and philosopher.

Monday morning: Eager to work.

Alex wakes up early Monday morning and slowly begins to stretch. He sees it's almost time to go to work. This thought infuses him with energy and excitement. In one swift movement, he gets up and jumps in the shower. He and his team have great things planned for today. There is a brainstorming session, a financial review, a team challenge, and an initiation ceremony. Alex begins to sing what he thinks is an opera aria in the shower. It's going to be that kind of day! His mind races, developing ideas for the team challenge. It will be a brilliant session with about ten coworkers with whom he feels privileged to work. They are smart, respectful, and extraordinarily skilled at their jobs. Together, they make an exceptionally high-caliber team.

On Thursday afternoon, Alex will be at a team's event. Each person in the organization belongs to a designated team. Every week, they compete for points in various events. People run, sing, solve puzzles, do challenges, and play games. This is one of the ways in which workers in

Alex's organization have a good time and become best friends. Even with playing, outstanding work is produced. Alex's organization constantly finds itself in the top ranks in patent creation, process innovation, and business financial results.

The organization is respected and appreciated. Its products and services are designed to improve the lives of people and directly benefit the community. It is no surprise that Alex's organization has a great following, with customers, suppliers, and other stakeholders actively participating in advancing the objectives of the organization and fostering its success.

There is nothing extraordinary about Alex's work. His job is just like any regular day at the office for you and me.

Not really, you say? Far from it? Perhaps it's been a while since you woke up in the morning and got in the shower singing, excited because you got to go to work that day. You may not remember the last time you wanted to stay at work out of enjoyment, not obligation or the lack of anything better to do. Your company may not be achieving the financial results described here, either.

Then allow me to ask this: Why couldn't this be your job or this your organization? Is it not possible?

If we were to work in such an organization, everyone would be better off. Workers would be healthier, live longer, and have better family relationships because it has been proven that satisfied and engaged workers do. Business owners and shareholders would reap higher profitability because it has been repeatedly shown that engaged workers not only produce more but also develop better and more creative innovations. Management would have a much easier job because it has been observed that engaged workers require little management. Everyone wants to be part of an organization that engages them, makes them feel proud, and constantly challenges them to become everything they can be.

Then, why doesn't it happen? What's missing? Instead, we are in a rat race that results in low job satisfaction, in business practices that create resentment with our communities and concerns with the environment, and in less-than-optimum business performance that often pushes companies into financial distress.

It doesn't happen because we are using the wrong approach. Nowadays, leading experts talk about motivation, organizational culture, job satisfaction, and engagement. We know now that organizations with these ingredients have more satisfied workers, persevere over changing market conditions, and exceed competition business results. We attempt to bring these missing ingredients to our organizations the same way an inexperienced chef adds salt to a cooked dish. The salt never becomes part of the dish! The goal of these organizations is the same: to get people to maximize profits, which eventually backfires and fails.

The business objective must be redefined. The reason for the business to exist must be to fulfill the needs of its workers. The business exists primarily to bring satisfaction and benefit to workers and their communities. One consequence of doing so, through the ways of the Driven Organization, is to have a powerful business machinery that overcomes its competitors and proves quite profitable.

Think about it! Imagine a classical composer who creates two pieces: a commercial one and one in which he poured his heart. Which one do you think he enjoyed creating the most? Which one will be the greater work?

Imagine two nannies. One believes that she is nurturing a future world leader, and the other one is solely concerned with the $10 per hour pay. Which one enjoys her work more? Which one is better for the child? Although nothing is as black or white as these examples, the fact is that there are "things" that affect how close we feel to our work. If the work connects with our needs, with something deep inside us, our engagement will be much higher; we will be happier; and our product, the outcome of our work, will be much better. Yes, we need the money, but it is an additional, almost secondary consideration.

If this is so easy to see for an individual such as a composer or a nanny, why don't we see the same for an organization, assuming it is appropriate for it to exist solely to make money? This incorrect approach produces less-than-satisfied workers and low business performance. We must put the needs of all the organization's stakeholders as the main objective of the business, and we must make sure the work is deeply connected with these needs.

It is true that the problem becomes complex when we think of groups composed of many individuals with different needs, skills, beliefs, and desires. How do we create a place that connects with all of them and makes them engaged? The purpose of this book is to help you understand how it works and why. After reading it, you will be able to build or transform your workplace into this organization that we call "The Driven Organization." You will see that it is not only possible but also easier than what it seems. There are many businesses already doing great advances in this area.

We can do so much better than today's business practices.

I grew up in a family of frustrated employees. I saw my parents, two well-intended and educated professionals, drown some of their biggest illusions and passions in their workplaces. I have wondered for many years how to make it better and I have taken that question with me through my academic formation and my business experience.

During this time, I have seen seeds and sparks of the Driven Organization here and there. I've seen great managers and small nimble companies (perhaps high-tech) that function in unorthodox ways and follow some of the ways of the Driven Organization. Rarely, there is an organization that understands its foundations and has structured a comprehensive system around it. Hardly ever, it is constructed so that the organizational activities support each other in an aligned manner, increasing exponentially its power. After many years, I have realized that creating such an organization is both more difficult and easier than what we think.

It is easy because some of the insights required are all around us. We simply must look at the needs and desires of workers, of managers, and owners, this is of human beings, which we all are. We will be able to draw some key conclusions from our own experiences, satisfactions, and frustrations throughout our work lives.

But to do so, we need common sense, which makes it a bit more complicated. Common sense is a skill that is developed from experience, observation, and self-reflection, but is not necessarily correlated with formal education. It's disappointing to see that some of the most educated professionals, such as doctors and lawyers, often display little of it. But something tells me we will be fine, considering that something prompted you to pick up this book.

What makes it difficult to create such a superior organization is that we have made it that way. We have developed beliefs that we never question, such as "the workday is from 8 to 5," "I am the boss; I know better," and "nobody likes to work; it is a necessary evil." We also use our working environments as tools to get away with certain negative behaviors, such as a way to accumulate power and belong to a superior class. The worst of it is that most of us consider it normal or even proper.

We have fought for democracy, for equal rights, for a voice and a vote, and for freedom. Then, we choose to make a huge exception for the activity that occupies the large majority of our time. Have you had to explain to yourself why working the whole day for years, doing something you do not find that appealing, all for a non-wealthy lifestyle, is that different from slavery? No, I am not trying to put the current system at the level of slavery, but to point out that often good workers feel this way, and when they do, they cannot be the best and most productive workers.

Productive systems evolve over time. Just as the feudal system was the most effective for its time and would be entirely unfit for today's needs and wants, capitalism is not standing still, either; it has evolved and will continue evolving. I believe that the organizations of the future will look progressively similar to the Driven Organization. As it so happens, they will cause a shift toward a better productive system that results in better quality of life for workers, communities, and other stakeholders, and higher and better business output.

If we are willing to question common business practices that make no sense, to use our experience as workers and human beings, and to appeal to our common sense, we have all it takes to start our path toward finding powerful ways to be happy, satisfied, and productive.

Attempting to fulfill "all" needs of workers.

The big idea of this book is so simple that I often questioned whether it still needs to be said. Sadly, the reality of our workplaces tells me it does. Organizations should attempt to satisfy all the needs of its workers; from the basic ones such as food and shelter, to those of higher levels such as life fulfillment and purpose. In doing so, workers and other stakeholders not only will be better fulfilled, happier, and engaged but also will produce superior results.

This book is for business owners, for line workers, for self-employed workers, and for everyone who performs work. We will all benefit by realizing how our job fits in our lives and what we need from it. We will all benefit by understanding the type of organization we can create, be it a 1,000 or 10,000 worker organization. We can all do it regardless of the level we have because each of us is a building block of the organization who has the capacity to move it forward toward a better place. No matter who you are, what you do, and with whom you do it, this book will help you reach your maximum potential at work, and thus improve your life.

I invite you to read with an open mind and see the possibilities, but I also ask you not to stop being critical because this work will be better understood if you perform constant sanity checks. I suggest you energetically reject what doesn't make sense, but in turn be brave to embrace what does.

This book is composed of five parts.

In the first part, we review and analyze current common business practices. Here, we put on our critical thinking caps. We ask questions. We compare. The objective is to bring forth our knowledge and common sense to study what we do at work and its effects. Here, we understand the problem, lack of engagement, and its consequences; and we contrast it with a Driven Organization and its capacity to affect the lives of its workers, communities, and shareholders. What is the potential of an engaged team? How to build a powerful brand? What is the role of money to create a great team? We will answer these questions in this first part.

In the second part, we explore our human needs as workers, managers, and customers. What do we want? What do we need? What tickles us? Using the most advanced psychological knowledge, but explained using simple stories and fables, we make sure that we get a solid understanding of this human being. We will understand what drives people and why we do what we do. We will also understand why we think differently from our parents and they from theirs.

Then, in the third part, supported by solid business insights, we create an organization specifically designed to connect with this human being, to fulfill his needs, and to form a cohesive group. We developed a framework, SPACES, to study the fundamental elements required to build our dream organization. These organizational elements are Salary, Purpose, Autonomy, Competence, Environment, and Strategy. These components work in a harmonious and complementary way to produce a driven and powerful business organization.

A great party starts by bringing in the right people. Some people like to dance, some to talk, and some to pray. How can we make sure that whoever comes to our party is the right match for us? In the fourth part, we will show how building a strong environment starts by bringing the right people into the organization. We will also discuss the role of management in this part. Management must promote certain behaviors and activities, but avoid becoming overbearing and controlling, which damages individual worker initiative. We will review how to do this while contrasting the best and most powerful leadership styles.

At the end, in the fifth part, there are examples of organizations that are applying components of the framework. We'll see how they are developing their own formula to use some of these concepts and the results they get. You may reference these organizations as you wander through the pages of this book.

I was asked once what my purpose for writing The Driven Organization was. I answered, "It's simple; to help everyone realize that work is one of the best vehicles to make people extraordinary."

"Are you bored with life? Then throw yourself into some work you believe in with all you heart, live for it, die for it, and you will find happiness that you had thought could never be yours." Dale Carnegie, author of *How to Win Friends and Influence People.*

The Driven Organization

Part I: Understanding the Basics.

At the end of this part, we'll have a good understanding of the potential of a workplace with engaged and driven workers. We will see how it becomes a powerful and robust organization, capable of tackling any problem. Workers become emotionally connected with the organization and focus their energy on its advancement and success. They see the organization as an important component in their life's satisfaction and happiness. Is this too far-fetched or too ambitious? Let's see.

Chapter 2:

Job Dissatisfaction Destroys; Engagement Builds.

"When the mind suffers, the body cries out." Cardinal Lamberto,
The Godfather.

I was dissatisfied with my job. Are you?

In the later part of the 2000s, I used to set up my alarm at 6:15 am every day. My commute was short, and even stopping by the fridge for a quick snack, I would get to the office by 8 am. I remember that every single day, I hit the snooze button all the way to 7 am. When I finally made myself get up, I did so feeling tired, not well rested, and often feeling ill. Slowly and in a quiet and serious mood, I got ready to go to work and perform my duties of the day. At the beginning, I attributed my bad feeling to physical illness, but later I understood that something else was going on with me. There was an intriguing clue. Saturdays and Sundays, I woke up at 6:00 am with no alarm, no feeling of tiredness or illness, and looking forward to doing many awesome things. The same thing happened week after week, month after month.

Only after many months of the same observations, I began to think about it and its possible causes. My job seemed fine. I had a good position, with a good salary, in a good company. I had been recently promoted, and my boss was an excellent manager. I was also working in the industry I liked best: automotive. Had somebody asked me whether I was satisfied with my job, I would have looked at it from afar where everything seemed well and answered "yes, of course." Still, underneath it all, I wasn't that happy. I often felt my job was too administrative and constraining. I felt it lacked imagination and purpose. I now believe that my body took upon itself to show this to me.

What do most people do in similar situations? We tough it out. We were taught to be responsible and carry on our duties. We don't have to be in love with the job; we just have to do it. We may remember our grandparents who worked hard on the land or in the shop. And those were hard jobs; ours are much easier. This way, I continued doing it for a while, until one day I finally couldn't do it anymore.

Taiichi Ohno, the creator of the Toyota Production system, uses the analogy of "lowering the water to expose rocks." The idea is that when there is a considerable amount of inventory in a system, the problems, or "bugs," stay hidden. In a river where much water flows, there seem to be no rocks. By limiting inventory in the process or "lowering the water," managers can see which processes struggle to keep up. This is where the rocks are, and this is exactly what happened to me. Because I felt ill, I had less energy to withstand a situation that was not working out for me anymore. The water level was down, and I was forced to see my rocks. I finally understood it. My job was not giving me what I needed. I needed to make changes, and fast.

Had I not had the "water level" down, I am sure I would have endured it and continued going to work every day, attempting to make the best of it, as probably you do and as many other people do. Unfortunately, the United States (and many other countries) seems to be plagued by the same disease. I am not referring to a physical illness, but one that leads to low job satisfaction.

The conference Board Research Group,[1] Harris Interactive, Inc.,[2] and other organizations report that satisfaction in America is at its lowest levels, at around 45%, in 2010. Although these numbers are particularly low because they are measured at the height of the worst economic recession since the Depression, these surveying organizations claim that worker satisfaction has been on a downward trend for more than two decades. They report that only about 20% of all the workers feel passidonate about their jobs. For the younger generations, the problem is even more significant. Only 37% of those younger than 25 report being satisfied with their jobs. The reports claim that these young workers are more distressed and feel the least amount of loyalty to their employers.[3]

When we are dissatisfied, we are not good workers.

Let us ponder for a moment. More than half of all workers in America are dissatisfied with their jobs! Two-thirds of the young workers are dissatisfied! How could a worker do a good job if he is dissatisfied; if he feels he has a regular, boring, must-be-done, or little-impact job? He may be trying to do his best out of the principles he was taught or perhaps from fear of losing the job, but his performance would be vastly less than spectacular, perhaps even mediocre.

When we are dissatisfied, our energy is low. Our inside pessimism sifts out. It shows in our attitude, the way we tackle problems, and how we react to new ideas and proposals. We have little initiative, and we are a drag on our teams. Instead of the goals or long-term objectives, non-engaged workers are focused on the tasks and requirements of the job, be it a number of hours on the chair or the number of work items completed.

Compare that performance with one of someone who is enthusiastic, connected, and engaged with his work. This person engages others and transmits enthusiasm and energy. His attitude helps him tackle any problem he encounters. He sparks the best in others.

Among all the dissatisfied, disengaged workers, there is a group at the bottom that is even more problematic. These workers are the ones who complain about the company's policies or actions. They see everything through a dark glass, and their mood permeates to other workers. They undermine the productivity and positive attitude that other workers bring. They plant the seeds of distrust, anger, and resentment with whomever they talk. They are the most dangerous workers for the organization.

The job satisfaction surveys also report that about 60% of American workers intend to leave if the economy improves. These workers are probably daydreaming about their new job and paying considerable attention to job applications and resume submissions. At the least, they have little interest in the long-term performance of the organization where they currently work.

"Job: Means by which at least 30% of your life is stolen from you to enrich the owners of a company making useless shit that some other poor idiot in a job will buy." UrbanDictionary.com

Is job dissatisfaction a factor behind the U.S. crisis?

In America, we have a crisis. I am not talking about the financial crisis; I am talking about the job engagement crisis. We cannot come up with leading products and technologies that create the way of life of the future if we don't care about what we do or if we are looking to leave our jobs.

We blame the economic crisis of 2008 on the sub-prime mortgage market, insurance-linked securities, and excessive consumer spending, subjects with which you are now quite familiar, but there may be another way to think about this crisis. When the Spanish conquered America, they traded objects with the American Indians. They traded small mirrors for large pieces of gold. In the Native American market, gold, although precious, was less scarce than mirrors. Today, we may laugh at them because they exchanged gold for mirrors, but the latter was the technologically advanced product that simply commanded a high price, even in gold.

Imagine you are the only person in a small isolated town who knows how to bake bread. Assuming you are able to keep your recipe a secret, your bread will command a high price. You will have a nice life in this town because you are the only one who knows how to make it. If most folks in the town farm potatoes, could they also command a premium price for their potatoes? No. If the price seems to be high, you'll buy potatoes from somebody else, but one loaf of your bread may be exchanged for several pounds of potatoes.

This can be explained with the value pyramid. This simple tool contrasts companies that produce complex and sophisticated products (and command higher prices) with others that produce commonly manufactured products (and cannot command a premium price). The technologically advanced producer resides at the top of the pyramid, where there are few producers; whereas the regular producer resides at the bottom, where there are many competitors.

We can use this tool with countries, too. If a country produces premium products that can only be produced there due to their technological sophistication and creativity, the country will command premium returns and will have a nice standard of life. If the country produces products that anybody anywhere can produce, the country will only be able to maintain the standard of life as the poorest of them. This may explain why the United States and other developed countries are in crisis. They used to produce almost every technologically advanced product, from engineering services to manufacturing equipment. If other countries, such as Brazil, Russia, China, India, and Korea, can nowadays produce products as technologically advanced as the United States, why would markets pay higher prices for the ones made in the United States?

In order for the products to command higher prices, they need to be better, more creative, better developed, and better manufactured. Functionality and capacity not only have to be higher but the product also has to grab the customer. Think about tennis shoes. Today, every country can produce top-quality tennis shoes, and these days, those that do must have a tangible labor cost advantage. It is impossible for the United States to compete, at least with the same product, but the product can be redefined with technology. Perhaps the tennis shoes, using acupuncture principles, massage foot nerve endings to address the customer's specific physical needs, which were determined by a picture of his iris, taken with his computer online. I don't know if this would work as I am not a doctor, acupuncturist, or iridologist, but if it did, it could redefine the market. The shoes would command a much higher price, perhaps enough for the United States to be a competitive country of manufacturing.

"You can't just ask customers what they want and try to give that to them. By the time you get it built, they'll want something new." Steve Jobs, founder and CEO of Apple Computers.

When we are engaged, we cannot but win.

When I was in college, I played water polo. I was not particularly talented and could only get to the "B" team. One day, in a tournament match, we were playing against the "A" team. They were superior by far; they had been playing for a lot longer than us; and they were faster, more organized, and more skilled. They had also promised they would crush us.

In the middle of the game, with the score heavily sided toward them, they made one mistake, and we used it to score. It was a silly mistake, and they became angry. They started yelling at each other, which made them even more upset. Our team celebrated the point. We felt united and enthusiastic. We started playing better, and they started playing worse. We kept scoring and they became more frustrated, arguing among themselves even more; such a dishonor it was to be accepting goals from us. We did not win, but we did level the score considerably. That day, I learned the importance of a united, enthusiastic team.

We see it all the time. Teams with strong players crumble down and are overcome by weaker players who suddenly become enthusiastic about the game. If it is so easy to see this in arenas, such as sports, why do we not see it in the business setting? True, in sports, we don't use the term "satisfaction" or "engagement," but it is the same thing. When team members are disenchanted with each other, upset that others are not doing their part to overcome their adversary, the team doesn't do well. When the coach keeps making strategic mistakes, the team feels demotivated. When the team believes they can't win, they won't. All these problems are psychological. In contrast, when team members feel united and coordinated, know what they want, and trust each other, they simply produce magic.

Remember a time in your working life when you felt passionate about your job. Something was at play that prompted you to get up every day full of energy, work for many hours without getting tired, and go home happy and satisfied with your work day. Perhaps, it was a new job, you just had a great time at work, or you felt your input had a significant and positive impact on the results of the organization. You were, in fact, "engaged!"

I want you to remember the interaction with other people at meetings, having an informal chat at the water fountain, writing a memo or email, or requesting help. I may not be wrong if I say that, at that time, you were doing remarkably well. When negotiating with others, you were able to get agreements, and it took less time. When you needed help, you convinced others to help you out. You also were proactive and tried to help with the challenges of others. You deployed creativity and came up with solutions that were brilliant. When you explained your ideas, you convinced others to try them out. A meeting that normally lasted two hours would be over in one because everyone would get on the same page more quickly.

Maybe you were not making much money at the time; you were only starting your career; or it was a time of crisis and change for the company, but you were engaged with the company and its problems. You were right there with everything you had. Now, perhaps you may make more money and you are more stable, but you don't feel quite the way you did then, and it shows. Position and money were not driving you, but you did achieve superior tangible results.

Am I wrong? Do you remember those days? Yes, an engaged employee can have such a positive impact on an organization. Now imagine that more workers were in the same state. This is the contagious energy that was behind Alex's workplace that we discussed at the beginning of the book.

Towers Perrin, a consultancy with specialization in human resources, surveyed 50 multinational companies to understand the link between employee engagement and performance. They found that companies with low levels of employee engagement had a 33% annual decline in operating income and an 11% annual decline in earnings growth. Those with high engagement, on the other hand, reported a 19% increase in operating income and 28% growth in earnings per share.[4]

A group of engaged individuals is a powerful machinery.

You may already know them, but let's make sure we remember the characteristics of truly engaged workers. An engaged worker:

- Is emotionally linked with the company, its challenges and successes.

- Is preoccupied with doing his part and looks for opportunities to improve the business, even when they reside outside of his area of responsibility.

- Is not easily tempted by higher salary offers or better positions from other companies.

- Is a builder and works toward the long-term success of the company.

- Strives to use his talents and creativity to improve the company and is naturally curious to acquire more skills to advance the company further.

- Becomes less concerned with himself, and more concerned with the welfare of the whole.

- Has found his place, and believes it is home. He thinks he has a better life every single day he spends with his coworkers in this organization.

A company with driven workers at the level of engagement we are striving to have in this book is an extremely powerful organization that overcomes every obstacle in its path. It works like the human body, in which systems, organs, and cells work in a coordinated, precise manner to achieve a grander purpose.

There are trillions of cells, and each one has its own purpose, be it to secrete saliva, enzymes, or sweat; move muscles; sense its surroundings; and more. Whatever its function, every single cell in this complex organization, the body, is 100% committed to its job. If one of the functions shuts down, the whole body resents it and may even face termination.

The body expects every single organ to do its job and do it well. We do not have a spare brain or heart, or a third leg. Not having spare equipment allows us to be efficient and quick. We can see, run, swim, jump, think, and manufacture tools, and all of it is thanks to our body cells that are doing their job. It is as if the cells were "convinced" that the purpose of the whole is bigger than their own self existence. They are organized in an extremely coordinated fashion with almost no supervision. We know they learn, too, such as with a vaccine that helps them acquire the capacity to identify unwelcome guests.

Imagine some cells doing something a bit different from what they are supposed to do. Let's say they start eating a lot and reproducing themselves. Their own small community grows and thrives. They seem to be doing well and don't let other cells interfere with their community. These cells no longer function for the well-being of the body. These cancer cells may eventually kill the body. The body cannot afford to have self-serving cells, only those that work for the betterment of the whole.

Now, as with the human body, imagine an organization with members convinced of the organization's purpose and willing to be part of its successes and troubles, organized in a strategic manner so that it can be nimble and fast. Imagine it fosters an environment that allows members to help each other, to teach and learn from each other, with minimal check points and management oversight. This organization would be able to run farther, think faster, and act better than its competition.

> "Engaged workers stay for what they give (through their work), and disengaged employees stay for what they get (a secure job in an unfavorable employee market, a desirable salary or bonus, favorable job conditions, or career advancement)."[5]

Do you think it is possible to have workers that care more for what they contribute to an organization than what they receive in terms of salary or perks? We may be asking too much. Is this "engagement" level really achievable? Can we foster it?

Some of the practices we have in our businesses lead to their own demise. The life of the modern corporation is just above 40 years. That of small businesses is even shorter. We are obviously not doing this purposely, but there are forces that drive us there. We must understand what these forces are and how to deal with them before we answer the previous questions.

1 Gibbons, John. *I Can't Get No … Job Satisfaction, That Is.* The conference Board, 2010.

2 Harris Interactive. *The New Employee/Employer Equation Survey,* 2008.

3 Gibbons, John. *I Can't Get No … Job Satisfaction, That Is.* The conference Board, 2010.

4 Towers, Perrin. *Employee Engagement underpins business transformation,* 2009.

5 Blessing White Research. *2011 Employee Engagement Report*, 2011.

Chapter 3:

A Focus on More Than Profits Leads to Long-Term Success.

"This American system of ours, call it Americanism, call it capitalism, call it what you will, gives each and every one of us a great opportunity if we only seize it with both hands and make the most of it." Al Capone, American gangster of the Prohibition era.

Our current system fosters growth and wealth creation.

When I was a young boy, I didn't understand why certain countries were poor. My reasoning was simplistic: If the country has natural resources, its people have the desire to work, and there is a need for products and services, what is missing? I later understood that government policies, capacity to trade, infrastructure, technical education, and investment have a pivotal role in kick starting and accelerating an economy. In a world of open markets, the latter ones are deemed to happen sooner or later almost automatically. Money and technical expertise will flow where there are natural resources, need, and government policies that allow them to operate. This way, the economies of countries such as Brazil, China, India, and Russia flourish once they open their markets to the flow of products, investment, and education.

Capitalism is good because it naturally fills voids and brings opportunities around. It naturally brings jobs, capital, and education to regions in need around the world. But it doesn't stop there. It rewards growth. The bigger the business, the more economies of scale from which it can benefit. Preparing 100 lb. of bread dough takes almost the same work as 50 lb. of bread dough, when we consider all the necessary activities such as buying the grain, transporting it, milling it, mixing it with water, kneading the dough, and cleaning the equipment. Whether we like it or not, the bigger business has better access to resources such as raw materials, equipment, distribution channels, and even talent.

Capitalism also rewards innovation as new and better products quickly replace the old ones and the businesses that produce them. The business that doesn't innovate stays behind, its margins get cut, and eventually faces financial trouble. Capitalism is set up to convince us that we need new products, even if we don't know about them. Businesses use advertising, marketing, and product development to create the need for their products. Capitalism also rewards efficiency and low-cost production. The business that is not competitive is soon out of the market. Producers of products and services must be constantly reviewing and improving their operations in order to remain competitive in the marketplace.

These characteristics of capitalism help us satisfy our needs for products and services, but they also foster short-term thinking. Market conditions may change in a snap, and unaware businesses may face dire consequences. Every opportunity is used to strengthen the business position. We have some of the best and brightest working exceedingly hard to develop successful business strategies, to react correctly to the frequent market shifts, and to maximize business results.

The market pressures companies into delivering ever better results.

Imagine a public company called Goodresults, Inc. Its management team has developed robust business strategies, and Goodresults is poised to grow 2% this year. The management has put strategies in place to keep the rate of growth at that level for the foreseeable future. The stock market analysts develop some calculations. Their calculations assume an enterprise value based on the expected revenue growth of 2% per year and the cost of money. They conclude, "The fair stock price of

Goodresults, Inc. is $50." It is a talented management team that weathers successfully many problems and maintains its promise; therefore, the stock price remains at $50.

John Investor Doe has bought some of the company's stock and wants to see it grow in value. The only way for the stock to grow is to increase revenue and profits beyond what is already expected.

Here comes John Goodmanager. He establishes skilled management policies, develops new products, cuts waste and unnecessary projects, refocuses the business, and is able to increase revenue 5% every year. What a fantastic manager! The analysts come back again, redo their calculations, and conclude, "Because Goodresults, Inc. is expected to grow 5% every year, considering inflation and the cost of money, the stock price should be $55."

John Investor Doe sells his stock and is satisfied he has made a profit. Here comes Jane Investor Doe, who has seen the stock price increase and decides to buy some stock, too. The only way for the stock to increase in value is by further increasing revenue and profit numbers beyond what is already expected, again! Jane Investor Doe, together with other investors, pushes the board of directors to hire an even more aggressive manager who can increase the revenue of Goodresults, Inc. beyond the 5% promised. She only wants her investment to yield a positive return. There's nothing wrong with that, right? And the cycle goes on.

I know there are additional considerations to truly determine how the price of the stock of a company varies, but this is the fundamental mechanism for a stock to change in value. My purpose in highlighting it is only to bring attention to the enormous pressure that managers receive to increase business results in the short term. It is not, therefore, unexpected that most of the company's resources are fully tied up in working out current problems or in developing new ways to grow, not in long-term concerns. These are not at the top of the management's priority list and are, in consequence, often neglected.

The pressure to achieve business results shapes company actions.

A business may have little real interest in making sure that the waste products it generates do not cause any long-term problem for the community where it operates. As long as it meets the government regulations, the business doesn't have an incentive to perform any further studies to understand other possible negative effects. From the shareholder perspective, going beyond the minimum requirement seems wasteful because it diverts resources that can be used to tackle competitive pressures and improve business results. Such expenses don't contribute to the bottom or top line of this or the next few years, and the manager that pursues them may be replaced for another, better-focused one.

The pressure to increase business results can be seen everywhere around us. Processed food companies add chemicals, use dubious suppliers and food sources, and engineer food to "fool" the brain into thinking we are ingesting nutrition-rich food, all with the purpose to sell more. Chemical producers creatively find new uses for their products and constantly fail to make sure these chemicals don't cause long-term health issues for those who use them. Farming practices produce food with a wide variety of chemicals. Multinational companies shift manufacturing, (and, increasingly, engineering work) to third world countries to lower their costs in the short-term while affecting the well-being of their home-country customers.

> According to a report by the Environmental Working Group, the average U.S. apple contains 53 different toxic chemicals.[1]

To maximize business results, companies have learned that affecting government legislation is much more cost effective than meeting it. With lobbying, businesses have found a way to steer government legislation away from policies they would find taxing or difficult to meet. Businesses spend countless hours packaging legislation to garner support from key allies such as politicians, unions, shareholders, workers, and influential associations.

> One of the top beer producers in the United States promoted a minimum wage increase for beer workers. Government officials applauded this producer for considering all beer workers. The worker's union, obviously, supported the measure, and politicians gained recognition and votes for the coming election. It was a win-win situation for everybody. Or was it? The major beer producer had studied wages across the state, and realized its wages were higher than most small

producers. These small breweries didn't have the scale and technology to produce beer as cheaply as the major producer, but because of their remote location and access to a local, cheaper labor force, they survived well by paying lower worker wages. By raising the minimum wage, the major producer eliminated a valuable competitive advantage these small producers had.[2]

Our current business practices hurt the business' long-term survival.

Is there any surprise that people have a general distrust toward businesses (think corporations) and that businesses are seen as a major cause of social, environmental, and economic problems? Is there any surprise that nongovernmental organizations (NGOs) are often focused on addressing the societal problems at the expense of businesses? What about the "Occupy Wall Street" protests across many countries in 2011? If you read the banners protesters carried, these protests were diverse, but if you paid attention, there was an underlying theme across the board: Corporations and government are failing to do what's best for society. Corporations are getting the lion's share of wealth at the expense of the many and at the expense of the environment, and government is not able or willing to help out with the situation.

Consider unemployment, the housing crash, Wall Street bonuses, credit default swaps, the Gulf oil spill, global warming, heavy metals in our food, extinction of species, increasing income gap, attempts to reduce union bargaining rights, mystery funding for political campaigns, and many others along the same lines. Corporations play a role in all of these issues, which causes people to distrust them and dislike them. Corporations must be concerned about this perception because it will sooner or later limit their capacity to exist and operate.

The ironic part is that companies cause their own long-term demise by focusing solely on their finances. This may explain why businesses have such a short life.

Fortune 500 companies have a lifespan of something between 40 and 50 years.[3] Of the 500 companies originally making up the Standard & Poor's 500 list in 1957, only 74 remained on the list in 1997.[4] For small businesses, the rate of survival is worse. Of those on the list today, less

Let's create a new system that strengthens our businesses.

In the last few years, the most significant leading thinkers have begun to emphasize the importance of other stakeholders (beyond shareholders) in the long-term survival of companies. It is now understood that a short-term focus causes companies to overlook the well-being of their customers, the depletion of natural resources vital to their businesses, the viability of key suppliers, and the economic well-being of the community in which they operate. It's in the interest of a company to consider these broader social, environmental, and economic effects. If ignored, eventually they will become significant enough to cause the demise of the business.

Since the '70, American automotive producers have resisted tighter fuel economy standards. They successfully lobbied the government, and in 25 years, from 1985 to 2010, the Corporate Average Fuel Economy (CAFE) requirement, which dictates fuel economy standards for vehicles sold in the United States, didn't move from 27.5 mpg. Although they apparently succeeded in their short-term objectives, these auto companies hurt their long-term probabilities of success. While other manufacturers, such as Toyota, Honda, and BMW developed higher fuel economy vehicles fostered by the fuel economy requirements of their home markets, the American producers successfully lobbied the U.S. government and didn't need to do much in that regard. At the end of the last decade, the big-three found themselves with most of their expertise and the majority of their portfolio of architectures (the underpinnings to build new vehicles) incapable of manufacturing fuel-efficient vehicles, along with a strong negative consumer perception that has played a significant role in their financial struggles of the last few years.

Why would a business invest in education, health, and social problems in the community it operates if these expenses don't clearly translate into positive business investments? Nowadays, most every significant business thinker has reached the same conclusion: The success of businesses and the long-term welfare of communities are closely intertwined. While businesses need communities for customers, resources, and talent, communities need businesses for jobs and wealth creation. This way, we have heard concepts such as "Shared Value,"[6] "Corporate Social Responsibility," "Conscious Capitalism," and "Purposeful Capitalism."

Activities that improve the business communities will improve the long-term prospects of the company, but this book suggests a slightly different point of view. Although the effects may point toward the same direction, the reasons for doing it, the fundamentals of how it works, and the overall results are all different.

This book suggests that by forming enterprises in which associates and all other stakeholders share meaningful values, purposes, and organizational ways, their work becomes much more engaging to them. Workers are happier and more fulfilled, and by consequence, their performance is much superior than that of other companies solely focused on growth and profits. By having alignment with what the company strives to achieve beyond financial results, the business stops being an exploiter of resources and people and becomes a community ally, promoting its welfare and quality of life. The business attracts the best people, doesn't have opposition by members of the community, and has access to many organizations, such as universities and NGOs that are willing to participate in the activities of the company and foster its success. In other words, everyone wins!

Note that I am not saying that the organization reduces its capacity to generate income or that generating high returns becomes less desirable. It is quite the opposite. We need to have sustainable businesses that generate income over the long run. We need the focused, driven, and passionate participation of every worker. We must improve today's current meager rate of business survival. We must reduce the excessive burnout and stress in workers and the social problems that today's businesses cause. It is the time to do it.

I believe that capitalism that fosters production and consumption will yield to capitalism with meaning, a system in which organizations not only generate income but do it in a way that improves the condition of human life. This capitalism with meaning is rooted in the company's workers and its communities. It generates income, not at the expense of its communities, workers, and customers, but with the objective to contribute to their well-being.

Who wants to eat food prepared by an upset and disgruntled cook? Who desires to give toys to children that were manufactured by people who didn't mind a manufacturing process loaded with toxic chemicals? Who wants to live in a house built by a builder whose main purpose was to squeeze out every penny from the project, never considering the dweller's long-term satisfaction?

Each of us has to decide if we want to join in or not.

This new production system cannot be a government-led system, nor can it be a dictated one. To start, government is clearly not able to police what every organization is doing, whether this is in the production of products and services, or in the creation and control of information (movies, advertising, etc.). Government cannot dictate what is good and what isn't. Doing so would be paternalistic and it may be interpreted as attempts to make citizens conform to a chosen model and to limit individual freedom. It is the individual drive to contribute to humanity that is the main driver for us to move forward to a new, more meaningful system. We will review later in this book how this is possible and why this isn't such a foreign idea.

I am certain than in the future, we will increasingly choose the products and services from the companies that go beyond worrying about their bottom line. We already do it, from grocery stores such as Whole Foods Market to air travel such as Southwest and JetBlue, from beer manufacturing such as New Belgium Brewing, to information management organizations such as Google and Wikipedia. The financial results of these companies exceed their competitors' numbers (often many times), and to top it off, these companies have satisfied, happy, and productive workers. In the future, this will be the majority of businesses. They will compose what today we call "capitalism with meaning."

But how do we choose to buy the product or service from one organization or the other? What influences this decision? Is it affected by the level of engagement we have in our organization? To answer these questions, we must have a greater understanding of brands and how they affect the customer's buying-decision process. We will review brands in the next chapter.

"A business that makes nothing but money is a poor business."

Henry Ford, founder of the Ford Motor Co. and sponsor of the development of the assembly line technique of mass production.

1   Environmental Working Group. *2011 Dirty Dozen.* Testing performed by Department of Agriculture and the FDA, 2011.

2   O'Dea, Raymond J. "The Determination of a Secondary Wage." *Journal of Industrial Relations*, 1968.

3   De Geus, Arie. *The Living Company: Habits for Survival in a Turbulent Business Environment.* 1st ed. Harvard Business Review Press, June 4, 2002.

4   Foster, Richard, & Kaplan, Sarah. *Creative Destruction: Why Companies That Are Built to Last Underperform the Market—And How to Successfully Transform Them.* 1st ed. Broadway Business, April 3, 2001.

5   Shane, Scott. *Illusions of Entrepreneurship: The Costly Myths that Entrepreneurs, Investors, and Policy Makers Live By.* Yale University Press, January 28, 2008.

6   Porter, Michael E., & Kramer, Mark R. "Creating Shared Value: How to Reinvent Capitalism— and Unleash a Wave of Innovation and Growth." *Harvard Business Review,* 2011.

The Driven Organization

Chapter 4:

Workers Build Your Brand.

"A brand for a company is like a reputation for a person. You earn reputation by trying to do hard things well." Jeff Bezos, Founder, Amazon.com.

No business can be successful without a brand that evokes positive feelings in its customers for its product or service. The brand is at the core of the customer's buying-decision process. If we are meant to build an extraordinary organization, we must ask how to create a great brand.

Brands influence our perception unconsciously.

A few months before graduating with my MBA, I had already signed on to join the strategic department of General Motors. Knowing that soon I'd be working there, I wanted to be as knowledgeable as possible about the car market. I often consulted my friends to give me their thoughts about car models, brands, companies, and the automotive industry.

Rebecca, a friend of mine, was not a car person at all, so I could ask her objective questions about the actual vehicles. Knowing that she could not identify their brand, I would surely get an unbiased opinion. One day, as we walked through the streets of Chicago, through a neighborhood that had restaurants with tables on the street, we enjoyed talking about the different vehicles we encountered. Eventually, I asked her about a four-door sedan. I didn't share with Rebecca that it was a BMW 3 series. Rebecca quickly told me that she did not like it and gave me several reasons for her evaluation. She said that the design made the car look too aggressive, the car was too showy and too low, and it did not seem practical.

I kept asking her about several other vehicles until we saw a four-door BMW 3 series of a different color. The car had about the same level of equipment as the previous BMW. I asked, "What do you think of this one?" And before she could see it, I added, "It is a BMW." Rebecca glanced at it for a quick second and said: "Ah, I love it." She gave me several reasons why the car was a great choice, "Well-designed, aerodynamic, fast looking, well built."

Later on, at GM, I spent some time with the folks in charge of the customer clinics. The clinics were normally used to determine how new vehicles would be received in certain representative markets. However, GM had run some special experiments. They showed people vehicles without badges, and then with badges. Interestingly, badges of American manufacturers tended to drag down the ratings. They even changed the badges around, putting the Japanese/European badges into American vehicles and American badges into Japanese/European vehicles. They compared these results with the evaluations of vehicles with the correct badges. Every time, Japanese- and European-badged cars came out with higher ratings, notwithstanding what the vehicles actually were.

The surveyed folks explained why the European/Japanese-branded vehicles were superior. They talked about the finish, the choice of materials, the colors chosen, the thickness of the steel used, the attention to detail, the sound doors made when closed, etc. They just didn't know that sometimes they were talking about an American car.

Just as with my friend Rebecca, the brand had changed the surveyors' perception of the vehicles. They sincerely and honestly believed that they were performing thorough, objective evaluations. They never thought that their objectivity was questionable, just as now you may be thinking that you would do differently if you were in those clinics. The truth is that we are all influenced by perceptions and brands that affect how we see the world on an unconscious level.

"I am irresistible, I say, as I put on my designer fragrance. I am a

merchant banker, I say, as I climb out of my BMW. I am a juvenile lout, I say, as I pour an extra strong lager, I am handsome, I say, as I put on my Levi jeans." John Kay, British journalist and author of *The hare and the tortoise*.

How do brands work?

One day, I met a manager who, as a hobby, practiced as a magician. Nick would sometimes entertain coworkers with magic tricks at parties and other gatherings. He was really good, and people would have a great time with Nick. One day, he told me that to make a coin disappear, he had to practice doing a specific exercise for 10 minutes every day for about 3 months. The exercise consisted of grabbing the coin with his right hand and passing it to his left hand, the way a person would normally pass a coin from one hand to the other. After these 3 months, he was able to perform the magic trick.

I didn't understand and asked, "How does passing the coin from one hand to the other help you do the magic trick of disappearing a coin?"

"Ah! But it is very important," Nick answered. "Imagine you are watching a movie. A movie can be built using still pictures that appear one after the other at a fast speed. If it is fast enough, your brain will not realize that it isn't continuous. It is the same with the magic trick. Your eyes are not able to see every single movement that I make with my hands, but your brain fills up the empty spaces. The brain, with the information provided, reconstructs the whole scene."

Nick continued, "I need to train my movements so that they are the right ones to signal to your brain that a coin is being passed to the left hand. Brains can be cheated, but the signals have to be right; otherwise, the brain thinks something isn't quite right. The basis of magic is to provide the right data points, and let our brains complete the scene."

I thought for a while about what Nick told me. Taking only a few data points is a way to save resources; it is a way for our brains to avoid analyzing the whole situation. By sampling information here and there, we free up brain power. Our brains are geared to do that: to develop shorter and shorter "thinking" routes. These routes help us react faster each time and do much more with the same available information. It is, in a way, like taking a brain shortcut.

Do you remember when you learned to drive? If you are like the majority of us, you had to think to keep the steering wheel in the right position, determine which pedal was the right one, remember to push pedals slowly, use the turning lights, watch other vehicles, and consider road conditions and traffic signals. For some of us who learned with a stick shift vehicle, we also had to push the clutch, put the car in the right gear, and synchronize it with the gas pedal. Some even had to manage a screaming parent in the background. Driving is a somewhat complex activity; otherwise, computers would be doing it for a while already. This may happen soon, but although computers help us control a significant amount of processes, machinery, and equipment, they are still not capable enough to drive in every condition. But we humans do it so easily. How come? We have managed to reduce that complex activity to a thoughtless, every day, and mundane activity. Our brains have developed shortcuts that allow us to keep the vehicle completely under control without thinking, stressing, or even paying attention to our movements.

A brand is exactly the same thing. It is a shortcut in life. Without brands, we would have to ask, measure, weigh, check, analyze, test, hit, stretch, push, bend, and more. We'd have to do it every time we buy a product to see if it meets our requirements. A brand speeds up the acquisition process by making our gaps in knowledge be of less concern to us. These gaps are still there, as there are things we don't know, couldn't know, or don't want to know, but with a trusted brand, we simply are not too concerned about them. Brands have freed us from spending resources in activities that don't add value to our lives. They provide a hugely important mechanism for our modern life to exist.

Companies struggle to have honest and differentiated positions.

In the mid-twentieth century, marketing managers thought they had discovered a good way to develop brands. They grouped the market on a whiteboard according to their buying characteristics, choose a segment of the market, think about the needs of customers in that segment, and launch an advertising campaign to convince this group that the product they offered met their needs and expectations. These marketing managers believed they had learned which pieces of information the customer used to make buying decisions. They wanted to be great magicians and feed us the data points we needed in order for us to feel a certain way about the brand, and effectively influence our buying-decision process. Brands became imaginary constructs of dream organizations that develop products and services exactly the way we need them.

It worked for a while. This way, companies developed many brands, each targeting a particular segment but covering the entire market.

In 2006, in its annual report, Procter & Gamble reported having 85 brands.[i] With the motto "a car for every purse and purpose," GM ended up having eight brands of vehicles just in the United States before its financial crisis forced them to get rid of a few.

Because we customers have become better and better at processing information, we can handle more data points. We have become better at catching the magician trick; although 30 frames-per-second were good enough for a picture 50 years ago, now we need 100 frames-per-second to be "fooled." We do know and want to know more about the brands, products, and services we buy. We want to know the origin and quality of the ingredients used, the chemicals used in the process, the conditions of manufacturing for people, the engineering specifications, safety standards, etc. These are the additional frames we need in order for us to believe the movie. For certain reasons that we'll discuss later in this book, we also have concerns about fair trade, use of natural resources, inputs and use of materials, labor policies, women and minority rights, fair worker opportunities, community support, and more. If this seems too far-fetched, think how you felt when you learned that Nike was using child labor in Cambodia and Pakistan in the 1990s.

Companies are always trying to fix the gap between what we need and the information they supply us. They pay close attention to what we want and try to incorporate it into their processes and marketing advertising. However, as time passes, they increasingly struggle to build the image they want in our minds. The situation becomes more complicated when they have multiple brands. How can they supply the right (and different) information for each and all of them? It becomes a challenge, especially with artificial positions. It requires a high advertising budget for each of them, which extracts valuable resources that could be used to develop new products or make prices more competitive. This is why artificial identities eventually tend to break down.

"It is not slickness, polish, uniqueness, or cleverness that makes a brand a brand. It is truth." Harry Beckwith, author of *Unthinking: The Surprising Forces Behind What We Buy.*

A brand that works is connected with our emotions.

A brand is a great vehicle to communicate product characteristics, but that is not all that happens when we choose a brand. There is a little rational thinking and a lot of unconscious emotional attraction. To understand this, we must first understand that we human beings are not as rational as we think we are.

Many high-end products that carry a steep price tag are manufactured with features and comparative quality similar to their much cheaper counterparts. This way, a purse may command a price from $50 to $3,000, depending on its brand. A more gender-neutral example comes from the Pontiac Vibe and the Toyota Matrix. These vehicles were engineered, designed, and built by the same people. The exterior sheet metal was modified a bit to accommodate the different brands, but no design was appreciably superior (according to customer clinics). Still, Toyota sold more units, at a noticeable higher price than Pontiac, when both were living brands. Remember that some of the most rational individuals in the world, guided mostly by cold and unemotional numbers, created one of the most important economic crises of the century due to their irrational behavior. Yes, Wall Street.

We want to believe that if we see something worth $1 million in front of us, we will recognize it. If we run into a sweater of our size made with the most refined fabric of the world, priced at $10, we would definitely buy it. We want to believe that brand is just a secondary consideration and we know when something is worth a lot, but we don't.

Joshua Bell helped test whether people can recognize when something is good or not. As you may know, he is one of the finest classical musicians in the world, an internationally acclaimed virtuoso, who has no problem filling up the music halls where he plays his violin. With the help of the *Washington Post*, he performed an interesting experiment. The violinist played his $3.5 million violin for 45 minutes in a hall outside the Metro in an indoor arcade at the top of the escalators. A few feet from where he was, there were people having coffee and breakfast at a couple of fast food restaurants. Many others were lined up to buy lottery tickets. Hundreds passed by him. The whole thing was filmed and can be seen in the Internet. Joshua Bell is extremely successful and his abilities can be readily observable. I mean, it is not like a DVD player, which even if I open it, I don't understand it nor can I really test it. But folks could listen to Joshua and in theory determine whether his performance was good or not, right?

Well... not really. The violinist, who performed for the soundtrack of "The red violin," had a total of 27 people making $32 in donations, and only 6 people stopped a few moments to take in the music (out of about 1,100 people who passed by during the 45 minutes he played). There was never a crowd. By the way, Bell played master-pieces that only few can perform and others that are better known, such as "Ave Maria." It seems that in this modern world of distractions and product proliferation, we need something to tell us how much things are worth; perhaps a recommendation, a price tag, or ...yes, a brand.[ii]

Once we know we are not that rational, the second thing we must understand is that brands help us, in turn, to brand ourselves. Brands communicate for whom the products were designed and who the buyers are. We use brands to communicate how much money we have, how worldly we are, and how technically oriented we are. We even use them to signal political affiliation, environmental concerns, sexual orientation, and hobbies. We use brands to tell other people who we are.

What do you think of these three women? The first one comes out of a Toyota Prius, wearing Birkenstock sandals and holding a Java latte in her left hand. The second one exits a Ford Escape SUV, wearing Oakley sunglasses and an Adidas Visor. A third woman comes out of a BMW 3 series, with a Versace handbag and Emilio Pucci sunglasses. What do these characteristics tell you of these women? Note that we are giving you only three brands of the hundreds that a person uses every day. If you knew the main 100 brands that a consumer uses, you would probably have a very good idea of that person's desires, tastes, needs, and problems. You may even be able to predict which brands she would acquire in the future. You may be able to determine a big chunk of his personality. When choosing a brand, we may not consciously intend to signal anything, but like the clothes we use, brands become an extension of our personality, and communicate very efficiently and effectively who we are.

Considering these factors, it is not surprising that we develop personal, emotional connections with the brands we use. They are like your preferred shoes, those jeans you want to take everywhere, or your old Jeep Wrangler. They are just what you like. We even have some kind of emotional connection with the brands we don't use. Think of Boeing. Very few of us have purchased jets, but if you dig deep enough, you'll realize you have some feeling toward the brand.

Reasons are less important than emotions when it is about brand selection and what the marketers call "buyer behavior." My friend Rebecca, who thought she was being very rational when explaining in detail the good characteristics of the BMW, was in reality strongly influenced by feelings she had for the BMW brand. She just was not aware of them. Companies know that emotions drive purchase decisions, so they very often appeal to them.

In 2006, United Airlines had one commercial made of cartoons. A guy gets up in the morning, shaves, combs his hair, and gets dressed. He is going to an important place because he spends some time choosing the right tie. He poses in the mirror with a determined face. Is he ready to face them? Finally, he feels he is ready and takes a cab to the airport, where he flies somewhere. At his destination, he goes into a very tall building, where he rides an elevator to a top floor. Suddenly, he realizes with concern he has chosen shoes of different pairs. He enters into a meeting room, where a few people are waiting for him. We can see he is being interviewed by some serious-looking people. After several long interviews, he is sent home with a simple handshake and inexpressive faces. The day has worn him down mentally and physically, and he shows it. As he is walking away from the building, he receives a phone call that makes him jump of joy. He's been offered the job! As he rests in the flight back, a message appears on the screen: "United will take you wherever you go in life."

United didn't show the specific features that made it a better choice of airline. It was only about a guy trying his best in a job interview.

Everyone who has been in that situation understands how he feels, and it seems that United Airlines understands it, too. It is not that consciously we believe it does, but somewhere inside ourselves we feel it does, and this is what is required to have a positive outlook for United. If there is a choice between similar-priced tickets, we may choose United. If they need a bailout from the government, we may be more inclined to have the government helping them. United understands it. A brand can be a powerful, emotional connection, and United wants us to develop such a connection with it. The problem may be that United, as brilliant as its advertising may be, may not have these values and structure throughout its organization to support this promise. We come back to the artificial construct that may not fulfill the needs of its customers.

"A great brand taps into emotions. Emotions drive most, if not all, of our decisions. A brand reaches out with a powerful connecting experience. It's an emotional connecting point that transcends the product." Scott Bedbury, American Advertising Executive who led Nike's campaign "Just do it."

The more brands, the more difficult to break through the clutter.

At the end of the twentieth century, the world started to change at lightning speed. With the advent of the Internet, information could travel to remote corners of the world instantly. Suddenly, to participate in the most intellectual discussion about art, a person didn't need to be in New York, for example. The Internet has helped to democratize information, making it available to everyone and disregarding country, religion, education level, or wealth. The informational boundaries have been reduced significantly.

In the same way, customers can peek into companies' processes, quality verifications, product development, branding, and values and work philosophies. We can see the kind of people the organization is composed of, and we can easily see whether it rings true to its promises. The Internet has decreased the importance of regular, planned advertising and has increased transparency between all stakeholders of a company. A company can no longer say something and do something else. We can now see the frames of the movie the company doesn't want us to see. A blog, a review, or even a tweet can create a difficult situation for the company, and eventually force it to refurbish important areas of its process. It happens all the time. Conversely, the same tools can also build and make a brand extremely famous and important. Information travels fast, and both good and bad things are recognized at the same speed.

To further complicate things, today there are hundreds of thousands of brands. Marketing houses report that the typical American consumer is exposed to between 1,000 and 5,000 brands each day!

Why does that matter, you ask? Have you wandered through the detergent aisle in a supermarket lately? You spend some time looking at the many options available, attempting to determine the best choice. After a while, you get tired, perhaps confused about what the most important considerations are, and decide to buy the brand that your mother has always bought. She bought it for a reason, right?

But, what just happened? With all these choices, you bought the usual brand, not giving an opportunity to anyone else. Apparently, this is the natural thing to do. Professor Alexander Chernev from the Kellogg School of Management has conducted a considerable amount of research about what is called "choice overload." He explains that the more options presented to the consumer and the more complex the decision is, the more likely consumers will rely on the single most important attribute (such as being the market leader, the highest-quality brand, or the one mommy used) and select the brand that is the best on that attribute.

This means that consumers will increasingly fall back to the "default choice" as the decision becomes difficult, in this case, by the many options available in the detergent aisle. In other words, as choices become more complex, people tend to follow the rule "nobody gets fired for buying IBM."

In the 1980s, when companies were in need of new computing equipment, it was easy to find suppliers at lower prices than those of IBM, but if the computers failed, the buyer would be at fault for buying substandard equipment. Instead, if he bought IBM computers and they failed, he would not be at fault because he had made the best, most

> recommended purchase. This gave room to the saying "Nobody gets fired for buying IBM."

Professor Putsis of the University of North Carolina gives us an idea of how powerful this dynamic is. He says that an increase in the number of brands increases the ability of national brand manufacturers to raise price.[iii] Isn't that counterintuitive? As more brands come into the market, the decision becomes more difficult for the buyer and he chooses the brand with most recognition or the one he's always chosen. As a result, because the number of competitive brands is exploding in most industries, the need for stronger, meaningful brands is even more important today!

If the old marketing model of sustaining a branding proposition designed at the whiteboard results too expensive to maintain; if customers are more discerning and need more and more difficult-to-fake data points; if the Internet increasingly lowers the walls between the company workers and its customers and exposes its true character, values and objectives; and if, in the brand clutter, there is a need for stronger brands, what is there to do? The answer is simple. Instead of advertising a dream organization, what if we actually build one?

"Nothing will kill a bad product faster than good advertising." Bill Bernbach, famous contributor to the advertising world.

"If you make customers unhappy in the physical world, they might each tell six friends. If you make customers unhappy on the Internet, they can each tell 6,000 friends." Jeff Bezos, CEO of Amazon.com.

These days, only workers can create a great brand.

When I was at GM, I sometimes ran into an employee who came to work with the objective of creating the best car ever made. He was so passionate for his work that it showed in everything he did. In meetings, he challenged his team, he asked questions, and his energy permeated to the rest of the team. He caught things that would have gone unidentified or created problems later on. He often asked "why not?" to new solutions for new and old problems. He wasn't happy doing a good job; he was looking for ways to make it outstanding. This was the type of guy who would spend hours at a friend's gathering talking excitedly about spark ignited direct injection and its impact on new products. Whoever heard him talking with so much enthusiasm would strongly consider a GM car for his next car purchase.

There were not many employees like him; perhaps only 1 of every 10, perhaps even fewer than that. I can't say. Still, their impact is quite significant. Notwithstanding GM's heavy bureaucracy, mistaken management decisions, excessive labor union cost, high health and retirement load, old brand legacy and whatever else you may want to add to the list of problems that GM faced, those 1 of every 10 people may have infused the company with so much energy to keep it afloat for a good chunk of its 100-plus-year history. They add product innovations, identify problems, increase product quality, reduce cost, and improve processes beyond what is expected from them. Thanks to them, GM continues to be a significant global competitor.

These successful folks derive their drive in spite of the obstacles mentioned previously, and they do so from their own personal sources. Perhaps it is their love for cars, their desire to have impact in a significant organization, or their enjoyment of automobile technology. It doesn't matter; what does matter is that their impact is so transcendental that they have kept this enormous organization functioning successfully for the majority of its history. Now, imagine that we could double the amount of driven people. Instead of 1 in 10, imagine there were 3 of 10, or even 6 of every 10.

Have you heard of the tipping point? There will be a point where these driven individuals imbue their enthusiasm to the rest of the people. Soon, every worker is working as hard as the rest. What would the capability of the organization be? What could this organization accomplish?

When they have the opportunity, driven and engaged workers create powerful machineries that sooner or later generate the attention deserved. These workers are constantly on the lookout for process improvements and creative uses of technologies that result in outstanding products and better ways to deliver them. These unique process improvements and product innovations become brand differentiators that are extremely difficult to copy.

There is no reason to spend hours and hours performing market segmentation analysis and consumer targeting clinics. The same activities that the engaged business performs to achieve its objectives naturally become brand differentiators and even free advertising. How many times have we passed along information that we find unique, such as 3M and Hewlett-Packard allowing its workers to spend 10–15% of their time doing what they want?[iv] How many times have we recommended great products, such as Google Earth or Napster? What about an amazing restaurant; did you see it advertised in the newspaper, or was it a friend who told you about it?

Without the need to pay customers or give away free products, the engaged business always gets amazing reviews. In the new interconnected world, the speed at which good or bad products, services, and experiences are recognized has exponentially increased, disregarding time zones and international boundaries. More than ever, superior performance speaks for itself.

"Take time to appreciate employees and they will reciprocate in a thousand ways." Bob Nelson, author of *1010 ways to reward employees.*

Use the power of reciprocation to build your brand.

Human beings have a natural appeal for talent and superior performance. Have you realized that you develop positive feelings for great actors or amazing performers? Although we may know little of their actual characters and personalities, we feel close to them. Something happens when we enjoy their performances that we develop certain appreciation. This happens with all artists, including musicians, painters, film-makers, and actors. The same desire to recognize talent is everywhere around us, and products and services are not exceptions. Customers want to be close to those who produce superior performance. They become part of the company, and because the company's products and services are part of their life, they share their experiences and beliefs with others like them. For example, Apple has a powerful force of followers who keep close attention to the company's products, who talk extensively about them, and who spend a big chunk of their discretionary income on the latest Apple product release. They have stopped being just customers and have become part of their organization's efforts. Who do you think has more impact on the company's success, its advertising or this group of hard core followers?

All human beings have a huge need to reciprocate when they are recipients of a gift. Psychologists say that this is a natural tendency and that only those who are mentally ill do not express it.

This story is about Ethiopia and Mexico, and is a great example of the powerful human need to reciprocate. In 1985, Ethiopia was suffering one of the most devastating famines in its history, and was in no shape to be helping other countries. Still, Ethiopia sent humanitarian relief help when Mexico City was struck by a powerful earthquake. When the Ethiopian leaders were asked about it, they explained that Mexico had sent funds to help Ethiopia fend off an invasion from Italy in the 1930s and was the only country to condemn Italy for the invasion at the League of Nations. Ethiopia felt the need to reciprocate, notwithstanding its dire situation.[v]

In a remote indigenous town, a Mayan girl gives visitors a flower at the plaza when she sees them coming. She goes away for a while, and then she comes back with some stuff to sell them. Many dislike the game she has played on them, but most people find difficult to say no and end up buying something from her. She knows the power of reciprocation.

When we enjoy a product or service, we have a pleasurable experience with it. If the product or service exceeds our expectations, we receive more pleasure than what we expected to receive. In a way, it feels like a gift. This is the reason why we feel the need to reciprocate and do something for the people who gave us such a gift. We become unpaid emissaries of their organizations.

A while ago, I found myself in need of a computer because my traveling got extended beyond my original schedule. Because it was only temporary, I went to the computer store and bought one of the cheapest computers—a small notebook. I enjoyed using it so much that I kept using it instead of my computer. I thought that it probably wouldn't last long because it was so cheap, but it has. The computer does its job really well, has never malfunctioned, and exceeds the reliability of the other "better" (and expensive) computer. And all in a small package that is convenient to carry around. It's just a good thing.

I have caught myself mentioning it to others a few times. Although I didn't know the brand prior to this computer purchase, can you guess which brand I will choose when it is time for me to pick up a new one? I want to show the company my appreciation, and through a purchase or a recommendation, I will.

In a similar fashion, the engaged workers are thankful workers. They feel that they receive more from the organization than they give to it. We will talk more about how this happens in the chapters ahead. For now, we can say that because they feel so appreciative toward the organization, they want to do more for it than what it is expected from them. There is an inherent desire to see the organization flourish and prosper. Besides a continuous focus on improving the organization and an overall better worker performance, telling everyone about their organization's efforts and achievements becomes natural. If customers become emissaries of the brand, wouldn't you expect the same from workers? Remember the worker talking about GM technology at the bar?

The engaged employee knows that although his job may not be the most exciting one (he may be only installing seats on a car, to continue with that example), his organization is creating products that bring enjoyment, satisfaction, and pleasure to people. He knows he is giving gifts to customers, especially when he is able to see the superb customer reception. He goes home tired but happy because the hard work he performed that day is appreciated somewhere.

"When you enchant people, your goal is not to make money or to get them to what you want, but to fill them with great delight." Guy Kawasaki. Former chief evangelist at Apple and author of *Enchantment*.

Be truthful. This is the best advertising.

To build a robust brand, the organization must be authentic instead of attempting to be something designed at the whiteboard. This means to be clear what it is, what it stands for, what it strives to achieve, and how it does it. Because workers are engaged, they believe it and do the right thing, even when no one looks after them. There is no risk of misspeaking or need of having a spokesman. There is little chance of misrepresenting the company, either with actions or with words. There is no need to hide parts of it, nor is it possible to do so any longer. What the organization is, what it does, what it fights for, and the way it does it eventually become its brand. This is the new transparent world. Advertising, if used, becomes only a loudspeaker to communicate and reinforce what is already there, and not to construct something artificial.

We now understand that we need to have engaged workers in the company in order to have a great brand. Every time there is talk about fostering engagement, the matter of money comes up. Money is today the single most used device to motivate employees and to foster engagement. But does it work? Is money as good as everyone makes it sound? In the next chapter, we will discuss the effect of money on motivation and as a tool to foster worker engagement.

> *"A brand is a living entity—and it is enriched or undermined cumulatively over time, the product of a thousand small gestures."* Michael Eisner, CEO of Disney.

---

i   Procter & Gamble. *2006 Annual Report,* 2006, p. 26.

ii   Weingarten, Gene. "Pearls Before Breakfast: Can One of the Nation's Great Musicians Cut Through the Fog of a D.C. Rush Hour? Let's Find Out." *The Washington Post,* April 8, 2007.

iii   Putsis, W. P. J. "An Empirical Study of the Effect of Brand Proliferation On Private Label— National Brand Pricing Behavior." *Review of Industrial Organizations 12,* pp. 355–37, 1997.

iv   Wikipedia. Retrieved January 2013. http://en.wikipedia.org/wiki/Bootlegging_(business)

v   Cialdini, Robert B. *The Power of Persuasion: Putting the Science of Influence to Work in Fundraising.* Stanford Social Innovation Review, 2003.

Chapter 5:

Money Doesn't Make Our World Go Around.

*"Money doesn't make you happy. I now have $50 million but I
was just as happy when I had $48 million."* Arnold
Schwarzenegger, Austrian/American actor and former governor
of the state of California.

Liza Minnelli and Joel Gray make an impressive argument for the
importance of money in the song "Money" for the filmed version of the
play *Cabaret*. The song's message is brilliantly delivered in a funny but
clear way: Money makes the world go 'round. If you are rich, you can
easily find companionship, fun, and love. If you are poor, you will face
hunger and cold, and even love will "fly out the door."

It seems that the song writers got it right. Money is perhaps the
main driver of today's world. For sure, it's the main driver of our
businesses. To attract quality workers, a substantial, competitive salary
offering must be presented. Bonuses and salary increases are given to
those workers that behave and produce in the desired way. Workers with
more responsibilities get paid much more than their base level
counterparts. In fact, there is nothing else that comes remotely close to
money to attract, reward, and drive performance in today's business
world.

But is it truly through financial objectives that human beings operate?

Economists already recognize several variables that matter in our search for satisfaction and happiness beyond money, but the latter still tends to occupy the top spot. In this book, we are creating the conditions for satisfied, happy, and productive workers. We must, therefore, explore the importance of money. To do so, we'll break this question into two parts. First, we ask what the capacity of money is to foster happiness, a state of well-being, or the capacity to have a full life. Second, we ask how effective money (or any other external reward) is to motivate people. Let us delve into the first question.

Money solves all problems and brings happiness, right?

Think about your biggest problem or your most important personal project. I may not be wrong if I say that money is somehow involved in the matter. Perhaps you are in the process of buying a house, arranging for children to go to college, or working on an exciting business idea. Whatever our problems or projects may be, we are constrained by insufficient money. If we had money to throw away, the problems would surely go away and we would be happier, right?

Imagine you win the lottery today. Let's say the jackpot is $50 million. With that amount, you can certainly solve the majority of the problems you have today. You can reward your family and yourself with some great gifts. That cottage in the mountains, the new Porsche, and a six-month road trip through Europe seem nothing but pure pleasure. You may retire early from work and dedicate yourself to painting, carving wood, or learning the intricacies inside of most electronics. With fewer problems and so much opportunity, life will certainly be better. Well... Maybe not.

Christoph Lau and Ludwig Kramer took on the task of answering the question of whether lottery winners are happier or not. The results from their study show that after a period of peak experience, on average the level of happiness (or unhappiness) returns back to what it was prior to winning the lottery. In fact, the authors argue that, in most cases, lottery winners are eager to come back to their ordinary lives. Several other studies support the same conclusion,[vi] which is certainly disappointing. What about all the problems that winning the lottery solved? Apparently having all our material needs and wants fulfilled is not enough.

"The happiness Paradox."

Winning the lottery is an extreme change of life. There must be many things happening at the same time that skew the results. We need to take a look at something closer to real life, closer to us, and perhaps more scientific; that is, with many more data points than the few millionaires available for research.

We enter the world of economics, a social science that is all wrapped around money. Because economics attempts to understand how economies work and how economic agents interact, it may be that every economist has asked this exact question: What is the relationship between happiness and money?

Richard Easterlin became a central part of the discussions with his research on the issue that used three different data analyses.[vii] First, he looked at differences in perception of happiness within a country. He found that, in fact, those with higher incomes are more likely to report being happy. Then he made international comparisons and found that countries with higher incomes reported being happier, although the differences in happiness were quite small. Finally, he looked at the United States and saw that income-per-person rose steadily for 30 years, but average reported happiness showed no long-term trend. This apparent contradiction is known as the "Easterlin Paradox," or the "Happiness Paradox."

Easterlin concluded from these results that we use peer-to-peer comparisons to establish how well-off we are. He explained using a height analogy. Imagine a country where the average male height is 5 ft. 4 in., or about 1.62 m. Let's say that John is a citizen of that country and that his height is 5 ft. 7 in. (about 1.7 m). Because he is taller than his peers, he may feel he is a tall person and be satisfied with being so. Within international standards, John is not a tall person. A 5 ft. 8 in. person in the United States may feel short even though he is, in fact, taller than John. Easterlin used the evolution of wealth in the United States to prove that more wealth in absolute terms doesn't translate into more happiness. A poor household in the United States today is probably better off than a middle class household 50 years ago, but according to the data, not happier.

After he published his study, many researchers and academics have proposed alternative explanations but the Easterlin Paradox seems to keep its ground. In 2010, Easterlin expanded his previous study with the evolution of happiness and income over time of 37 countries. The conclusion is the same for each of these countries: Over the long run, getting richer doesn't make a country happier.

Life satisfaction is not Happiness.

There is something that doesn't quite make sense. In my mind, having money when we see our neighbors struggling does make us feel fortunate, but not exactly happy. Having more money than our peers seems to be a thing of prestige and respect, but not happiness. If I am correct, this may explain why when I think of rich people, I don't perceive them any happier than the rest of us. Let's see if we are on to something.

Nobel laureate Daniel Kahneman and Angus Deaton from Princeton University may help us get clarity on this. They conducted a study with 450,000 responses in the United States.[viii] These researchers distinguished between two aspects of subjective well-being. First, they defined "emotional well-being," or "day-to-day happiness," which they called the frequency and intensity of experiences of joy, sadness, stress, anger, and affection that make our daily life pleasant or unpleasant. Secondly, they defined "life evaluation," or "life satisfaction," which they used to describe the thoughts that people have when they think about their life.

They found that positive emotional experiences (joy, affection) seem to go up, and negative emotional experiences (anger, sadness) seem to go down as income levels rise, but only to a point. At a household income of about $75,000, emotional experiences seem to flatten out. Does this make sense? Surely, those who are struggling to feed their family, to have access to health-care services, and to live in a safe neighborhood must be experiencing more negative emotions on a daily basis. It is sad and upsetting to live in difficult conditions, and people must have fewer opportunities to experience positive emotions.

What about the other side, the one about life satisfaction? Kahneman and Deaton did find a relationship between life satisfaction and income. They concluded that the reason people think money makes them happier is that chasing it leads to conventional achievements such as getting that coveted promotion and being able to afford that big house, both of which bring life satisfaction. In other words, it is related with prestige, respect and social status. It is related with "winning the game." We were onto something, and we were right. Rich people may feel pride with their riches, but they don't laugh any more than you and I.

In summary, does money makes us happy? No! But the lack of it does make us unhappy. After reaching a household income of about $75,000, we only increase our level of "overall satisfaction in life," but not our happiness. By the way, according to Kahneman and Deaton, higher income is correlated with higher levels of stress. This is interesting as it suggests that we trade day-to-day happiness for life satisfaction. The manager of an engineering team is more stressed than the engineers working for her, but she may feel prouder of her position and salary.

Is money the only way for us to achieve life satisfaction?

One day, I attended a talk by Charlie Trotter, the owner of Charlie Trotter's restaurants in Chicago, some of the finest restaurants around. One thing he said became stuck in my mind. He explained he would never be able to provide a superior experience if he fulfilled the desires of his customers.

"I know my business much more than they do, and it is my business to amaze them," Charlie said. "I don't even ask what they want because they don't know it." Unfortunately, this is quite true. We are terribly deficient at knowing what makes us happy, what delights us. Because Charlie is the expert chef and owner, he knows which preparations, dishes, service, and atmosphere must be used to create a magnificent dining experience. This philosophy is at the core of Charlie's restaurants.

Beyond a dining experience, do we know what truly makes us happy, what truly brings life satisfaction? Perhaps we don't know that, either. We give considerable importance to money, power, and fame, perhaps because they are the easiest for everyone to see, but there are other more effective ways to build life satisfaction. We can achieve it by doing excellent work, pursuing personal goals, becoming better at what we do, helping others, and creating something innovative. In Part II, on human needs, we discuss why these are significantly better at bringing life satisfaction.

Even if money, power, and fame, are not the most effective ways to produce life satisfaction and happiness, they may still be powerful motivational tools. Let's remember that they are the primary reward mechanisms used by most modern companies to motivate their workers. Work hard and you'll be rewarded with a bigger paycheck, authority, and a position with higher visibility. But does it work? The majority of our modern businesses cannot be all wrong. This is the second question we explore in this chapter: how effective is money at motivating people?

Eight concerns of using money to motivate workers.

Many prominent researchers, academics, and scientists have struggled with this question and have conducted experiments with students, children, and adults.[ix] From their work and conclusions, we list eight concerns of money and other external rewards when used as drivers for motivation. These are:

1. External rewards may cause people to lose interest in their work.
2. External rewards, which often make people feel controlled, may result in feelings of incompetence and dissatisfaction.
3. The other side of the coin of an external reward may feel like punishment.
4. External rewards may hurt teamwork.
5. External rewards ignore reasons.
6. External rewards may encourage risky behavior.
7. External rewards may limit creativity.
8. External rewards may diminish intrinsic motivation.

We will review each one in the sections that follow.

1) External rewards may cause people to lose interest in their work.

An experiment was conducted by a scientist named Edward Deci.[x] He used Soma puzzle cubes, which as you may know, have seven pieces, which each composed of three or four fixed small cubes. The objective of the puzzle is to arrange the pieces so that they look like a given shape. One of the easiest challenges is to put the cube back together, for example.

To compare the power of financial rewards, Deci divided the participants into two groups: the money group, who were offered money for each completed puzzle, and the unpaid group, who were not offered anything.

When the experiment started, each participant came into the room and found three drawings of puzzles to complete, the Soma puzzle pieces, and some magazines. Deci sat in front of the participant to measure the time it took him to finish each puzzle. Between solving puzzle 2 and puzzle 3, Deci let the participants have some free time, telling them he needed some time to input data into a computer. They were free to do what they pleased, he told them. This was just an excuse for him to get out of the room and leave the volunteers alone. The participants didn't know this was the actual experiment.

After he left the room, Deci observed what the participants did. Did they continue playing with the puzzle, did they look at the magazines, or did they sit back and wander into their own thoughts? Those who had been offered money spent more time playing with the puzzle in their "free time," which is somewhat expected. They probably wanted to get a head start on their next challenge.

The following day, Deci told the paid group there was no more money to pay them. The structure of the day continued as before: Two puzzles, then some free time, and then one more puzzle. The results were different. Those who had never been paid spent a bit more time than in the first day, about 5 minutes of their free time, on average, playing with the puzzles. However, those in the previously paid group spent less time than their counterparts, and much less time than they spent the previous day.

The money group folks had lost interest in the Soma puzzles. Somehow, Deci had managed to make an activity that was interesting much less engaging for them. An interesting activity had become work, and to do it, they needed to be paid!

There are several other researchers who have performed similar versions of the previous experiment with a variety of external reward variations such as avoidance of penalties, deadline stress, or competition stress.[xi] In all cases, external rewards seem to hamper long-term interest in the activities. Alfie Kohn, who has studied it in detail, summarized it perfectly, "If they have to bribe me to do it, it must be something I wouldn't want to do."

2) External rewards, which often make people feel controlled, may result in feelings of incompetence and dissatisfaction.

Because rewards are usually designed to foster certain behaviors that normally would not take place (otherwise, they would not be required), the subject feels he is being controlled and has no autonomy. Another group of researchers performed a study to understand the effects of teaching styles on student motivation and self-image.[xii] They studied 35 classrooms of fourth-, fifth-, and sixth-grade students, and their teacher's teaching style. Some of the teachers tended to support their students' autonomy, and some of the teachers had a more controlling style. The team of researchers assessed students' level of curiosity and preference for challenge. They also measured their perceived competence and feelings of self-worth. They found that in the classrooms of control-oriented teachers, the students had less curiosity, had fewer preferences for challenges, perceived themselves as less competent, and felt less good about themselves than the students of autonomy-supportive teachers.

A psychologist explained it to me. She said that when people feel controlled, they feel they are not trusted to make the right decisions and to complete the task the right way. The message they receive is "You don't have the capacity to do it correctly." If workers feel they are not trusted to do it correctly by themselves, they conclude it must be because of lack of capacity. She finishes, "When a person is constantly told he isn't smart, eventually he won't be smart, even if he was."

3) The other side of an external reward is punishment.

Imagine you are an employee in a small company and you suffer from something that I have struggled throughout my life: being late. Your boss, a progressive businessman who has the best intentions for you, makes a deal with you. "If you come on time every day for the next month, I'll let you take one day free," he tells you. It so happens that you want to go hiking with your friends to the mountains next month, and you need one free day to make it a long weekend. This is extremely good news for you!

Every day, you wake up one hour early and arrive at the office with time to spare. You do so for many days, and the end of the month is approaching. On the 27th day, you can't make it: There is an unusual amount of traffic that extends your commute, forcing you to arrive at the office 20 minutes past the agreed time. Your boss is considerate, but a deal is a deal. You cannot go on your planned getaway.

You tried hard, but somehow you didn't get the reward. Even if you believe that your boss's decision not to let you go is fair, somewhere inside you feel robbed, perhaps even punished unjustly. All the effort you invested went down the drain. How come a positive reward turned into a negative feeling? Will you try again next month?

4) External rewards may hurt teamwork.

In a classroom, the teacher says, "The first 10 kids who finish the problem correctly will go to break early." Susie knows how to work through the problem. Peter asks her for help. Will she help him? That would mean forgoing the prize; not a suitable proposition. Perhaps if, Susie had explained the problem to him in her own words, he would become more interested in math, and Susie would learn to explain things to others. An opportunity, as small as it may be, is lost.

The same situation takes place at our workplaces. Each of us is focused on our own specific responsibilities. We want our bosses to recognize our individual efforts and make us recipients of those nice yearly bonuses, but the product that customers buy from the company is the sum of all our efforts, with one customer in mind. We often forget that the company is only as strong as the weakest one of us, who may be a customer care representative, a manufacturing operator, or a quality control inspector. This worker will be coached and assisted when other workers see their fate is linked to his.

5) External rewards ignore reasons.

Let's say I am a salesperson with a sales goal to reach. If I reach it, I will receive a considerable bonus. I need one more sale to reach the bonus level. I only have one possible customer, Specialcustomer, Inc., that is interested in the product. I know that in 25 days, we will launch a new product that will better meet the customer's needs. If I tell them about it, they will certainly wait for it, and I won't meet my bonus quota. If I don't tell them, they'll resent my company when they find out. Note that I worked hard on meeting the quota, and the reward of my effort hinges on an issue of morality.

This is the classic problem of the goal justifying the means. We have seen this problem with certain public corporations, whose CEOs and CFOs perform creative accounting in order for the stock price, which is used to calculate their compensation, to move in the right direction. Every time there are external rewards in play, this dynamic takes place, making workers struggle between the right thing and the sweet rewards.

6) External rewards may encourage risky behavior.

Two words: Wall Street. Investment bankers and other finance professionals were incentivized to generate as much profit as possible for their financial institutions. What did they do? They performed risky transactions such as developing creative financial services (e.g., collateral debt obligations) and extending the mortgage market beyond what was financially sound. The riskier the transaction, the higher the expected return. What was the worst that could happen? They could lose their jobs if things went badly, but the upside potential was exceptionally attractive: In one year, they could earn a bonus equivalent to several years of salary. Some of them became extremely rich, but caused an enormous amount of damage to their organizations and the entire world.

7) External rewards may limit creativity.

Teresa Amabile, a researcher from the Harvard Business School, researched the other side of the coin of taking too much risk.[xiii] She had a group of art evaluators assess the works of 23 artists. Each artist contributed 10 commissioned and 10 non-commissioned works for the study. In terms of technical mastery, there was no perceivable difference between the commissioned and the non-commissioned works, but the commissioned works were judged to be significantly less creative.

Other researchers have found similar problems diminishing out-of-the-box thinking. Sam Glucksberg used a Candle Problem experiment to learn about the effect of incentives. In this problem, there are a box of matches, a box of thumbtacks, and a candle. The objective is to fix the lit candle to the wall. Most people try to tack the candle to the wall or to melt some wax and use it to attach the candle to the wall, but none of these solutions works. After a while, the answer is found: The thumbtacks box is emptied, tacked to the wall, and used to hold the candle.

To solve the candle problem, you must come up with a creative solution. Glucksberg gathered his participants in two groups and said, "I'm going to time you. How quickly can you solve this problem?" To one group he said, "I'm going to time you to establish norms and averages for how long it typically takes someone to solve this sort of problem." To the second group he offered rewards. He said, "If you're in the top 25 percent of the fastest people you get 5 dollars. If you're the fastest of all of today's participants, you'll get 20 dollars."

It took the second group, the rewards group, 11 minutes to solve the problem on average, about 3 1/2 minutes longer than the non-rewards group. The conclusion is clear. Rewards will make us get there faster, like in an actual race, but only if the solution is right there. When the solution requires a creative, conceptual solution, rewards make us miss alternative solution paths. In other words, with a large enough reward, we will drive faster with our heart pumping on adrenaline, but we'll surely miss those shortcuts that may cut our trip in half or a street vendor selling delicious crepes.

In the business world, when a manager is motivated to find a solution or to achieve a goal with an external reward, he will look for the simplest, most straightforward path. He probably will take the usual beaten path and solve the problem exactly as it has been solved before. The solution from that approach may lack creativity and be unimaginative. It won't provide new insights about the nature of the problem or create new ways of solving it. Most probably, it won't move the businesses significantly forward. The alternative is to find the problem challenging and opening exploration opportunities. From the fun and intrigue of something new, solutions may come that are more creative and may advance the business to a whole new level of performance.

8)   External rewards may diminish intrinsic motivation.

Intrinsic motivation comes from our inner desires. It may come from the desire to do the right thing, to perform civic duties, to pursue challenges, or to investigate the not-yet understood, among others. It comes from self-determination and normally results in behavior characterized by concentration and engagement. It is simply an interest for something. How is this affected by financial or external rewards?

Unfortunately, in a negative way.

Even back in 1970, Richard Titmuss from the London School of Economics advanced the idea that paying for blood donations causes people to feel less inclined to donate blood. It wasn't until 2005 that two Swedish researchers tested Titmuss's belief.[xiv] They divided people into three groups. The first group was not offered any monetary incentives. The second one was offered SEK $50 (about US$7), and the third one was offered the same amount with the possibility to donate the money to charity. Forty-three percent of the non-paid group agreed to donate blood, only 33% of the paid group agreed to donate blood, and 44% of the charity group donated blood. Monetary rewards had managed to take the civic duty value out of donating blood, and folks felt less inclined to do it.

Another study found that high school students in Israel collected less money for charity if they were offered a small monetary incentive. The study divided the students into three groups. The first one received a speech about the importance of the activity. The second and third groups received a reward comprised of 1% and 10%, respectively, of the collected money (paid by the research team). The speech group did the best of all, followed by the 10% reward group, and finally the 1% reward group. In yet another study, subjects answered fewer questions correctly on an IQ test if they were paid a small fee per correct answer.[xv] Monetary rewards kill the challenge, reduce the value of civic duty, and make things look just downright materialistic.

When should financial (and other external rewards) be used?

We know now that money is not particularly effective in improving performance or job satisfaction,[xvi] but there is one instance where it works well. Psychologists use the term *algorithmic* activity to describe those activities that follow a process with a set path to complete the objective, and *heuristic* to describe those activities where the solution requires cognitive sophistication, open-ended thinking, and creativity (there is no set path to complete the objective). Designing a car, solving an engineering problem, finding what's wrong with a patient, taking care of children at a daycare center, solving a customer complaint—all these are heuristic problems. Painting one side of a 10-inch metal piece, assembling two components, and drilling a hole are classic algorithmic activities.

Financial rewards are extremely effective at fostering higher output for algorithmic activities. For a welder, who performs the same weld hundreds of time a day, financial rewards help him weld more pieces per day. With this incentive, he focuses his entire attention on the operation, eliminating wasteful actions and making every movement with skill and efficiency. As soon as we add heuristic activities to his responsibilities, such as product quality inspections, team management, or team training, financial rewards will cause problems for the operation.

A bank teller may have algorithmic activities such as cashing checks and depositing money, but she may have several heuristic activities as well, such as customer service and selling bank services to customers. In this case, an external reward will hamper the non-algorithmic activities and any activity not directly incentivized. The bank teller may be so focused on those activities for which there is a reward that customer satisfaction, relationship fostering, and overall performance will suffer. There are several organizations that have stopped paying commissions to their sales force, reporting positive results over the long-term.[xvii]

We are often doing it wrong.

"Most of our jobs have a financial reward component and they are mainly heuristic," you may say, and you'd be exactly right. This is precisely the disconnect between business and common sense that causes many problems everywhere around us.

What do we foster when we reward teachers if their students get higher test scores, program managers if they complete projects faster than usual, professors if they are highly graded, or engineers if they design more gadgets per year?

What about doctors getting paid more if they perform C-sections instead of helping mothers deliver naturally[xviii] or by the number of tests they have their patients endure?[xix] Even NASA got it wrong with the *Challenger*. Incentives played a determinant role in dismissing significant concerns voiced by some engineers who wanted to delay the launch.[xx]

Money is an important component of our lives. We need to have it. We need to work for it. This is clear for everyone. However, just as we know that it is not correct to devote our lives to get money (we know there are other "things" that are significant in our lives), money should never be used as a reward for behavior or as the main motivator for our work. We will discuss in subsequent chapters how to deal with money in a way that doesn't destroy engagement, but builds it and fosters a stronger bond among the members of the organization.

> *"One might think that the money value of an invention constitutes its reward to the man who loves his work. But... I continue to find my greatest pleasure, and so my reward, in the work that precedes what the world calls success."* Thomas A. Edison.

So far in this book, we have highlighted some of the ineffective practices that are often used in our modern organizations. We now know the dangers of using money as a way to control behavior. We have also seen how organizations with a complete focus on profits eventually get into trouble with their stakeholders, risking what they so actively seek. On the other hand, we have learned the capacity of an engaged organization to enthusiastically and energetically deal with problems and challenges. Its brand, an asset envied by its competitors, naturally transpires from what the organization strives to achieve with every action and decision. We also know that using engaged workers is the surest, easiest way to build a great brand.

But do we know what this Driven Organization looks like and how it differs from others? How does it feel to work there? It's time to go on a tour to visit these organizations. See if you find your workplace in the pages of our next chapter.

vi   Eckblad, G-F., & von der Lippe, A. L. "Norwegian Lottery Winners: Cautious Realists." *Journal of Gambling Studies* 10(4), 305—322. 1994.

Falk, Pasi, & Mäenpaä, Pasi. *Hitting the Jackpot: Lives of Lottery Millionaires.* Berg, 1999.

Kaplan, H. R. "Gambling Among Lottery Winners: Before and After the Big Score." *Journal of Gambling Behavior* 4, 171–182, 1988.

vii   Easterlin, Richard. *Does Economic Growth Improve the Human Lot? Some Empirical Evidence.* University of Pennsylvania, 1974.

viii   Kahneman, Daniel, & Deaton, Angus. "High Income Improves Evaluation of Life but Not Emotional Well-Being." *Proceedings of the National Academy of Science.* Data from the Gallop-Healthway Well-being Index, August 4, 2010.

ix   Kohn, Alfie. *Punished by Rewards: The Trouble with Gold Stars, Incentive Plans, A's, Praise, and Other Bribes.* Boston: Houghton Mifflin, 1993/1999.

Amabile, Teresa M. *Creativity In Context: Update To The Social Psychology Of Creativity,* 1996.

Lepper, Mark. "Undermining Children's intrinsic interest with extrinsic reward: A test of the 'Overjustification hypothesis.'" *Journal of Personality and Social Psychology* 28(1), pp. 129-137, 1973.

Ariely, Dan. *Predictably Irrational: The Hidden Forces That Shape Our Decisions,* 2008.

x   Deci, Edward. *External Rewards on Intrinsic Motivation,* 1972.

xi   Good player rewards (Lepper, Greene, & Nisbett, 1973); Avoidance of Punishment (Deci, & Casio, 1972); Deadlines (Amabile, DeJong, & Lepper, 1976); Imposed Goals (Mossholder, 1980); and competition (Deci, Betley, Kahle, Abrams, & Porac, 1981)

xii   Deci, Edward L., Nezlek, John, & Sheinman, Louise. "Characteristics of the Rewarder and Intrinsic Motivation of the Rewardee." *Journal of Personality and Social Psychology* 40(1), pp. 1—10, January, 1981.

xiii   Amabile, Teresa M. *Creativity In Context: Update To The Social Psychology Of Creativity,* 1996.

xiv   Mellström, Carl, & Johannesson, Magnus. "Crowding Out in Blood Donation: Was Titmuss Right?" *Journal of the European Economic Association,* 2008.

xv   Gneezy & Rustichini. *Pay enough or not pay at all,* 2000.

xvi   Judge, T. A., Piccolo, R. F., Podsakoff, N. P., Shaw, J. C., & Rich, B. L. "The Relationship Between Pay and Job Satisfaction: A Meta-Analysis of the Literature." *Journal of Vocational Behavior* 77(2), pp. 157—167, 2010.

xvii   Examples: Microchip Technology, GlaxoSmithKline, Fog Creek Software.

xviii   Childbirth Connection. "Cesarean Section: Why Does the National US Cesarean Section Rate

Keep Going Up?" *Childbirth Connection*, 2011.

xix   Pines, Jesse M., & Meisel, Zachary F. "Why Doctors Order Too Many Tests (It's Not Just to Avoid Lawsuits)." *Time Magazine,* February 25, 2011.

http://www.time.com/time/health/article/0,8599,2053354,00.html#ixzz1jjl4bpFE

xx   Berkes, Howard. "Challenger: Reporting a Disaster's Cold, Hard Facts." *National Public Radio,* January 28, 2006.

Chapter 6:

Three Different Organizations.

At this point, can you imagine how it feels to work for a Driven Organization? Not yet?

Let's go on a visit and observe the practices of three organizations that achieve vastly different results. We call them *Goodworks*, *Okworks*, and *Crummyworks*. Find your current workplace in their descriptions. Imagine how you would feel working in these organizations.

You may find organizations such as Goodworks too good to be true. This feeling should go away as you understand how it works and we study real examples of organizations implementing similar practices. You may re-read this chapter later to see how your point of view has changed. The mechanisms and dynamics that make Goodworks work will be clear when we discuss SPACES, the framework for building a great organization, in Chapter 9.

Crummyworks stinks!

At Crummyworks, Inc., workers believe their situation is far from optimal. In fact, people gather together to complain and make each other feel better. They talk about management, how they are exploited, their tough job, their desire to work anywhere but at Crummyworks, the market that doesn't "get it," or the new market conditions that have become extremely tough after the Chinese incursion. There is always a good reason for workers to feel they have been dealt a bad hand. This feeling permeates all levels of the company, from manufacturing workers to executive senior managers.

Workers at Crummyworks do their jobs because they have to and perform only the minimum requirements for the job. But even at the end of the workday, they go home feeling extremely tired. They work hard because it is very hard to perform a job people that doesn't energize them. In Crummyworks, folks tend to feel that people have to work to live, and there is no way around it. We have to pay our dues to the world and then perhaps we can have a few hours of real life with a little enjoyment at the end of the day.

Crummyworks' environment is characterized by low initiative and little imagination about the future. The air is often a bit heavy, and people tend to be serious. People are obedient. They do what they are told to do, and do so without much questioning. Management, in turn, tends to be a rigid entity that isn't very accessible by those outside its borders, by those who don't belong to the elite. These are the smart guys who know what is going on, and one day might come up with a strategy that actually works.

At Crummyworks, workers may punch time cards. Leaving the office during the day requires a written permit by a manager. There are metal detectors at the organization's entrance. Sending product samples to customers requires the signatures of a number of managers to make sure that the samples are going to the right place.

Unfortunately, this description of Crummyworks mirrors the reality of some businesses, especially those in developing countries. They have been able to survive because they are located in a low-cost labor market or because they have a monopolistic position. This is also the case with many government jobs. The government's retrograde ways produce a low morale among workers and a very inefficient structure. Eventually, new competitors come in, labor wages equalize, or governments restructure. Those organizations that remain like Crummyworks are doomed to become history.

You may be familiar with Okworks.

The second organization I want you to imagine is Okworks, Inc. This is an organization that probably resembles more closely a "good job" for most of us. Okworks has the classic corporate America model. People in Okworks are professional, educated, and somewhat progressive. They say good morning and good evening, and celebrate colleagues' birthdays.

At Okworks, although people don't need a permit to leave the office, a manager, who normally oversees about four base-level workers, keeps an eye on the worker, making sure that he is spending the necessary amount of time at the office and that he is working during that time. A good manager at Okworks is hands-off and becomes involved only when necessary.

Managers pride themselves on treating workers well. They thank workers for their efforts and sometimes allow them to rate managers and their management skills. Workers are able to do their jobs with certain independence, but still, when issues arise, managers jump in to control the situation and make proper decisions. This is, of course, to make sure the company achieves the best result. Often managers get involved when base-level workers from different functional units cannot find a suitable agreement. The issue moves higher in the hierarchy until it finds an appropriate compromise between functions.

Don't get me wrong; in general, managers and executives at Okworks are brilliant. These leaders exude security, are charismatic, and have a huge drive. They surround themselves with people who value and admire their outstanding capacity and are able to execute their initiatives as they need.

Information at Okworks is often shared to involve workers with the company's efforts. One example of this is the quarterly financial presentation of the CEO. She says things like, "We need to reduce expenditures, while increasing productivity," or "Every employee is an asset, which is why we have decided not to lay off anyone this quarter." The senior manager of the function also prepares presentations for her own workers, who will most likely stay in this function for their entire employment with Okworks. This may have something to do with why workers often complain about the ridiculous demands of other functions or foreign offices.

Different personalities seem to interact in Okworks and form small packs of people with their own little environments. While most workers do their job in an okay professional way, there are some who work really hard. These are the ambitious folks, often graduating from top MBA programs. These folks are well-dressed and tend to work much longer hours than others. These are the fast-paced characters, the stars, the aspiring managers-to-be. They feel that the rest of the employees aren't motivated or sufficiently smart. They believe they can make the organization work with 30% of workers if they were like them: active, practical, progressive, and efficient. Some of the star individuals keep escalating functions and acquiring responsibilities, but many of them eventually suffer burnout, joining the pack of typical workers.

Okworks has made sure that there is a comprehensive database for manuals and regulations, which attempt to regulate internal behavior and conduct. These manuals describe what acceptable behavior is and describe what is considered to be out-of-line behavior. Job descriptions establish the responsibilities of a position, and a periodical evaluation by the workers' manager takes place to measure the workers' performance and compare it with the job description.

Innovation at Okworks is highly determined by management. From strategic analysis, management determines the viability and expected benefits of certain projects. Even when projects come from the bottom, they must still pass through several management approval gates to gather the necessary funding. Often when management decides to incursion into certain business area, they do so only by acquiring other companies.

Okworks has a mission that is similar to this: "Okworks and its employees strive to operate a profitable and successful company fostering values of excellence and quality at all times." This mission statement appears as a screen saver in every computer at Okworks. People tend to believe that while the company makes money, the mission is being fulfilled. Okworks takes pride in positively affecting the communities in which it operates. The last few years, it has matched employee donations for disaster relief assistance for events such as the Japanese tsunami or the Haitian earthquake.

Okworks is really not a bad organization, except that it often fails to yield the desired results and causes certain problems. Some people get really stressed out, others aren't engaged, and others feel alienated and not quite at home. Okworks is designed to exhaust resources, be they natural or human, and is focused on achieving business results in the short term. In fact, Okworks will eventually dispose of a large chunk of workers who age past their youth.

Goodworks is getting close to a Driven Organization.

The third organization I'd like you to imagine is Goodworks, Inc. When you visit Goodworks, you quickly realize that instead of polite smiles, there seem to be actual laughs. As you walk around, you may see a couple of workers playing ping-pong at 10:30 am and another fixing his bicycle. There is a lot of informal chatting everywhere. It is only through careful listening to their conversations that you see that they are actively having discussions and making agreements about work issues.

Today happens to be Ron's birthday. Because he doesn't care for cake and celebrations, his colleagues are not throwing him a party... at work, that is. They are having a small gathering at Ron's house with lemon pie. Workers are always looking for excuses to hang out together and tend to spend the majority of their social time with other workers from Goodworks.

When you attend a meeting in Goodworks, you see that everyone participates actively. There isn't one person who dominates the discussion. The contribution of each person is expected. Looking at the participants of the meeting, it isn't obvious who the managers are. No one has a commanding tone. Nobody is looking at other people, waiting for them to make the final decision. Workers seem to be friends, instead of bosses or subordinates.

Still, managers are consulted about difficult issues, not so much because the org chart says so, but because they often bring a wise perspective that helps the team move forward. Managers at Goodworks play the roles of facilitators and experts, but decisions are made by the teams. Management does make sure that employees understand the important aspects of the business. It isn't rare to see a new worker spending eight weeks working side by side with one or two managers.

At Goodworks, functional boundaries are soft, and people seem to move to different positions quite frequently. Offices are designed so that workers have ample opportunity to interact with many others. In addition, they often interact in the intranet social network application that brings them even closer. These foster great relationships that help solve problems in short order.

Workers believe their coming to work does benefit the world. Goodworks exists for two purposes: to bring forth a great product and to make sure their organization improves the lives of human beings. Each worker feels responsible for fulfilling these two purposes. They have distilled values from the company to guide their daily decisions. This way, they have avoided using rules and regulations.

When a worker has an idea, it is easy to get others to form a team and study it. Others provide assistance and attempt to get the most information without spending any funds. The value of the idea speaks for itself, notwithstanding who the originator is. Eventually, when these projects need funds for experimentation and pilots, the projects are evaluated by a committee of workers and managers.

Workers at Goodworks feel they are special, not because when Goodworks posts a job, it receives hundreds of applications or because they beat the market by a mile, but simple because they feel the best at Goodworks. Here, they have many friends and a great time. Workers are focused on protecting their organization as much as possible and want to be part of its success. It would be disastrous for them if it went away.

Goodworks resembles the environment of the most progressive organizations (or, I should say, the ones with the most common sense). These organizations have beaten the market considerably by most measures, including profitability and employee satisfaction. Although there is not a perfect example, there are several companies that are attempting to play in the realm of Goodworks. I refer to companies such as Semco (a Brazilian producer of a variety of industrial products), Zappos (the biggest online shoe retailer), New Belgium Brewing (the third-largest craft brewery in the United States), Whole Foods Market (the largest retailer of natural and organic products), Southwest (the largest U.S. airline by number of passengers), JetBlue (a fun, low-cost airline), Starbucks (the largest coffeehouse company in the world), Google (the largest provider of Internet-based services), Davita (a Fortune 400 provider of dialysis services), Great Harvest (producer and retailer of bread products), and Guayaki (a leading producer of yerba mate tea).

It's clear that workers at Goodworks (a.k.a. a Driven Organization) are capable of amazing performance, they outperform the market, they have a great brand with a large following, and they impact the world in a positive way. But how do we go about creating such organization? What are the foundations behind it? To answer these questions, we must first have a clear understanding of the worker behind the uniform; of the human being who shows up at the company's door every day. What does he want? What does he need? How does work relate to it? These are questions we'll answer in the next chapter.

"There are two ways of being creative. One can sing and dance. Or one can create an environment in which singers and dancers flourish." Warren G. Bennis.

The Driven Organization

Part II: Our Human Needs.

If we are to design a superb workplace, if we are to construct an organization in which its practices and objectives echo in the heart of its workers, we must first make sure we understand them. What do these workers need to be happy and satisfied? What do they need to be engaged with their everyday work?

In this part, we take a look at the human being behind the worker. We attempt to understand how our needs motivate us. We'll see the effect of these wants and needs in our every decision, our society, our work, and our lives.

The Driven Organization

Chapter 7:

What Do We Need to Be Happy, Engaged, and Productive?

"A table, a chair, a bowl of fruit and a violin; what else does a man need to be happy?" Albert Einstein.

What do we need to be happy, engaged, and productive?

This may be the question that every psychologist, philosopher, and thinker has pondered. One way or another, possibly every human being has tried to answer it. We all have an idea of some kind of answer when we are faced with the multiple decisions that affect us. Perhaps the question is underneath our choice of girlfriend or boyfriend, of profession, and even of something as banal as choosing our breakfast or the movie to watch at the cinema.

Satisfied, happy, fulfilled, engaged... Do these things go together? It seems the happy employee usually enjoys his work. The highly productive person tends to be happy and satisfied. We've seen that folks who have fun are able to keep a high level of productivity for a longer period of time. But, what causes one or the other? What makes an employee happy? In this chapter, we strive to get a brief journey through what we want and what we need in life. We attempt to get a glimpse of what motivates us, what fulfills us, and in what order. We may learn why some folks manage to have a fuller life than others. At the end of the chapter, you may have one or two more tools to answer the question posted above.

What we do at work has to play a large role in our lives. To start, it is the activity that uses the majority of our available time. Directly or indirectly, it determines how much money we have, how we spend our days, which kind of friends we have, what we achieve in life, and what we learn. Whether we want it or not, work plays an enormous role in making us satisfied, happy, and fulfilled with our lives. This book is about businesses and workers, but in order for us to understand the worker, we must understand the human being behind it. When we do so, we may know what we need to achieve our entire potential and how to help other workers do so, as well.

Maslow's Pyramid is a great tool to understand our human needs.

Abraham Maslow proposed a theory of human motivation that is one of the most influential works on the subject.[1] You may have heard about "Maslow's pyramid," the "Pyramid of needs," or the "Hierarchy of needs;" all graphic representations of Maslow's theory, which he developed with extensive clinical observations. The theory has kept its ground throughout its seven decades of existence.

As opposed to Freud and other prominent psychologists who focused on the ill and troubled, Maslow used the healthiest and most successful people in his studies. Some of these were Albert Einstein, regarded as the father of modern physics; Jane Addams, the first woman to receive the Nobel peace prize; Eleanor Roosevelt, the first lady who was an important civil rights activist; Frederick Douglass, a significant abolitionist; and Abraham Lincoln, the U.S. president who led the country through the civil war. We will start our journey to understand human needs with Maslow's theory.

If you have not seen a Maslow's hierarchy of needs, imagine a pyramid composed of eight horizontal levels, where the one on top is always smaller than the previous one. Each level represents a set of needs. The size of the level refers to the attention we put on this set of needs.

The most complete version of the Pyramid of Maslow

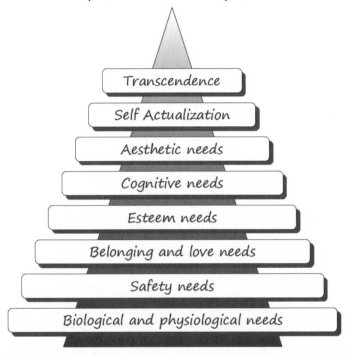

The original theory had only five sets of needs, but Maslow revised and strengthened his theory all the way to the end of his life. In fact, some of his latest thinking was published after his death. This evolution is understandable because it reflects the continuous learning of this brilliant student of man. However, the unintended consequence is that the most complete version of his work is not what is commonly known. I attempted to use in this book what I found is the latest and most complete thinking of Abraham Maslow: a hierarchy of needs composed of eight sets or levels. I believe that Maslow would be satisfied with how it is described and depicted here.[2]

The first four levels of the pyramid are the deficiency needs.

Human beings are complex entities who have several competing needs at any given time, but in general there are some needs that must be satisfied first due to their pressing nature. Maslow called the first four sets of needs (or pyramid levels) "deficiency needs." When the individual feels a deficiency need that lacks fulfillment, he focuses his attention on fulfilling that need first. When this is done, the previously deficient need stops being a motivator for the individual, and other needs, higher in the pyramid, become new motivators. The first four sets of needs are physiological, safety, belongingness and love, and esteem needs.

At the bottom or base level, we find physiological needs, such as hunger, shelter, and other bodily needs. Maslow said that a person who is suffering from hunger, for example (and we are talking real hunger, not a midnight desire for cheesecake), will not think of anything else other than food. This dangerously hungry person will dream, think, and become emotional about food. For this person, Utopia is a place that primarily has an abundance of food. We rarely see somebody with such focus because for most of us it is rare to find someone suffering from extreme hunger. In this first level, we find shelter and health, too. When a person loses his health, he suffers a tremendous setback that most often takes precedence over anything else in life. Most of us would dedicate ourselves to solve our health concerns before continuing building our empires, learning about new ways to measure fluid dynamics, or looking for a lover.

Once the hungry person is satisfied with a regular supply of food, shelter, and the other bodily needs, he may find himself in need of something else. This *something else* refers to the second level, or safety needs. These needs refer to security, stability, protection, order, law, and freedom from fear and chaos. This may explain why in violent neighborhoods, there is less interest for learning and enterprising, and for other less-pressing needs.

> A Detroit woman interviewed on the radio said, "I was told I'm not eating right for my diabetes, but how can I be concerned about it when I am constantly ducking down for bullets?"

The same dynamic applies all along: after the belly is full, and she is not running constantly for her life, she will want to have friends, to have a partner, and even a family. This new set of desires is the third level, which Maslow called "belongingness and love" needs. Maslow comments that the need to belong, to be part of a group, is so strong that people sometimes develop artificial means to achieve that objective. He mentions youth rebellious groups that, driven by the profound hunger for group feelings, for contact, for real togetherness, and to feel a bond among themselves, often find common enemies in the face of other gangs, older generations, and people with different behaviors.

The fourth level is esteem needs, which comprise self-esteem and esteem from others. Self-esteem is the desire for strength, adequacy, achievement, mastery, competence, independence, and freedom. It is to have confidence in the face of the world. It is the "I know I can do it" confidence. Esteem by others refers to the desire for reputation or prestige, status, fame and glory, dominance, recognition, importance, and appreciation.

Remember the discussion in the previous chapter about money? We found out that more money, in absolute terms, doesn't make people happier or any more satisfied with their lives (at least after the basic needs are met). We also learned that more money in relative terms; that is, more money than our peers does result in a good life evaluation. Do you see it now? Money in this case is serving the role of a satisfier for the fourth level. It is bringing prestige, respect, and recognition of achievement. It helps the person feel proud of what he has accomplished. It is acting as the vehicle to show others that we are to be respected, but in truth, it is only one of the many possible vehicles to get respect, status, prestige, importance, recognition, and appreciation.

Maslow says that we should satisfy both, the self-esteem needs and the esteem by others. When there is an imbalance, a deficiency is generated. This makes me think of singers and actors, who feel little self-worth even when adored by many. Somewhere inside their heads, they attribute their fame and achievements to luck, to their looks that they didn't earn, or to having the right connections in the business. This imbalance may be a key reason why their lives often feel empty and purposeless, even when they are highly successful.

I just heard on the radio the story of a 22-year-old American woman who is the legal guardian of 13 girls in Uganda. She is trying to adopt them. I am sure that she is working in good faith for the benefit of the girls; I would never try to minimize her altruistic intentions. We'll talk about these altruistic needs a bit later in the chapter. However, as she was interviewed on NPR and I heard her having interactions with the girls, I couldn't stop thinking about the level of prestige and respect that she has in their house. She is, in effect, the "Big Mama," respected and adored by the girls, and most probably deservedly so.[3]

Consider those folks who embark themselves in challenging enterprises that may not necessarily reward them with esteem by others, but that may help them with self-esteem. Consider mountain climbers, sailors, Ironman athletes, and many other sportsmen who will never be famous, but work extremely hard to prove to themselves how capable they are.

The upper four levels of the pyramid are the growth needs.

Just as the first four sets of needs were called "deficiency needs," the upper four are called "growth needs." In contrast with the deficiency needs, the growth needs don't go away when they are fulfilled. They become an integral part of the individual and help him keep growing. It is said that an individual who doesn't satisfy needs beyond the deficiency needs engenders a sense of boredom, emptiness, and meaninglessness.[4] We can see this when looking at famous, rich people who have money and friends, are admired for their skills, take pride in what they do, and still feel empty. The upper four needs are the need to know and understand, aesthetic needs, self-actualization needs, and selfless actualization.

"The man who regards his life as meaningless is not merely unhappy but hardly fit to live.[5]" Albert Einstein.

The fifth level is the need to know and understand. It refers to the natural curiosity, desire to learn, to experiment that all humans have. It is about acquiring knowledge and systematizing the universe. This need to know and understand comprises our attraction to the chaotic, unorganized, and unexplained.

Harry F. Harlow proved that even monkeys have a natural desire to experiment and learn that isn't motivated by external rewards at all. Harlow proved that monkeys enjoyed solving puzzles, especially when they weren't offered food as a reward for solving them.[6]

This set of needs explains the Einsteins, Galileos, Newtons, Darwins, Da Vincis, and all other researchers, thinkers, and philosophers of the world. Thanks to this need, we have all the scientific and technological advances that afford us to have our modern life. Maslow says that the healthy individual is always attracted to the unknown or unexplained. Cynicism, low morale, loss of capacity, submission, and lack of initiative are some of the consequences of not having this set of needs met.

Consider the many workplaces in which workers are supposed to do their job without any capacity to learn. Imagine receiving the order, filling the documentation, filing it, sending an e-mail to the production department, invoicing, and performing many other dull activities hour after hour, day after day. If this employee is not learning something after work, after a few years, he will show some of the behaviors that Maslow anticipated: cynicism, lack of initiative, and lack of capacity. Maslow says that we cannot be taught to be curious; we naturally are. He says that we can be taught not to be curious, as we just described.

The sixth level is aesthetic needs, which refer to the need for beauty, order, symmetry, closure, completion of an act, system, and structure. When I first read about these aesthetic needs, I almost disregarded them as unimportant, but I later realized how they are related with many of the activities we perform. These needs may explain why we paint our houses, why we mow our lawns, why we wash our cars, and why we like to vacation on the mountains. They explain why we feel somewhat distraught when our house is a mess and why we feel better in a clean, nice-looking office. They also explain why design has become such a vital part of our lives, touching almost every product we use. But they still go further than that! By fostering systems and structure, the aesthetic needs help us learn, understand, communicate, and produce better. They help us build over previous thoughts, raising the overall level of thought. They help us improve over previous technologies and developments.

Those who have studied music can attest to the importance of structure just as much as those who design buildings. This set of needs is probably related to the mathematical beauty that nature offers, shown in simple equations or ratios that repeat everywhere.

One example is the golden ratio that is often used in visual arts, music, and architecture, and is seen in nature. Adolf Seizing found the golden ratio expressed in the arrangement of branches of plants and veins in leaves, in the skeletons of animals, in the proportions of chemical compounds, and in the geometry of crystals.[7] Volkmar and Harald Weiss have concluded from their research that the golden ratio underlies the clock cycle of brain waves. This area must still be studied in order for us to understand it and make sense of it. There are many questions that still need to be answered, but today we recognize that nature is highly structured, with order, symmetry, and beauty everywhere; characteristics for which we look in our lives.[8]

The need to self-actualize is about reaching our entire potential.

The seventh level refers to the need for self-actualization or self-fulfillment. It refers to the need of the individual to reach his entire potential in life. Maslow called it "fulfillment of mission," but colloquially we refer to it as "vocation" or "call." Meeting this need entails doing what we must do and to the maximum level to which we are capable. The path to fulfill this need forces us to understand and accept who we are. This path is also a constant trend toward the integration or unity within the person through all the activities she performs; she may be a professor, parent, and community organizer; or perhaps a football coach, engineer, and amateur race car driver.

When going for a walk in the evening, we sometimes run into a house with a perfect front garden. A multitude of flowers and plants were set up in precise and beautiful arrangements. It's easy to see that this garden took many, many hours of work. The person living in this house may be using this activity to satisfy some of his self-actualization needs. Working in the garden provides for him a level of enjoyment, spending hours with no concern for anything else.

Self-actualization needs encompass creativity in whichever form the individual expresses it. The musician will make delightful music, the painter will paint extraordinary scenes, the engineer will develop creative solutions and outstanding products, and the businessman will find creative business propositions. To self-actualize, the individual chooses what to do and how to do it.

We can see self-actualization from the enabler perspective: What needs to be there in order for us to satisfy this need? If we believe that humans are naturally active, growth-oriented organisms, we need only to have the autonomy necessary to pursue the activities that help us grow. *Autonomy* refers to the capacity to choose what to do, how to do it, when to do it, and with whom.[9] Autonomy will result in creativity, independence, and self-reliance, all of which are needed to achieve self-actualization.

The need to self-actualize also compels us to make use of all our talents and abilities, and to advance and improve them. This need is the internal fight to reach our entire potential. It is an ongoing process, in which each activity, every time, takes us closer to where we need to go. We may be able to get to a state of exhilaration and a deep sense of enjoyment when our bodies or minds are stretched to their limits by attempting to accomplish something that is difficult and worthwhile. We are working exceptionally hard, but we don't get tired, and afterward we are even more energized. This is what psychology professor Mihaly Cziksentmihalyi described as "Flow," a concept that has become widely known throughout the world.

Most of us have experienced the state of Flow a few times in our lives, but although we all have the capacity to reach it, certain individuals (those closer to self-actualization) achieve it constantly. In a state of flow, the mind or body works at a much higher level of performance. There is complete focus on the activity, and the person, in effect, turns off everything happening around him. Those who can do it at work not only feel great but their output is also much better than that of regular workers, both in quantity and quality.

The selfless-actualization needs place the focus outside of us.

At the end of his life, Maslow added selfless actualization (as opposed to self-actualization), also called self-transcendence to the top of the pyramid.[10] This set of needs has two parts. First, it refers to the need to work for the benefit and welfare of others; second, it comprehends our spiritual needs, the needs that refer to a creator or a divine power. I won't go into this latter one; I will only point out that throughout history, people from all cultures and regions of the world, exhibit an imperative need to believe that there exists an intelligent force underlying what takes place in this world.

The first part, the need to work toward the benefit of others, reminds us of the altruistic love that human beings sometimes exhibit. It comprehends the various forms of humanitarian and selfless actions such as those of Mother Theresa, Gandhi, and Martin Luther King. It is the need to help others, to work toward something greater than oneself and not for our own benefit, and it takes place here on this earth and now in this life.

"But I have no aspirations or need to be like Mother Theresa," you may say. Well, some of us are working on lower levels of the pyramid, and some of us work in simpler ways to satisfy these needs, but all of us have selfless actualization needs. Remember when somebody has asked you for help and you have given, with no ulterior motive or agenda, as much help as you were able to give? Why did you do that? Did you feel satisfied afterward?

If you think that only those like Mother Theresa have this need, how do you explain why Bill and Melinda Gates donated the majority of their fortune? Or that Warren Buffet, George Lucas, Mark Zuckerberg, and many others have promised to give away billions?[11] I know what you will say, "They have so much that they can give billions away without even noticing it!" You may be right, but they don't have to do it, do they? And how do you explain that on any one day, more than 27,000 individuals provide assistance to others in Doctors without borders,[12] or that in 2010 about 63 million Americans performed volunteer work at a rate of 52 hours per person?[13] This is more than one in every four American adults. If almost everyone is busy with their lives, and there are so many ways to use that one week's worth of time productively, why would so many people dedicate it to work for other people who are frequently strangers?

"The true meaning of life is to be found in the world rather than within man or his own psyche." Viktor Frankl, existentialist, humanist, and author of *Man's Search for Meaning.*

Bruce Headey and team, from the University of Melbourne in Australia, found a relationship between altruistic behavior and happiness. They led a 25-year effort surveying between 3,000 and 60,000 people per year to understand the factors that improve people's satisfaction and happiness. They found that people whose annual survey responses changed to place a higher priority on altruistic behaviors and family goals were rewarded with a long-term increase in life satisfaction. Those who prioritized career and material success experienced a corresponding lasting decline.[14]

Do an experiment for me. It'll be easy. Next time you are about to pass through a toll booth, see how you feel. You may be preoccupied with getting somewhere on time or with work pressures. When you get to the toll both, pay for your vehicle and pay for the next vehicle coming after you, without even looking back. When you do so, see how you feel.

Another experiment is at work. Find something you like or appreciate about one of your coworkers. Observe them carefully, looking for something that is especially commendable. Once you find it, tell them about it. Perhaps you might say, "You know, Tom, I like the fact that you always try to include everyone in our meetings"; or "Susie, your running shows in your healthy skin color." These are simple, selfless purposeful actions, but even these, as plain as they may be, are capable of affecting our mood for the better.

If you still don't believe how much importance we place on how we affect others, imagine the following. You are a tailor. Your business has been somewhat soft, but today at 8:00 am, John comes to your workshop and orders a shirt, a good solid shirt. You'll finish it today by 5:00 pm. Later that day, he comes to pick it up. He checks it out and pays you. He tells you that the shirt is fine. Then, in front of you, he takes out some scissors from his pocket and cuts the shirt into little pieces. Then he asks you if he can borrow your trash can. You naturally ask him what was wrong with the shirt. He answers that nothing was wrong, that you did a fine job. You don't understand what just happened, but let it go. He must have had some reason to do that.

The following day, John comes at 8:00 am again, and orders the same shirt. You really don't understand what's going on, but this is your job, so you do it. At 5:00 pm, he comes to pick it up. He checks it out, pays for it, and performs the same scissors deed. You are less happy, but you let it go again. John repeats the same routine for a couple more days, until you are downright pissed off and respectfully tell him to take his business somewhere else. You prefer to forgo the income you receive from his business than to continue with this dynamic.

They question is why. Why would you feel upset if you are getting paid and you do an adequate job? Even John mentioned that the shirt was fine. How different would you feel if you delivered the shirt and then later on, in a gathering of important people, you see that your customer is one of the speakers and is wearing the shirt you made for him? He tells you that because you made the shirt with detailed care, he feels special every time he uses it, which has boosted his confidence and helped him perform well at his business events. It doesn't feel the same. This time, you like it. The truth is that we want (and need) our job to have a positive impact on the lives of others.

In our companies, how do we expect that workers are satisfied when they work on projects that don't go anywhere? I have seen widespread frustration within entire functional departments of large corporations with thousands of people because decisions are made arbitrarily.

> Planning is the function at GM that helps determine which type of product should be developed, which characteristic it should have, and for which market. To do so, it needs to understand consumer preferences, competition, capacity, product profitability, and more. I witnessed that GM leadership made decisions on which product to build, not based on Planning's recommendations, but on a full-size vehicle model depicting a gorgeous but unnecessary vehicle. Notwithstanding how many reasons Planning had not to build that model, it was just so beautiful and had to be built. This was the case with the Chevy SSR, Pontiac Solstice, and Chevy Camaro. Instead of building these premium, niche, and often unprofitable vehicles, Planning's recommendation was to heavily invest on small and medium-size cars to successfully compete with the Corolla/Civic and Camry/Accord, which belonged to vehicle segments where the majority of Americans resided. The effect of this "what-are-we-doing-here-then?" feeling was dissatisfaction and tiredness across a worldwide functional department composed of some of the most brilliant folks I have ever met.

Understanding happiness with Pleasure, Passion, and Purpose.

Two researchers, Stephen Lehmann and Stefan Klein, developed a simple formula to achieve true happiness.[15] The "Magic triangle," as they described it, is composed of three types of happiness: Pleasure, Passion, and Purpose. The first type, Pleasure, comes from eating a chocolate ice cream, enjoying a romantic night with a partner, and driving at 140 mph on the Autobahn. This is the type of happiness that is exhilarating, rock star happiness, but its ephemeral nature makes it difficult to maintain. Even rock stars who have pursued it by using drugs have learned that it cannot be maintained.

The second type of happiness is derived from Passion. It is the pursuit of those activities that take us to the "zone." It is around what Cziksentmihalyi referred to as flow and what Maslow described as self-actualization. This type of happiness is less ephemeral than Pleasure. We can enter such a state often and stay for a while. It is about working on something that seriously grabs us. It is the engineer passionately creating a powerful and robust, yet simple and elegant mechanism or the painter capturing the most beautiful scenery with impressionistic touches.

The third type of happiness comes from Purpose. Finding the way to work for the welfare of others or for something bigger than ourselves is the least ephemeral of all the happiness types. It stays with us and gives us a stable and long-lasting feeling of "good." It's Maslow's top level. It's so powerful because of two reasons. First, it forces us to be less concerned for our own needs, shifting our attention toward the welfare of others. It is as if by focusing our attention on the welfare of others, we forget the needs of our own.

> Let's say you are enjoying a delicious chocolate bar, satisfying a craving (or need) that had been there for a little while. You then realize there are several starving children around you. You would readily, with no further thought, give them the chocolate bar, and perhaps whatever else you've got! You immediately forget the craving you had.

When we forget our needs, we have fewer reasons to be unhappy. We can more readily appreciate the goodness of life and be happy.

The second reason why Purpose is so powerful is because we naturally enjoy making others feel good. It's what you feel when you hear the sincere "thank you" given by the stranded driver appreciating that you went out of your way to help him. It's also what you feel when you see the 129 jumps your daughter does after learning she will go to Disney World this year. It's the feeling of seeing the exuberant happiness of your dog after receiving a delicious meaty treat.

When we build our life with a structure based on Purpose, working for something in which we believe, then we add Passion, doing the type of work that makes us excited; and to top it off, we have occasional Pleasure, such as eating chocolate or receiving a handshake from a good friend, we are guaranteed to have a much more fulfilling life. I feel that I understand Mother Theresa more and more.

The seventh and eighth levels are the most significant ones of Maslow's hierarchy. This is where all the other needs converge. It is often believed that these two levels are interrelated and represent the highest goals in life. Maslow says that as one becomes more self-actualized and self-transcendent, one becomes wiser and automatically knows what to do in a wide variety of situations.

Maslow saw that those who are working on the growth needs, the upper four levels, seem to have greater longevity, less disease, better sleep and appetite, and so on. For sure, the satisfiers for the upper needs bring more profound happiness, serenity, and richness of the inner life. Maslow believed that the self-actualized person is characterized by a superior perception of reality, increased acceptance of self and others, spontaneity, autonomy, fresh appreciation, kindness, ethics, humor, creativity, and stronger and truer individualism. Of course, we must not forget that in order for the individual to work on the growth needs, the deficiency needs must be fulfilled first.

"This is all great theory, but I want to use it in reality, to understand people better. I want to see it applied to see how good the theory is," you may say. I agree. Let's take our Maslow's pyramid for a ride and see whether it holds its ground with complex problems. We will use it at work to understand why a customer care representative is happier in India than in the United States. We will use it at home and we will see how we can explain generational preferences with it. We will do so in the next chapter.

"To fulfill a dream, to be allowed to sweat over lonely labor, to

be given a chance to create, is the meat and potatoes of life. The money is the gravy." Bette Davis.

1   Maslow, Abraham H. "A Theory of Human Motivation" (originally published in *Psychological Review*, 50(4), pp. 370—396, 1943.

2   Maslow, Abraham H. "A Theory of Human Motivation" (originally published in *Psychological Review*, 50(4), pp. 370—396, 1943.

    Maslow, Abraham H. *Motivation and Personality*. New York: Harper, 1954.

    Maslow, Abraham H. *The Farther Reaches of Human Nature*. New York: Viking Press, 1971.

    Maslow, Abraham H., & Lowery, R. (Eds.). *Toward a Psychology of Being*. 3rd ed. New York: Wiley & Sons, 1998.

3   Report by Bonnie Allen. "In Uganda, American Becomes Foster Mom To 13 Girls." *National Public Radio,* July 9, 2011.

4   Csikszentmihalyi, Mihaly. *Beyond Boredom and Anxiety,* 2000.

5   Assagioli, Robert. *The Act of Will*. New York: Arkana, p.112, 1973/1992.

6   Harlow, Harry F., Harlow, Markaret K., & Meyer, Donald R. "Learning Motivated by a Manipulation Drive." *Journal of Experimental Psychology,* 40(2), 228—234, April 1950.

7   Padovan, Richard. *Proportion*. Taylor & Francis. pp. 305—306, 1999.

8   Weiss, Volkmar, & Weiss, Harald. "The Golden Mean As Clock Cycle of Brain Waves." *Chaos, Solitons & Fractals* 18(4), pp. 643—652, November, 2003.

9   Deci, Edward L., & Flaste, Richard. *Why We Do What We Do: Understanding Self-Motivation*. Penguin, 1996.

10 Maslow, Abraham H. *The Farther Reaches of Human Nature*. New York: Viking Press, 1971.

11 Information from givingpledge.org.

12 Doctors Without Borders/Medecins sans frontieres. *What Is Doctors Without Borders/Medecins Sans Frontieres?* MSF Fact Sheet.

13 U.S. Department of Labor, Bureau of Labor Statistics. *Volunteering in the United States, 2010*. Economic News release, 2011.

14 Headey, Bruce, Muffels, Ruud, & Wagner, Gert G. "Long-running German panel survey shows that personal and economic choices, not just genes, matter for happiness." *Proceedings of the National Academy of Sciences*. DOI: 10.1073/pnas.1008612107, 2010.

15 Lehmann, Stephen, & Klein, Stefan. *The Science of Happiness: How Our Brains Make Us Happy—And What We Can Do to Get Happier.* Tra ed. Da Capo Press, March 29, 2006.

The Driven Organization

Chapter 8:

And This Means What, Exactly?

I don't believe there are perfect explanations for human motivation. No explanation encompasses every single human being or explains our every need. Frameworks that attempt to be that comprehensive can become so complex they are not understandable. I like Maslow's theory because it is a solid, clear, and practical framework for understanding what is most relevant for human beings. It helps us understand how our motivation evolves at the individual level and also at the level of society.

> In previous times, most people were concerned with fulfilling the lower levels of the pyramid. Food wasn't easy to get and people often struggled to get enough of it. Many classical books of the time, such as *Lazarillo de Tormes*, or *Oliver Twist* revolve around food because it was a central issue of the time. By contrast, in today's modern life, we rarely see written books that revolve around food. Even when the characters of a film, book, or TV series may face hunger, the writers often choose to emphasize other struggles beyond the simple need to eat. Think, for example, about the *Lost* TV series.

Our generation thinks differently than our parents do.

In general, what satisfied our grandparents may not be enough for us. Perhaps our grandparents were happy having a job that allowed them to bring home enough money to eat well, to have a decent place, and to live in the company of their wife and children. Remember, this is the Greatest Generation that saw two major international conflicts and a long financial crisis. The whole focus of the generation was on the first levels: physiological, safety and security, and friends and family needs. It meant security in your country, a safe place to live, enough food to eat, a loving wife, and a good family at home. Life was simple but good.

This, however, didn't satisfy our parents. They strove to go further. Our parents went looking for the fourth level. They looked for power and respect from their peers. We can see in films of the time that this Baby Boomer generation began to pay much more attention to what others thought of them. The term "popular" acquires significance. This generation fought hard to get some standing in the world.

Many of the Baby Boomers saw in money and power the capacity to fulfill the fourth level, which is the reason why they are often described as the generation that lived to work. They were great builders who built international mega-corporations and went to the moon.

This search for recognition and respect can also be observed in the search for equal rights of women, who fought in masses for a standing equal to their male counterparts in family, at work, and in social environments. More women attended universities, traveled, and took part in organizations dominated by men than ever before. Women created a way of life that allowed them to explore their entire capacity and surrounded themselves with products that supported them in their fight, such as contraception products, which diminished the risk and disadvantages of unwanted pregnancies, household cleaning products, ready-to-eat foods, and microwaves, which promised to reduce the time women spent tied to the kitchen.

Even the civil rights movement has a large component of breaking down the institutions that blocked minorities and disadvantaged groups from achieving their own standing in life. It was a time of rebellion and the many institutions—religious, governmental, corporate, and social— were in the way of Baby Boomers. They fought enthusiastically to break down the "establishment."

Remember that we are making generic observations. In truth, there are many people in every generation who work on the upper parts of the Maslow's pyramid. We must also notice that as a generation becomes older and experienced, more of its members tend to seek to fulfill higher levels of the pyramid.

Things keep changing for Gen X and Gen Y. At least in the United States, these folks grew up in a world in which everyone had a house, a couple of cars, a few TVs, and at least one video game console. In regular suburban neighborhoods, nobody was starving or fighting for their lives, and almost everyone seemed to belong to a large middle class. The first two levels were of absolutely no concern to them. Most had access to friends and family, and this generation understood that the esteem needs could be achieved in many different ways beyond merely money and power.

Because no one was struggling with money in a significant way, it became less relevant as a differentiating tool to get respect. Gen X is the first generation for whom the upper needs, or growth needs, are, in practical terms, within reach for an entire generation, not only for a few privileged individuals.

The needs for knowledge and understanding, aesthetic, self-actualization, and self-transcendence begin to play a vital role in daily life for Gen X and Gen Y. Gen X is the first one to ask in a significant way, "What do I want to do and how do I want to do it?" This is the generation of constant change, of trying different professions, of voluntarily moving to different places. Thanks to this generation, there is an explosion of activities led by creativity, diversity, beauty, and other self-actualization efforts.

For example, let's see how sports have changed. In previous generations, American people used to practice the classic American sports such as baseball, basketball, swimming, and football. The newer generations practice these and many more. Just to name a few that are seriously played: sky surfing, hang gliding, air-snowboarding, snowboarding, river-boarding, mountain biking, BMX, bungee jumping, radio control racing, demolition derby, drag boat racing, freestyle motocross, drifting, ultimate Frisbee, and wave jumping. This is a very short list compared with the hundreds that Wikipedia produces when prompted for "list of sports."

The newer generations, and especially Gen Y, is statistically much more inclined to search for jobs where they can be creative; where their work is meaningful and impacts their world. Gen Y also puts much less emphasis on accumulating traditional things like homes, cars, and years of service at a company; instead, it puts much more energy into acquiring experiences, such as traveling; working abroad; and living different majors, jobs, and professions.

Gen Y is the first generation that finds it unimportant to distinguish between nationalities and races. Distance and remoteness become obstacles with little relevance as Gen Y finds it easy to establish and maintain close relationships across the world. Gen Y also easily understands the idea of "shared fate" or "linked fate," which purports the notion that what happens in Siberia has some kind of an impact in New York.

These generational differences may explain why our parents have often had difficulty understanding some of our decisions, and why sometimes we fail to understand our children. Our values, driven by what we think matters in life, are different.

We can also understand regional differences.

Maslow's pyramid may be also used to explain why in the United States, people struggle with certain professions that are perfectly respected in other countries. Consider the job of a phone customer service representative. With only a few exceptions, this job in the United States is normally scripted, merits little power or respect, and pays a small salary. For folks in the United States who may be working on the upper four needs, this job will not be fulfilling. Even those in the United States working on the third or fourth levels will find it to be lacking. Now let us imagine a developing country, in which such a job pays enough money to fulfill the first two levels, food and safety, and allows the individual to have a family. His job may command respect because it is a serious, respectable job, which fulfills the fourth level, too.

In a country in which most are still on the lower part of the deficiency needs, such a job may be pretty decent and result in a satisfied worker. The same job leads to entirely different levels of satisfaction, depending on where the focus on the pyramid is for the person performing it.

Do you remember that those who are satisfied and engaged in their work are statistically much more productive? The developing-country customer service rep will be, not only less expensive for the company, but more productive, too. This assumes everything else is equal, which is often not the case; the American worker may have more formal or informal education, experiences, and understanding of American customers.

What does this say of the business competitiveness of the United States? If we are doing the same jobs that folks at other countries are doing, we may not be competitive. They may perform better, even after adjusting for salary differences and working conditions. However, the U.S. advantage lies exactly in the other extreme. Most people in the United States need (let me emphasize the word *need*) opportunities to fulfill their upper needs. These folks will be satisfied and engaged if business owners and employers provide them with opportunities to do so. They want to be creative, achieve results, be part of a bigger effort, and have an impact on their profession, their companies, and their communities.

Leaving our needs out isn't professionalism, but lack of authenticity.

In modern America, we tend to leave a substantial chunk of our sack of needs, desires, goals and quirks outside of the company. Entering the company, we become professional, say "Good morning," do our job the best we can, say "Good night," and leave. Some of us are black, Latino, white, tall, short, chubby, skinny, Ivy-League educated, community-college educated, idealist, realist, guitar player, dancer, mountain biker, home beer maker, video game star, quilt maker, kombucha brewer, organic farmer, specialty cook, etc., but we leave all of this outside of the company. Inside, we put our suit of the engineer, manager, admin, accountant, doctor, or whatever it is we do. It is as if we segment our needs and personality in two sets: at work and out of work. With the objective of having work environments free of prejudice and racism, we have asked our workers to leave all their personal characteristics outside of the professional environment. We don't ask; they don't tell. Sound familiar?

This compartmentalization has two problems. First, it doesn't work because our prejudices, beliefs, goals, and so on go with us wherever we go, even when we don't realize it. Project Implicit,[1] composed of researchers at Harvard University, Washington University, and University of Virginia, is an excellent way to find out our hidden biases, attitudes, and stereotypes. By presenting associations between good and bad, black and white, young and old, thin and fat, and several more; and by measuring our reaction time to classify them in the right bucket, they have an amazingly effective way to determine how much bias we have. For example, Project Implicit has found that 75 to 80% of self-reported Whites and Asians show an implicit preference for whites versus blacks. They also found that the big majority of people who showed a preference believe they don't have any bias at all. Unfortunately, most of us do, and the Project Implicit researchers are able to ferret it out because the biases are always there ready to come out. Not talking about these prejudices doesn't mean that we don't act on them when we hire people, prize good work, choose with whom to hang out, or choose people for promotions.

> Researchers have confirmed our beliefs. A study by Rice University, University of Houston, and George Mason University found that hiding who you are at work is linked with lower levels of job satisfaction,[2] while Canadian researchers found that authenticity at work is linked with well-being.[3]

A better alternative could be to see the problem, recognize it, and treat it. For example, if John grew up in a predominantly white neighborhood, and hasn't had the opportunity to deal with other cultures, wouldn't it be expected that he doesn't feel as relaxed with African American folks as he is with white folks? He is just less familiar with them. In an adult intelligent world, couldn't we get John a "tutor" that takes him into African American life, events, and other opportunities to explore African American incredible cultural richness and warmth?

The second problem, and probably the most significant one, is that by asking people to keep it professional, we miss out on who they are, what they need and want, and what their aspirations are. We miss out on discovering the beliefs, prejudices, desires and needs, and quirks of the workers with whom we perform the biggest activity of our days.

Let's say that John is an environmentalist and organic farmer. He spends some of his free time learning about the environment. On weekends, he likes to go camping to pristine, natural places. He also leads a group of volunteers to restore local state parks, where he has acquired the reputation of a natural restoration guru. As we can see, he is actively working on the upper needs, the growth needs. He learns about the environment, enjoys the beauty of natural places, becomes self-actualized as a restoration expert, and feels great by helping the environment.

His job as an accountant for an appliance producer, however, doesn't have anything to do with his being an environmentalist and organic farmer, with his achievements, or with his dreams and goals. His job pays the bills, but has nothing to do with his upper needs. John spends almost the entire day working to fulfill his financial obligations. At 6:30 pm, he goes home and eats a quick dinner because he happens to have a restoration meeting with a volunteer group in the evening. His family won't see much of John today. He feels guilty. Every day he goes home after 6 pm, to see his children for only a couple of hours. On top of that, he spends one night a week away in these meetings, and some additional time replying to emails for the volunteer organization. Weekends are torn between house cleaning, family stuff, children, wife, and the actual restoration events that happen once a month.

John's wife, Mary, understands the situation and is considering reducing her working schedule in order for the family to stay afloat. However, the partner at the law firm where she works has given her indications that reducing her work schedule isn't a smart career move. On top of that, she has a few upper needs of herself she is pursuing. She is quite involved with a group of sculptors that gather at local sceneries to get inspired. She hasn't been able to do so lately as much as before because her work and the kids absorb all her free time. The family does well economically, and with some restrictions could probably live off of one salary, but John and Mary are concerned that no job is safe with the financial crisis. They feel that their personal activities, as restoration leader and active sculptor, are taking time away from their family and their work responsibilities. Both feel they need those activities to be part of their lives in order for them to feel happy and satisfied. They are torn between these two apparently separated worlds.

Unfortunately, this is the situation most workers face. They spend almost their entire day working, fulfilling the first two sets of needs: money to live and pay the mortgage in a safe city. The unlucky ones go home at 6 or 7 pm, still with six needs to fulfill, but little time left to do it. The luckier ones have some capacity to fulfill more of their needs at work, but doing it is not easy. Most often workers are forced to choose between achieving power and respect at work and having a family, working full time and having a purpose in life, or doing a fulfilling job and achieving financial security.

What if we could fulfill most of our needs at work?

The question is why. Why do our modern productive systems make workers struggle this much to fulfill their needs? Is it not possible to conceive a workplace that allows its workers to fulfill the majority of their needs, from the basic ones such as money for food and shelter, to the needs for self-actualization and self-transcendence?

Continuing with John's example, imagine he finds an organization in which most of the workers are concerned about the environment. The company fosters workshops, camping outings, observation trips, and other similar events. It may be that the organization invests 5% of its workers' time in these activities, but consider the engagement that John feels of being part of such organization. He respects and admires his coworkers, spends time with them, and is their friend. They work together effectively and efficiently. What John finds in this organization is unique. He will work to protect it with all his capacity.

This isn't a utopia, a we-are-all-together, hippie chanting, unreal idea. There are some notable examples of organizations doing what we are talking about here. These organizations outperform the market in every case. I believe it is not only possible to have such a place; it is the natural evolution of our productive systems. We already know that satisfied, engaged, and driven workers produce more and with higher quality than regular workers. We already know that consumers are attempting to develop stronger relationships with the brands they use. We already know that both consumers and workers have needs that must be satisfied, and that workers have a natural desire to be productive and useful. In the next chapters, we will start looking at how we can organize such an enterprise.

You probably have seen how fast businesses are evolving. What used to be outstanding customer service has made its way to many companies and has become "expected" customer service. Great brands of the past used to be those that produced the same product consistently and with solid quality, such as Coca-Cola or Jell-O. These days, leading brands seem to do several more things besides producing a consistent, good quality product. Think of Whole Foods Market, Apple, or Virgin Airlines. Each one of them seeks to establish a strong multi-linked relationship with their customers.

Producing for the sake of producing, disregarding the impact it has on consumers, the environment, or other stakeholders is no longer viable as an acceptable business practice. Businesses are expected to be more connected to the communities in which they operate and the consumers they serve. They are no longer operating in a vacuum, throwing products at "the other side of the wall." What we discuss here today will be the normal way of the future. This is the new business reality.

Maslow coined the term "Eupsychian." It comes from the Greek *Eu* – good (as in euphoria), and *psychian*, mind or soul. The term means of good mind or toward good mind. Maslow used this term to describe an organization or place in which good people work. He said that in this place, "The conditions of work are often good not only for personal fulfillment, but also for the health and prosperity of the organization, as well as for the quantity and quality of the products or services turned out by the organization,... [for] man has a higher nature which is just as 'instinctoid' as his lower nature, and that this higher nature includes the needs for meaningful work, for responsibility, for creativeness, for being fair and just, for doing what is worthwhile and for preferring to do it well."[4]

"*No enterprise can exist for itself alone. It ministers to some great need, it performs some great service, not for itself, but for others; or failing therein, it ceases to be profitable and ceases to exist.*" Calvin Coolidge. American president, 1923 to 1929.

1   Projectimplicit.net

2   Madera, J. M., King, E. B., & Hebl, M. R. "Bringing Social Identity to Work: The Influence of Manifestation and Suppression on Perceived Discrimination, Job Satisfaction, and Turnover Intentions." *Cultural Diversity and Ethnic Minority Psychology* 18(2), pp. 165—70, April 2012.

3   Ménard, Julie, & Brunet, Lec. "Authenticity and Well-Being in the Workplace: A Mediation Model." *Journal of Managerial Psychology* 26(4), pp.331—346, 2011.

4   Maslow, Abraham H. *The Farther Reaches of Human Nature.* New York: Viking Press, pp. 237—238, 1971.

Part III: S.P.A.C.E.S.

We have learned that work is a great vehicle to fulfill several of our needs. We learned that, in fact, work can help us fulfill every level of Maslow's pyramid. Work is that powerful. But how do we make sure that our organization is capable of such great tasks? How do we build a workplace that help each of us reach our maximum potential, providing "things" that we don't even know we are missing? How do we foster a daily gathering of amazing people ready to do great things and have a great time?

We will do so through *SPACES*.

Remember, it doesn't matter what level in the organization you attain or the number of people you direct. You are a significant influencing member who can effect important change in your organization. The seed of a giant Sequoia is only about 4 millimeters long. You are what, 5 ft. 8 in., 5 ft. 11 in.?

Each of the letters of SPACES corresponds to a very important element of our Driven Organization: Salary, Purpose, Autonomy, Competence, Environment, and Strategy. We will study these components in the next few chapters.

It is my firm belief that no matter what we call this new type of workplace and its elements, this type of organization is the future. There is significant pressure toward having organizations that help us do more with our lives, from learning interesting things to creating a positive change in the world.

Years ago, only a few companies understood the importance of customer service; now everyone does. Similarly, the number of companies that understand the need to have engaged, satisfied, and driven workers is increasing exponentially. Just as today's organizations that don't pay attention to customer service fail, those that don't take employee engagement into account will soon do so, too. Unfortunately, even those that care for engaged workers do not necessarily know how to do it. We will learn it in this part.

There was a time when democracy was impossible, when it was only a farfetched dream. But one day, society matured. A few visionaries helped us see that democracy was not only possible but it was also a right for which we had to fight. After most of us believed it, it was just a matter of time for it to become our way of life. In a similar way, we must ask. Is this the right time for SPACES and the Driven Organization (or whatever you want to call it)?

Today, we see the emergence of democratic workplaces, of purpose-driven organizations, of companies focused on the well-being of their workers. We see unhappiness and discontent with the corporation model that used to be so successful. We see corporate greed causing significant negative consequences in every part of the world. We see large corporations with "brilliant" managers who drive their companies to the ground and cause significant financial problems for everyone. We see small organizations that change the world from a garage because of their new ways to solve problems (think Google). All of which makes me believe this is the right time for a new system.

Where did SPACES come from? It comes from years of gathering the findings of scholars, researchers and thinkers in organizational and human psychology, motivation, marketing, and leadership. It comes from observing, interviewing, and studying organizations that do things differently than most, from observing our regular workplaces, and from the firm belief that they can perform better.

Each of the components of SPACES could be implemented by itself and may be quite powerful on its own, but the synergy and reinforcing power they have together increases their effectiveness exponentially.

Let's see what SPACES is about.

Chapter 9:

S Is About Salary.

"All Dancing Deer employees are stakeholders in its profitability and share in the rewards of a well-run, growing company. We believe that if people love what they're doing, it shows in the food. We developed this philosophy from the earliest days when we observed that baking 'angry' would ruin a cake.[1]" Dancing Deer Baking Company.

Salary is important. There's no question about it. It helps us cover the first two levels of Maslow, the physiological and safety and security needs. It allows us to eat and wear clothes. We are able to pay the mortgage for a house in a safe place. But it may also be used to fulfill the fourth set of needs, the esteem needs. Money has traditionally been the easiest, fastest, most visible way to command respect.

In the last few years, it's become less effective as countries have become richer and people have climbed up Maslow's pyramid. Having a lot of money isn't that unusual anymore. There has also been an explosion of activities that can be used to address the esteem needs. Therefore, money commands less respect than before and it's a less effective tool to address these needs.

Even so, as we discussed in Chapter 4, money is still an extremely delicate matter and it can be damaging to the workers' level of engagement and motivation. In fact, nothing else is as powerful to destroy worker engagement as money can be. This begs the question, how do we go about assigning salaries within the company? How do we deal with this matter so that it promotes and never hurts engagement?

Large differences in compensation makes us not feel part of the team.

Let's imagine you are a teller in a bank. You perform your work trying to tend to your customers' and organization's needs. You are professional, responsive, and try to help your customers solve their problems. After work, while you take the bus home, you reflect on your annual compensation of $24,000. This year, the bank has done really well. You are happy there will be a bonus for you. You will receive 3% of your annual salary or about $720. A coworker tells you that the total compensation of your company's CEO will be 70 million dollars. In other words, he is making more than 2,800 times your total compensation. Do you believe that somehow his output is 2,800 times that of yours, that it would take him about 40 minutes to achieve the same output as it takes you to achieve during the whole year? You probably feel that you are not on the same team as he is.

Obviously, the decisions of the CEO affect thousands of people, so his training, experience, and education must be superior. His leadership, common sense, knowledge of the industry, and grasp of the information must be extraordinary. But 2,800 times? Unfortunately, the numbers I am using aren't unusual. A bank teller makes about $24,000, and it isn't unheard that bank executives receive compensation in the tens of millions of dollars.

According to the Bureau of Labor Statistics, in 2010, the median annual wage for bank tellers was $24,100.[2] In contrast, in 2007, total compensation for top executives was (in millions): From Goldman Sachs: Lloyd C. Blankfein, $70.3; David A. Viniar, $58.5; Gary D. Cohn, $72.5; Jon Winkelried, $71.5; Edward C. Forst, $49.1. From Bank of America: Kenneth D. Lewis, $24.8. From JP Morgan Chase: James Dimon, $27.8. From Merrill Lynch: Gregory J. Fleming, $27.4.[3] If you think this happens only with banks, you may like to see the compensation of Tim Cook from Apple at $378 million in 2011 or Philippe P. Dauman from Viacom at $84.5 million in 2010.[4]

Apparently this situation is more common than we expect. The ratio of CEO pay to average worker pay throughout the American business world has wildly widened. In the '60s and '70s, the ratio oscillated between 25 and 35 times. In 2010, the ratio was 243 times, down from a peak of 299 times in 2000.[5] Remember that this ratio includes organizations of all sizes, and not only Fortune 500 companies.

Most workers feel this is unfair. Instead of being inspired by their leaders to feel good about their organization and its objectives, they often feel forgotten and resentful. Even those who may think the CEO is something of a divine figure who deserves to make 2,800 times their salary would find it difficult to identify with him and follow his leadership.

> In 1982, GM negotiated certain concessions from the workers' union and then attempted to give large bonuses to their executives. Such an outrage occurred that GM had to cancel the bonuses.[6]

Large compensation differences create gaps that are too difficult to bridge and damage the possibility for worker engagement.

Not equal and not too different.

In society, when the big fish has the capacity to eat the small fish with no remorse or penalty, the overall national wealth is reduced. There are many names for systems with this description: imperialism, state monopoly, or totalitarianism; and the big fish takes the form of a corporation or a government. In such a system, antitrust laws are almost non-existent, which leads to monopolistic behaviors. Prices of services and products are high, service and product quality are low, and technological advances become rare events. All thanks to the fact that competition can be eliminated with no remorse or legal control. The few owners of the production operations are rich and powerful, and their workers are poor with few rights and little decision-making power.

The same is true inside a company. Those organizations in which some receive all the benefit and all the power become stagnant, slow, bureaucratic, and are doomed to fail. Workers take little ownership for the company and its products, services, and actions. Workers aren't engaged, and stakeholders exert little to no creativity. Why would a worker spend countless hours developing new products or services if he knows the decision about which products to pursue will be made to benefit some people, not the whole organization? Even if his proposal is accepted, most likely he won't take part in its rewards.

At the other extreme, we can picture an egalitarian organization in which everyone receives the same salary regardless of their output, function, and experience. Will a worker do her best when she knows that no matter what her level of expertise is, the responsibilities she has, and the effort she exerts she'll receive the same salary as everyone else? If Karla studied 18+ years to develop mastery in a critical process required for the company to produce certain products, would she feel it's fair that Jenny, who attended basic schooling and has been in the company for 6 months, earns the same? An egalitarian system doesn't work because it diminishes creativity, doesn't prize unique skills and advanced expertise, and dampens individual motivation.

We must not forget that there are several ways to recognize exemplary performance and effort; that is, it doesn't have to be with money. Those who are clearly performing better could be offered more responsibilities, may have access to higher positions, would be invited to teach and coach others, and simply would play a bigger role in the success of the organization. We must also remember that the organization we are building, considering the principles and thoughts of this book, does have intrinsically motivated workers. This means that workers are engaged and motivated to do their work for reasons other than external rewards.

We discussed in Chapter 5 that these external rewards are not effective in motivating workers. The unmotivated worker who doesn't give his entire potential to the organization must be helped, assisted, offered alternatives, and, if necessary, removed from the organization before his lack of motivation infects others.

The fact is that compensation is still the quickest, easiest way for workers to compare themselves with their peers, and (as we learned from Easterlin) to determine their satisfaction level. Compensation will also help determine their perception of fairness of the organization and their coworkers. But how do we set up compensation properly?

Before joining Goodpay, Inc., Susie used to regularly make $10 per hour.

In this company, Susie makes $15, which makes her feel good. She then learns that John, who has less responsibility, makes $18. Susie isn't as satisfied as before. She may feel her work isn't valued, she's being exploited, or this organization makes compensation decisions arbitrarily. What to do about this problem?

Management should stay out of compensation decisions.

"Who, if not management, will set these compensation numbers?" you may ask. Management should set the rules (ranges, allowances, levels, and exceptions) and then stay out of it as much as possible. The idea is simple. For a worker to become proficient in his job, he needs a certain amount of time, skills, and effort. Assume we have engaged workers and the effort is already there. Acquisition of skills and time are the main variables left to acquire proficiency in a job. These two variables also account for how interconnected within the organization the worker is, how much expertise he has, how productive he is, and how much fit he has with the organization.

For example, for a welder there is a range of proficiency levels, from novice to expert and master. Those at the high end of expertise are much more productive because they can weld faster, they can coach others, they can teach the new crowd, and they can improve the whole "welding department." Imagine that management has determined that novices start at 60% of the highest level of salary, which is raised every 6 months, assuming they pass certain proficiency levels such as (I am going to come up with a few things here) welding by tact, reduced space welding, gas, arc, spot, tig, and wire feed welding. The welding department can determine by itself which skills are needed to be proficient, how fast workers can get them, and how to certify for them. After 5 years, and after all requirements are met, salaries are topped off. Because the rules are fair, published (internally), and available to all, there is no perception of unfairness.

Management's job becomes the sole responsibility to make sure the salaries are comparable with other companies and with the social circle of the worker. For example, Jeremy is a logistics associate and works almost entirely with his multidisciplinary team. He will compare himself not only with his logistics friends at other companies but also with the guys from manufacturing, purchasing, and other departments who work constantly with him in his company.

Jeremy works in a company that produces several different products: it produces scissors for children and rocket components. Workers are divided by product. Jeremy, who happens to be in the rocket component team, knows that buying products for rockets takes much more care, expertise, and knowledge. He cannot be making the same amount of money as the scissors logistics person. In Jeremy's case, only because there is a big difference in complexity, there has to be an adjustment, which is also published and available to all.

In the same way, the CEO, who has more responsibility and can affect in a much bigger way the lives of the workers, the fate of the company, its customers, and its community, should make more money than folks with fewer responsibilities. Most workers would accept that he earns more. Surely not 2,800 times more, but more nonetheless.

Jeremy will be paying more attention to the salary of his teammates even when they work in manufacturing, purchasing, and other departments than to the salary of other logistics professionals at other companies. This means that in our Driven Organization, we have much more freedom to determine our own rules and for workers to accept them and believe they are fair if they make sense within the company. Even the highest position, the CEO, should still be attuned to the salaries of Jeremy and all other coworkers.

Let's take the issue of money off the table.

In our chapter about money, we learned that money causes distress and unhappiness when it is insufficient to cover the basic needs. We said that workers who feel they are barely making it think about it constantly. They spend quality energy trying to solve this problem that is significant in their lives. This effort is wasted because it doesn't provide any benefit to the organization or themselves.

The organization must attempt to take the issue of money off the table. This way, other needs can play a bigger role in the workers' life. They can now occupy themselves with the growth needs, working on competence, beauty and structure, self-actualization, and self-transcendence needs. When they do so, they are much more creative, productive, satisfied, and happy.

It is my belief that different people have different thresholds of what is sufficient to stop worrying about money. This may have to be addressed at the moment of hiring to see what the worker's needs are. Based on what the company can pay and what the social circle of the worker makes, will the worker perceive his salary as sufficient and decent? If so, money won't be in play anymore; the worker can move on to higher needs and attempt to be everything he can be.

A mentality of "we are all in this together" is the best.

One way to promote a strong cohesive environment is through the concept of "shared fate." The simple idea is that all the company's stakeholders share together in the good and in the bad times, from the top level to the bottom one. Remember the story from Guy Kawasaki about Mexico and Ethiopia, where Ethiopia sent money to Mexico while it suffered one of its worst famines? Well, the same situation can take place with the workers. Workers are thankful, develop strong bonds, and do their best to make the company successful if they feel the company is loyal to them.

With the shared fate concept, only actions matter. Words without actions may actually hurt. Financial compensation is a great way to carry out this concept because it is observable and measurable, which makes it meaningful. Shared financial fate also works in the bad times. As a matter of fact, bumps and struggles are great opportunities to show loyalty to the organization's workers and to create incentives for those who don't feel this sense of loyalty for the company to leave. For those who stay, as with partners in a marriage who decided to stay together through happy and difficult times, the bond only solidifies with the shared experiences.

Even when many corporations say they share in the good and the bad times, the opposite often happens, and financial rewards mark stark differences between management and workers. There is nothing more demoralizing than seeing your compensation be out of tune with the great times the company is experiencing or reduced disproportionally when things are difficult. And the damage tends to stick.

Workers of most corporations have become so skeptical of management sharing their fate that, even when the corporation's CEO decides to accept only $1 of annual salary, as was the case with the Chrysler's CEO in 2008, workers don't believe it. They feel that the CEOs will get even within the next opportunity in a substantial way, and they are the only ones carrying out the load of the entire recovery.

A simple shared fate arrangement could be to tie salary increases and bonuses to company performance. For example, if profitability increased 5%, all workers of all levels get a bonus of 5%. Another example comes from Whole Foods Market that "limits the compensation (wages plus profit incentive bonuses) of any Team Member to nineteen times the average total compensation of all full-time Team Members in the company." They also reward teams, not individual workers. It's important to remember that any compensation program is meant to promote shared fate, as opposed to a goals-above-means mentality that would cause significant damage on the long run. This must always be emphasized in communications with workers.

Performance reviews are to learn, not to determine pay.

Many companies tie performance reviews with pay. Is it wrong? To answer that we need to remember what the purposes of management and peer reviews are. If they are correctly done, they should provide constructive feedback that helps identify actions and behaviors that can be improved. The worker uses the feedback to interact with others in a better way and increase his level of expertise. This is also a good opportunity for the worker to ask questions, to request help, and to give feedback to the company.

When we add the financial reward component, there is an implicit message. If you do what we tell you to do, you'll be prized. If you don't, you'll be punished. We all need feedback and help, but when feedback is tied to financial rewards, things get murky. Remember the concerns we discussed when we reviewed the use of external rewards. Folks lose interest in their work, feel controlled, punished when they don't get the reward, lose creativity, become competitive with other workers, and engage in risky behaviors with eyes only on the goal. We are treating this worker as a child who wouldn't, through his own choosing, do what is best for the organization unless he is rewarded or punished.

Financial rewards cause a reaction, but never create intrinsic motivation. It's the opposite, in fact. When we tie peer and management reviews with financial rewards, peer and management reviews lose their honest character and become formal institutions for reward and punishment. While they can be sincere, true learning opportunities, they lose their capacity to foster new understanding and development of skills based on a platform of intrinsic motivation. Taking the money out of the equation, peer and management reviews can provide help, direction, and feedback, identify issues, and provide an open platform to discuss them. If we are truly looking for feedback and an environment that allows for improvement, reviews shouldn't have financial reward components.

Some organizations don't have formal peer or management reviews, but workers have coaches, sponsors, and friends who are constantly providing feedback and helping them achieve their potential. If the environment of the organization allows it, workers have ample opportunity to help each other, learn from others, ask for support, and improve overall working conditions. The environment, which will be discussed later, provides the arena for workers to be the best they can be often without the need for formal reviews.

If the organization cannot afford him, don't have him.

There are financial competitive concerns for all businesses that may limit our capacity to pay a sufficient salary. We must then decide whether we can afford a worker or not. A worker without a sufficient salary may be destructive for the organization. Can we solve the need by equipping other workers with more sophisticated tools? Can we ask other workers to pitch in to do the work without hiring the additional head? Workers should be in the center of these discussions, proposing solutions for the problem.

Summary of Salary.

- Excessive differences in compensation damage group cohesiveness. Egalitarian practices don't foster it, either.
- Management should attempt to stay out of the compensation decisions as much as possible.

- A worker's wage must be related with his social peers and secondarily with his peers from other companies.

- The rules to determine salaries must be the same for all and (ideally) published.

- Salaries must promote shared fate mentality, in which everyone shares in the good and the bad with others in the organization.

- Peer and management reviews shouldn't affect salary levels. They should be part of a sincere conversation focused on learning.

- When salary is sufficient for a decent life, the worker moves on to higher needs that provide better and higher quality output. Efforts used by workers trying to improve their financial standing don't provide benefits to the organization.

- If the company cannot afford a worker, don't employ one. See whether workers can absorb the job, perhaps with the use of better tools.

---

1   Dancingdeer.com—About Us.

2   Bureau of Labor Statistics. Year 2010: Median Pay.
http://www.bls.gov/ooh/office-and-administrative-support/tellers.htm

3   CNN.com. http://money.cnn.com/news/specials/storysupplement/ceopay/

4   Thurm, Scott. "Apple's Cook Tops the List of Highest-Paid CEOs." *The Wall Street Journal,* May 2011.

5   Bivens, Josh. "CEOs Distance Themselves From the Average Worker." *Economic Policy Institute,* November 9, 2011.

6   Freeman, Richard B., & Medoff, James L. *What Do Unions Do?* New York: Basic Books, 1984.

Chapter 10:

P Is About Purpose.

"True happiness ... is not attained through self-gratification, but through fidelity to a worthy purpose." Helen Keller, author, political activist, and first deaf-blind person to earn a bachelor's degree.

A worthy purpose lightens our load.

Today, you are on Chicago in a business trip. A coworker heard you'd be in Chicago and asked you to pick up a spare part for his classic motorcycle that can only be found here. You cross town to get to the store, and while you do so, you become familiar with the traffic of the windy city. You wonder why he decided to ruin your afternoon instead of paying the $40 that it costs to have the part shipped. You spend a few hours in this endeavor and when you come back to the hotel you feel exhausted and drained. Somehow, this activity has made you tired.

Two months ago, your wife signed you up to volunteer driving elders to get free health screenings. You agreed reluctantly. You spent the entire day doing it and you dealt with the same traffic and a job similar to the motorcycle-part task. But when you saw how much you helped the older folks and how much they appreciated it and needed it, your heart got into it. You remember that when you went home, you were energized and satisfied. At dinner, even your wife noticed how enthusiastic and full of energy you were.

This memory brings another one. A few weeks ago, you drove 300 miles to get two lobsters that your brother had caught for you and again, you weren't tired; you were excited with the prospect of eating the freshest lobsters prepared with your grandfather's recipe.

These activities require a similar amount of work, but interestingly, different levels of effort. It's all related to the purpose of the activity. To make it bearable, to energize us, the purpose has to be worthwhile in our eyes. For you and me, crossing town to get a motorcycle part to avoid the shipping cost may not be a worthwhile endeavor, so it takes a lot of effort. Driving folks to the clinic may be worthwhile, so it takes little effort. Getting those two lobsters may be important for you and me, but perhaps not for most people. A worthy purpose energizes and excites us, and afterward brings a sense of fulfillment and satisfaction. Imagine how we would feel if our everyday work had a genuinely worthy purpose.

To feel energized, we first have to relate to the purpose of the organization. But what is it? It's the answer to the following question: If the organization disappeared from the face of the earth, what would be missed? What would the world not have? The purpose is the reason why the organization was formed in the first place. As human beings, we have the right not to know our purpose for existence. A couple didn't sit down and plan to: "create an individual to advance scientific knowledge." But this *is* the case with organizations. They are conceived to fulfill a need and to achieve something specific. This is their purpose for being.

Any purpose will do, but choose one that is meaningful to you.

Are all purposes good? No purpose is wrong unless it actually refers to immoral activities. Assuming the purpose is well intended, the organization is free to pursue it. For some, it takes the form of helping the environment, helping disadvantaged groups (like children in Ghana), pursuing an idealistic goal (like democracy or emancipation), among many others. You may believe that classic music is conducive to elevating one's spirit and because you believe it so strongly, you may participate in an organization that fosters the dissemination and expansion of classic music. Your organization may wish to create the best vehicles in the world, advance astronomical knowledge, or help folks create wealth for retirement by providing sound financial advice.

An organization with a significant purpose may help us satisfy the growth needs, the upper levels of Maslow's pyramid. Working toward a worthy purpose may help us with our desire to know and understand (fifth level), self-actualization (seventh level), and self-transcendence (eighth level). Even the aesthetic needs (sixth level) may have a shot. For example, imagine an organization whose purpose is to "develop scientific and technological solutions for a cleaner environment." If the workers are the right match, they will fulfill their desire to know and understand when they research and learn methods and techniques to reduce pollution and clean the environment. They will attain their entire potential by being great biologists, managers, or accountants. And because the organization works toward having a positive impact for humanity, by restoring the environment to its natural order, workers may be able to satisfy self-transcendence needs, too. They also work in an orderly fashion, in a clean working environment, taking field trips into nature, all of which may help them with their aesthetic needs.

Not every purpose will help us satisfy the upper needs. Imagine another company whose purpose is to provide expensive loans and get a very high return. Although this is certainly a purpose, putting aside any legal concerns, workers at this organization will have more difficulty finding opportunities to fulfill the upper levels. The purpose of the organization resides within the lower levels of the pyramid; therefore, the workers in this organization will find satisfiers for the needs from the lower levels as well, at least at work. It's easy to understand that in such an organization, managers are not interested in fostering knowledge, order, beauty, or assistance to other human beings, or to maximize their entire professional capacity.

In the SPACES framework, the letter *P* is the only opportunity to consider the self-transcendence needs. It is now known that these needs are extremely important to us, which is why we have started to see organizations that use terms such as purpose-driven, socially responsible, community-oriented, fair trade, ethical sourcing, and so on.

For most of us, the fulfillment of these transcendence needs is mostly channeled through working with non-profits, volunteering, and attending religious institutions that act as distractions from work and family. Imagine that it's possible to satisfy these needs within the work we do every day; that we work with 200 other people who care about the same thing and who have joined forces in this organization to have grander impact.

The purpose should be at the core of what the organization does.

The purpose doesn't have to be divorced from productive activities —quite the opposite is true; it can and should be, as much as possible, intermixed. Think of two companies that produce bread. The purpose of one is solely to generate shareholder return. This company chooses ingredients and produces bread performing the minimum required activities to achieve a perceived quality level and cost objectives. They use chemicals and add flavoring, color, and vitamins to improve a product that would otherwise have poor flavor and nutrition.

The other company has chosen a purpose "to help improve the general health of people through the manufacture of nutrition-rich food." The company's self-imposed mandate requires it to produce nutritious bread and avoid polluting actions. Their bread is recognized as nutritious, which causes their brand to strengthen and increase profits. Consumers believe that workers at this company choose the best ingredients to produce their bread because their purpose matches what they, the consumers, want. They feel they can trust this bread maker.

Workers in this nutritious-bread company go home feeling proud of their work, knowing that somewhere, somehow they are averting illness and suffering by providing people with proper nutrition. If they decide to expand to other food items, their mandate, like an umbrella, extends to the new products. Note that purpose and brand are entirely intertwined.

A company that manufactures tennis shoes might have the purpose of providing athletes with the tools to stay healthy and become better at their chosen sport. This hypothetical company could develop tests and medical programs to help athletes improve their joints while gathering research and test data for their product development. A bank might have the purpose of expanding the middle class and reducing poverty. The bank may assist customers in saving more and using loans properly so that they increase their financial standing while the bank gets to know the members of its community intimately. A research institution can link its efforts to benefit humanity by establishing ways for the medical professionals to access their research and use it for helping people.

Discovering the next scientific frontier may be a purpose in itself, but linking it to benefiting humanity makes it great.

These examples are not meant to suggest purposes for businesses, or businesses for purposes, but instead to illustrate that the purpose, whatever the company's stakeholders decide it to be, can be intertwined with the business of the company. The specific actions of the organization may change over time, but they must always strengthen the organization and its capacity to fulfill the organization's purpose. Even if you and I don't think their purpose is meaningful, the organization's stakeholders must believe so. The purpose must make all stakeholders feel, deep inside, that they are good people doing good things in the world.

Seemingly opposed purposes still lead to a better society.

Our purposes may take us in opposite directions, even if they are meaningful. Imagine that Abstemious, Inc,. an organization that exists only in the pages of this book, believes that alcohol is a substance that should never be consumed, so it wants to work toward the decrease of alcohol consumption. This is Abstemious' purpose; you and I may not agree with it, but we don't have to as long as the company is happy with it. It so happens that one core value of a real organization called New Belgium Brewing is to foster the "responsible consumption of alcohol,"[1] which in this specific case goes against our imaginary Abstemious organization's purpose and efforts.

"If different purposes oppose, what is the point?" you may ask. "Are we just fighting each other? Is one purpose better than the other?" All people have unique needs, experiences, and beliefs that may lead them to make different conclusions and identify with different philosophies. This is the part of living in a democratic society that respects our individual beliefs and values, even when we may not necessarily understand them. For some, Abstemious, Inc. is right. For others, it is New Belgium Brewing. Because the latter fosters the responsible enjoyment of beer,[2] I can see that the combined effort of these two organizations would decrease the irresponsible (and destructive) consumption of alcohol. Society will be better off by the existence of both companies, even when they seem to have opposing values and purposes.

Workers must feel the purpose matters.

If Charlie, a regular worker, likes to have a beer every day or so, can he be a good fit for Abstemious? Imagine he has a good job there and his job is appreciated. Still, he finds himself thinking once in a while, "These people are prudes with a silly purpose." Now, imagine that Charlie works for New Belgium Brewing. All else being equal, Charlie would enjoy with delight having that coveted beer at the end of a workday with his New Belgium Brewing friends. How much more satisfaction will this variable by itself bring to Charlie? How much more connected will he be with his coworkers at New Belgium Brewing?

I remember from my early days as a project manager the importance of establishing personal relationships with people at work. One time, we had been battling through difficult issues for the entire day. We had the participation of folks from overseas facilities, and the issues proved difficult to solve. At 7:30 pm, someone said, "Let's go out for dinner. We can justify the company picking up the tab." At dinner, after enjoying a good meal and a couple of drinks in a relaxed atmosphere, issues that couldn't be solved in 10 hours of discussion magically went away in 20 minutes. The next day, we showed up at work, summarized our agreement from the previous evening, and were ready to move on to the next topic. I've repeatedly witnessed this process. The fact that we were able to solve problems in a more effective way is because we lowered our functional walls and began to communicate as human beings. We related to each other, spoke openly, and understood our needs. This is the type of interaction that Charlie could enjoy with his friends at New Belgium Brewing, not only after work but also during his work days. This is just one way in which Charlie would be much more productive there.

This brings us to the reason why organizations should have clear purposes from their early beginnings and make sure that every new worker is aware of the purpose and fits with it. Once the company is big, and they have hired people who have hired people who have hired people, the newer workers may not even know why the company was formed in the first place. It is possible for a company to grow big and have a strong sense of purpose well ingrained in its people, but the focus on the purpose must be a conscious effort through its growth.

The Driven Organization

"Success demands singleness of purpose." Vince Lombardi, Green Bay Packers coach.

If workers don't share the organization's purpose, what could have been a great tool for workers to be engaged and satisfied could be taken sarcastically and destroy the very morale it is trying to build. In other words, people must want to smoke from the same pipe, whatever that is. If they do so, it will cause them to like themselves better and to respect each other in a much more significant way. Have you been in a situation in which you respected somebody very much? Do you remember that you tried your best to never disappoint them?

We respect those who believe what we believe.

After getting my MBA, I went to work for the strategic department of GM. The hiring process had been long and complicated. In one of this hiring process' sessions, we had spent a whole day of tough business cases, incisive behavioral interviews, challenging group exercises, and flash presentations. The competition had been tough with folks coming from all top business school programs. We knew how difficult it was for us to be there, and felt really lucky to have been accepted into the program. I'm probably not wrong if I say that each of us felt the others were the good ones, that we were the lucky ones to have been accepted, and that we should always try to give our best to try to match the others.

Respect commanded our best effort. We never wanted to disappoint those whom we respected. This is why it's important to highly regard others with whom we spend the majority of our time. And the easiest way to respect others is to see that their beliefs hold value for us.

It is embedded in our DNA to surround ourselves with people whom we trust and respect. It so happens that when we find others believing what we believe, we develop trust for them. Even when others have come forward when needed in the past, we may only find them reliable, but not necessarily trust them. Trust is a gut feeling that gets developed when we find that, after following a whole different path in life with its unique experiences, some people have developed the same beliefs and reached the same conclusions that we have. We feel we know them. We feel close to them and we trust them.

You may have concluded that the rate of usage of natural resources these days is excessive. Or the opposite: that these fears are led by some who benefit by inspiring fear. When you see that other people have reached the same conclusions, and have, in fact, founded organizations around those beliefs, you identify with them, develop trust, and readily become a potential customer or even a potential employee.

We can easily see the importance of having people on board who share the same values. We understand how the hiring process must explore the values and beliefs of the candidate. The candidate must clearly see the values of the organization. If the match is good, it is like a match made in heaven. If not, well ... you already know.

> Early in my career, I was the project manager with a multidisciplinary team. There were folks from different paths of life—some brilliant, some just ordinary. Some had experience; most of us didn't. We did some great things. Along the path we learned that it didn't matter how much brains, experience, and support an associate had. The attitude toward the work and toward others is almost the only thing that matters.

A group of people with a shared purpose gets there faster.

When the purpose is understood and accepted by the members of the organization, the organization becomes easy to manage. There is less friction because the direction of the company is clearer to everyone, and everyone accepts it as such. Those who fit well, stay; those who don't, leave. This is the difference between fighting the war in Iraq/Afghanistan and fighting the World War II. There was no doubt in anybody's mind that the latter needed to be fought with everything there was. People in many places sacrificed at all levels to make sure that the soldiers had what was needed to win. People bought war bonds, ate less meat, donated metals, and enlisted. Women became workers in factories and heads of households. It was a time of shared sacrifice. Were people in the United States doing the same thing for the war in Iraq/Afghanistan? I'm not making a political statement; only pointing out that differences in the valuation of the purpose cause dissent, which diminishes the capacity for the organization (or country) to succeed.

When the purpose-driven organization needs to make difficult choices, such as those required by a downturn in business results, it will be better accepted by folks in the organization, even if they are hard. If the top objectives are accepted, the hard decisions will be easily determined and understood, and the organization will reach consensus faster and with less friction.

The human body can help us visualize an organization where all stakeholders believe in its purpose. Steve is running in the annual New York City Marathon. Every organ of his body, and therefore every cell, is contributing to the effort of the whole entity, which is to keep Steve alive and help him succeed. Not one cell is saying, "I don't think that it's fair that Steve makes us go through this. Because I believe Steve should sit down, I'm not really going to do my part." Every cell in the body has accepted Steve's purpose, and the body will give all it has until it is dangerous for the body to keep doing so without damaging the prime imperative, which is to keep him alive.

A few days later, Steve must spend 16 hours at the office, sitting on a chair while working on his computer. The cells act accordingly and attempt to give Steve what they have to help him in his task. Not one cell will be thinking, "Folks, I believe it's time to run," even when that may not be a bad idea. The purpose, which is to keep Steve alive and help him succeed, keeps his cells motivated to do so.

A group of people convinced of its purpose develops intuition.

It has happened to all of us at one time or another that we taste something that seems "off." For some reason, we keep eating it only to later find out that we have become ill. After a couple of these experiences, we learn to listen and follow what our body tells us. The body uses intuition that even experts cannot match. It uses all its sensors to consider its own state and determine whether what we are about to do is good or not. This is why when the body's sensors identify the food we just ate may have a few bad bugs, we don't become hungry for a while. The body determines it doesn't need to complicate the situation by adding more food when it is struggling to process something bad.

Our organization does something similar. When stakeholders believe in its purpose and have free access to information, they become intelligent sensors of the organization, gathering information that helps make the right decisions. Just like human cells that bring information to the body no matter their function and location, organization stakeholders identify threats and detect market opportunities with their unique relationships, contacts, and functions.

In the human body, scientists have observed cells in the gut with similar capacities to brain neurons. They learn and act on their own accord. They make their own decisions to foster the body's health based on the information they have. There are many cells throughout the human body with similar capabilities. In the same way, in a purpose-driven organization, provided they have access to organizational information, every stakeholder can act as a capable agent who makes decisions and acts properly notwithstanding function, location, or level.

It's easy to see the organization develops intuition. Like the body that today doesn't seem to like cheesecake, the organization moves cautiously toward those areas where it feels unsure, where it has detected dangers, or where the benefits aren't substantial. The organization, as a matter of fact, has developed organizational wisdom.

My job connects with the purpose.

Every worker must be able to connect his daily job activities with the overall purpose. One of the main roles of management is, in fact, to make sure that every worker clearly understands how his specific input affects the organization's capacity to reach it. When a stakeholder loses the capacity to see the link, no matter how powerful and enlightening the purpose is, the worker won't feel his contribution is adding anything to it. To him, it would be as if the purpose wasn't there at all.

If the purpose is not meaningful, it will hurt us in the long run.

Now that we understand how important the purpose is, why not manufacture one so that workers are happy? I'm sure that some managers, perhaps MBAs with their self-perceived brilliancy, can come up with purposes that seem truthful, but in reality are designed to further advance the organization's image, branding, and employee productivity. This unfortunately doesn't work. The real objectives and worries of management come out with the daily decisions or when things get tough. People notice, and the consequences are quite the reverse. A negative perception develops, and cynicism and disappointment follow. People feel the company is trying to deceive them and use them. It's much worse to do so than to do nothing at all.

Often when the organizations grow, the purposes that prompted their very existence are forgotten or relegated to secondary or tertiary priorities. There are three main signs to detect when this happens. The first one is lack of passion. When workers don't have passion for their work any longer, they simply aren't connecting with the purpose. The second one is when the organization starts becoming too concerned with its competition. They begin excessively watching competitors' moves, their product development and their merger and acquisition activity. The third sign is when the company starts asking its customers who they should be or which products they should pursue.[3]

When this happens, senior management begins to differ about brand positioning, products development, customer targeting, etc. Customer surveys are performed, which only helps add fire to the discussions. Unfortunately, this internal struggle is soon perceived by customers too. In some of these cases, by the way, the company may be posting excellent financial results, for the moment.

If an organization wants to add or modify their purpose, ideally, it should do it with the participation of its entire workforce in order for the purpose to be meaningful. Each individual worker should start by answering a few questions such as: What is significant enough to devote my life? How can we do it through the product or service our company produces? Which needs in our community are best suited for our company to meet?

This is not a two-week process. It may take much longer, but step by step, the organization finds its place in the world. Soon, people volunteer, take the lead, and vote to see these ideas become reality, and these efforts infuse the organization with a new kind of energy. If done well, the effect on the bottom or top line is minuscule, while the benefits to the organization and its workers is quite large.

Mission, vision, values, principles, beliefs, attitudes?

You may have heard about companies stating a mission and a vision, others talking about values and principles, and some others talking about beliefs. Some organizations are very specific when they write their purpose. Others are more generic, but accompany their purpose with core values. Others don't use purpose, but use instead principles and beliefs. Which one is best?

As long as the statement of purpose serves stakeholders to clearly understand why the organization exists and what it strives to accomplish, it is fine to use any of these different ways.

See, as an example, Whole Foods Market:[4]

What:	How:
Purpose(s):	Healing America through the use of better nutrition and lifestyle. Creating a more sustainable agricultural system that also has a high degree of productivity. Helping end poverty across the planet. Spreading conscious capitalism.
Values:	Selling the Highest Quality Natural and Organic Products Available. Satisfying and Delighting Our Customers. Supporting Team Member Excellence and Happiness. Creating Wealth Through Profits & Growth. Caring about our Communities & Our Environment. Creating ongoing win-win partnerships with our suppliers. Promoting the health of our stakeholders through healthy eating education.
Motto	Whole Foods, Whole People, Whole Planet.

Its four purposes are objectives toward which they work, but may never achieve success. In its values, Whole Foods Market specifically explains what it actually commits to doing to pursue its purpose. Finally, it has a motto that puts its entire philosophy in a simple line that is linked to its name, purpose, and values, and is easily remembered by each and every stakeholder. Notice that Whole Foods Market does not provide specific solutions that may constrain the organization.

A word about mission and vision. There are two schools of thought regarding mission. First, some think mission and purpose are interchangeable, the same thing. Some others consider mission to be the actionable effort derived from purpose. As in a military conflict, mission has a specific objective. In this thinking, while the purpose of the organization may never change, the mission has a mid-term plan. It doesn't matter which school of thought you subscribe to, as long as there is a solid purpose toward which the organization works.

To finish with definitions, vision is the ideal future of the company, describing what the company can achieve in a certain time horizon.

Different organizations describe themselves in different ways. See examples at the end of this chapter. Note that not all of them encompass self-transcendence needs.

The purpose is the northern star.

Like the northern star, on which sailors always count to guide them through turbulent seas, the purpose is always there to influence minor and major decisions of the organization. It reassures us that we are doing the right thing because our everyday actions are aligned with a true worthwhile objective. It provides us with a way to respect each other and have a better time working together. It helps us carry the load with more energy and satisfaction; and it helps everyone, workers, shareholders, and customers, improve the world.

"In organizations of the future, it will be much more important to have a clear sense of purpose and sound principles within which many specific, short-term objectives can be quickly achieved, than a long-range plan with fixed, measurable objectives." Dee Hock, CEO and Founder of VISA®.

Summary of Purpose.

- Every organization should have a clear and spelled-out purpose, which is its reason for being. If it is worthwhile, it acts as a great source of enthusiasm and focus for workers that lightens the load and increases job satisfaction.
- If the purpose targets Maslow's upper needs, such as self-transcendence, the workers of the organization have a better shot at fulfilling them through work.
- The purpose should point the organization toward a distant far-reaching objective.
- Seemingly opposed purposes still lead to a better society.

- The purpose should be intermixed with the productive activity of the organization, and by consequence, with its brand.

- The purpose can be spelled out via values, principles and beliefs.

- We respect those who believe what we believe, who value what we value, and who share our purposes.

- Each worker should clearly see how his or her work contributes to the overall organizational purpose. This is one of the most significant roles of management.

- When things become difficult, decisions are unclear, or there is confusion, the organization can count on its purpose to find guidance. If stakeholders are fully on board with it, there is little friction and discussion.

- A false, manufactured purpose eventually breaks down, causing worker cynicism, dissent, and anger.

Company	What it's Called	What it Says
Charles Schwab Corp.[5]	Purpose	To help everyone be financially fit.
	Values	Provide the most ethical financial services. Be fair, empathetic and responsive in serving our clients. Strive relentlessly to improve what we do and how we do it. Respect and reinforce our fellow employees and the power of teamwork. Always earn and be worthy of our clients' trust.
BMW[6]	Vision	In 2020, we will be the leading provider of premium products and premium services for individual mobility.
Wikimedia (foundation behind Wikipedia)[7]	Purpose	A nonprofit charitable organization dedicated to encouraging the growth, development and distribution of free, multilingual content, and to providing the full content of these wiki-based projects to the public free of charge.
Hy-vee[8]	Mission	Making lives easier, healthier, happier.
	Sustainability mission	To promote the well-being of our customers, employees, communities, and the global environment.
Google[9]	Mission	To organize the world's information and make it universally accessible and useful.
	Core Principles	Focus on the user and all else will follow. It's best to do one thing really, really well. Fast is better than slow. Democracy on the web works. You don't need to be at your desk to need an answer. You can make money without doing evil. There's always more information out there. The need for information crosses all borders. You can be serious without a suit. Great just isn't good enough.

1   http://www.newbelgium.com/culture/our-story.aspx

2   http://www.gettips.com

3   For more information, see Sinek, Simon. *Start With Why: How Great Leaders Inspire Everyone to Take Action.* Portfolio Trade, December 2011.

4   http://www.wholefoodsmarket.com/company/corevalues.php

5   http://www.aboutschwab.com/about/purpose/

6   http://www.bmweducation.co.uk/coFacts/view.asp?docID=26

7   http://wikimediafoundation.org/wiki/Home

8   http://www.hy-vee.com/company/about-hy-vee/default.aspx

9   http://www.google.com/intl/en/about/index.html

Chapter 11:

A Is About Autonomy.

"As our business grows, it becomes increasingly necessary to delegate responsibility and to encourage men and women to exercise their initiative. This requires considerable tolerance. Those men and women, to whom we delegate authority and responsibility, if they are good people, are going to want to do their jobs in their own way. Mistakes will be made. But if a person is essentially right, the mistakes he or she makes are not as serious in the long run as the mistakes management will make if it undertakes to tell those in authority exactly how they must do their jobs. Management that is destructively critical when mistakes are made kills initiative. And it's essential that we have many people with initiative if we are to continue to grow." Laid out in 1948 by William L. McKnight, president of 3M.

McKnight turned down an idea that Richard Drew, a young technician, developed on his own time and with no support. Allegedly, McKnight rejected Drew's idea three times, which eventually led to masking tape. McKnight determined to never repeat this mistake again.

Excessive control causes us to be dissatisfied and perform poorly.

Think about people that you perceive as excessively perfectionist, meticulous, controlling, or rigid. Tell me, how is their leadership style? Are they great leaders, admired and followed? Do people wish they were in their groups? The answer almost always is a conclusive "no."

Note that I didn't say they don't have positions of authority, as their attention to detail and rigidity are often confused with focus on the work and self-confidence, qualities often desired in our organizations. Even when they may be exceptionally smart, they aren't the best leaders, the ones that inspire others to do their best, the ones that spark the most enthusiastic performance. This happens simply because no one likes to be controlled or overly limited. Excessive control is so negative it even causes a feeling of lower self-worth.

Remember the study in chapter 5 about the effect of the teacher's style on student motivation and self-image? The researchers found that those students with teachers who had a more controlling style had a lower level of curiosity and preference for challenge. The students perceived themselves as less competent and felt less good about themselves than those with autonomy-supportive-style teachers.[1]

I saw an example of the effects of excess control a few years after graduating from engineering school, when I began working for a German company in Mexico. In this company, almost every manager was a German on international assignment in Mexico. All working levels, with the exception of a few interns, were composed of local folks. I remember witnessing mix-ups and basic mistakes happening frequently. I started to wonder why. It was excessive.

I realized there was an unspoken dynamic. Management implemented strict procedures as a way to establish control and reduce mistakes. These procedures allowed them to keep track of every process, request, audit, and result. This is a fairly normal management reaction, but it is based on a lack of trust for workers to do the job as required. Local workers sensed it. They felt they were of "lower class," and they knew their future couldn't be too bright there. Eventually, they became disengaged and showed less interest for the organization's objectives.

Obviously, the number of mistakes and mix-ups wasn't reduced, which made management confirm their belief that lower levels couldn't be trusted. Unfortunately, the focus of the organization on following procedures did make the organization slow and bureaucratic.

As an added consequence, many of those with potential (and self-esteem) left the company because there was no place to go in this organization. Obviously, local personnel were of low value to the company because they were "prone to make mistakes," which caused the company to offer only low salaries. This, in turn, assured a good supply of the less well-trained personnel and a further perception of lower class, which only helped fuel the cycle all over again.

The group I was hired for served as a good example of contrast. We were more carefully hired, offered better salaries, and were fully accountable for our jobs. My boss at the time didn't bother too much to keep track of what I was doing, but I couldn't have felt more responsible to achieve the required results. I learned then the importance of hiring the right people, furnishing them with tools and responsibilities, and leaving them alone to complete the job. People do better when they are fully responsible and accountable for their work.

Several researchers have found a positive relationship between job satisfaction and internal "locus of control,"[2] defined as the extent to which an individual believes he can influence his future state. Consider a person that notwithstanding what he does and how much effort he exerts to get ahead and progress, has no control over his future. Naturally, he becomes demoralized and unmotivated. The same studies find a positive relationship between performance of different types and this "locus of control."[3]

Monarchies don't work anymore. Why do we have them at work?

Throughout history, we have made revolutions and overhauled production systems because we find it unacceptable that a few "chosen ones" make all decisions and receive all the benefits, as in a monarchy. These often-costly conflicts attempt to give people more decision-making power and a better share of the earnings. The U.S. Constitution was developed with the specific intention to limit and distribute power. The United States has become such a powerful country in great part because it has been the place where whoever has good ideas, works hard, and is blessed by a touch of luck, can make it. It's been the place where good projects naturally bubble up and where people achieve results from the sole merits of their creations.

However, most of our modern corporations, with their hierarchical structures of power, still look like monarchies. Senior management has all the power, and most workers have little or none. The CEO makes millions, and workers at the lowest levels struggle to pay the heating bill. Senior management decides which ideas to pursue, and most associates have no say at all. The question I have is simple: How come we decided to forgo the very rights we fought so hard to get, spending the majority of our days in organizations that are contrary to our dearest beliefs?

I have worked with senior management in hierarchical corporations, only to find out they lack the power to influence their organizations, too. Unfortunately, even those close to the CEO don't have much say, either. This happens because in these organizations the good ideas don't necessarily bubble up. Those that do so align with the mentality of the person at the top. And he is expected to be consulted on … well, everything. Everyone else must follow his direction. The organization isn't set up at any level to act autonomously, and the top is not the exception.

In today's modern corporations, decisions are also made in the wrong places. Let's talk about something simple: brooms. Most often, brooms are acquired via a buyer that purchases supplies for all offices of the company. He gathers options, evaluates them, performs value/cost analyses, negotiates with suppliers, and decides. He probably didn't ask the people who actually do the job. We do it this way because we save a few dollars per piece, but we don't consider the impact on job satisfaction for those sweeping the floor.

"If we ask them, they'll ask for expensive brooms," we may think, but I don't think so. Most folks are reasonable and understand value versus cost, but even if they did, what if their broom choice is $8 more expensive? In reality, $8 is little when we consider how much better or easier he'll do his job. Even in the worst case, if there were little practical measurable benefit, the worker satisfaction, using his shiny broom, would be enough to pay for it many times over.

"The person who sweeps the floor should choose the broom!"
Howard Behar, former president of Starbucks.

A hierarchical organization is as smart as the top guy.

In hierarchical organizations, a project or idea runs the risk of being "disliked" by each subsequent higher level of management it encounters as it looks for the necessary support. The difficulties to reach maturity for a newborn project are enormous. But this concern goes away when the organization acts less hierarchically, when people act with autonomy. There isn't a power structure that rejects projects. The best ideas make it, notwithstanding whose proponent they have, but by their own merit. Innovation then becomes a way of life and it is a great competitive advantage.

"Our plan is to lead the public with new products rather than ask them what kind of products they want. The public doesn't know what is possible, but we do. Products like the Walkman captured imaginations and provided credibility." Akio Morita, Sony's visionary founder.

In a hierarchical organization, those who are higher in the power structure are expected to know more and be able to make decisions for all those lower than them. However, we know that expertise and managerial capacity reside at all levels of the organization. We know it isn't true that those higher in the power structure know better. Thinking so would be closing the door to great resources. Instead, it's essential to find the way to use the entire capacity and wisdom of every stakeholder wherever he resides.

Think about the reasons people go into entrepreneurship. On one hand, it's a choice with considerable financial risk, with low initial salary and no benefits. It also doesn't take advantage of the power of teams to accomplish more substantial objectives than the ones few people can accomplish. Entrepreneurship is often lonely, with little, or at least less capacity to socially mingle with other folks on a daily basis. And it's definitely hard work. On the other hand, entrepreneurship has a great upside potential; the business may do well, but this isn't the main reason why people go into entrepreneurship. Entrepreneurs have the capacity to decide for themselves. There are few rules and regulations to block them, more capacity for originality, freedom to make their own decisions, flexibility, and a rational salary that is closer to the value they provide to the market. They are finally able to pursue the good ideas and make them flourish.

> According to a study by the Small Business Association, small patenting businesses produce between 13 and 14 times more patents per employee than large patenting firms.[4]

The good news is all these good characteristics of entrepreneurship can be experienced in a bigger organization with all of its added advantages of belonging to a larger team, with the use of Autonomy.

"None of us is as smart as all of us." Ken Blanchard, author of *The One-Minute Manager.*

Autonomy is an enabler of the entire Maslow's pyramid.

In 1960, more than 50 years ago, Douglas McGregor proposed in his book *The Human Side of Enterprise,* two ways in which we can think of workers. Theory X assumes that people are lazy and need to be pushed to do their work, that they dislike it. It assumes workers have no self-ambition, don't care about anything other than themselves, don't want to change for the better, and aren't particularly intelligent. Trying to motivate employees with rewards (or any other bribe) is based on theory X.

On the other hand, theory Y assumes that folks are self-motivated to do the best they can, want to go to work to achieve results, and need to work as a child needs to play. Theory Y also assumes that if they have opportunity to fulfill the upper needs of the pyramid, they will look for responsibility, exert effort, and use creativity and ingenuity in their work.

These are old news today, 50-something years later, but seemingly, most of our organizations are still working under the same philosophy following the precepts of theory X. We keep "attempting" to motivate people as if they were children or horses, with bribes.

Theory Y would call for a supportive environment in which workers are able to have a decent life, be creative, look for challenges, search for learning opportunities, reach their entire potential, have a great time, and even improve the world. Autonomy would help give workers the capacity to do it and to satisfy these needs, which by the way, correspond to every single level of Maslow's pyramid.

Autonomy is an enabler of the entire pyramid because it allows for the satisfiers of each level to take place. This is quite powerful.

You may be familiar with the concept of the democratic organization, which is becoming more and more popular. According to Worldblu, a non-profit organization that certifies democratic companies, there are about 230,000 people working already in Worldblu-certified organizations, and there are an estimated 500 million people who have read about Worldblu in the media around the world. Who are some of these Worldblu-certified organizations? They include Davita (a Fortune 400 provider of dialysis treatments), Zappos (the biggest online shoe retailer), Hulu (TV online), Groupon (the popular e-commerce marketplace that offers goods and services at a discount), New Belgium Brewing (the third-largest craft brewery in the United States), and WD-40 (the famous lubricant and metal protector). Note that these businesses belong to a variety of industries.[5]

Autonomy needs a shared purpose and free access to information.

In the last few years, the U.S. Congress has shown how two groups with strong opposite beliefs can come to a halt. People are tired of this bickering and would like them to start working toward what makes sense for America. Is this a risk for democratic organizations? How do we make sure it doesn't happen to us? Simple. While this is impossible to do in the United States, we can make sure that only those who fit with what the organization stands to do and stands for belong to the organization; only those who believe in its purpose.

In our organization, we will not get into gridlock as long as we share the same purpose. If a worker does not believe in the purpose, he isn't a proper fit for this organization and must be let go. When workers agree on the purpose, all discussions take place only in light of how much they advance the organization toward it or not.

In previous parts of the book, we compared a well-functioning organization with the human body. We said that the body's organs never decide to do something different from what the rest of the body (or organization) needs. Remember Steve, who was running the New York City Marathon? It isn't as if the cells in his lungs say, "If I slow down, maybe Steve will stop performing this activity that doesn't bring any benefit to me." Does this happen in organizations? For sure. Remember when managers "spend" all their budget dollars in the current year so that next year's allowance isn't reduced?

There is one case where the organs and systems of the body act to the detriment of the body. Think about the immune system attacking the body when the person suffers an allergy or an autoimmune disease. Think about a certain part of the body growing and growing beyond what is healthy, like in a cancer. In these and other cases, the body's informational system is failing. Somewhere between the sending, transmitting, and receiving of the information, the signals aren't reaching their destination in the proper form. The cells decide to act in a different way from that which fosters the well-being of the whole. In an allergy, the immune system incorrectly "believes" there is an enemy to overcome. In cancer, the cells are given instructions to reproduce and reproduce, as if they were part of a growing embryo.

Organizations are alive and susceptible to the same problems. Every area of the organization needs to have access to information so that it makes the right decisions and performs the right actions. Otherwise, it may act on incorrect information and perform actions that hurt the whole entity.

> In one organization, the marketing department was tasked with achieving sales growth goals. It developed marketing advertising and product promotions such as rebates, price reductions, and free promotional extras and gifts. The department wasn't given product profitability information, even though each of these activities affected it. They didn't know whether the product was making money or not. Finance, on the other hand, was tasked with maintaining product profitability. This is, the more money that each product unit made, the better the department believed it was doing its job. It wasn't concerned with brand building, customer retention and satisfaction, and other measurements with which marketing was concerned and rewarded.

These two departments bumped heads constantly. They literally hated each other. Of course, they were blocking one another's goals. The very objectives toward which they went to work each day opposed the objectives of the other function. Wouldn't it make sense that they work together to come up with strategies and programs that make the product profitable, while promoting brand-building and long-term sales growth? Of course, to do so, they needed to share information.

You may be thinking this is an isolated example, but if you look around in your organization, you'll find similar examples. It's so ingrained in our minds that information should be kept hidden from others, and information is so important to develop sensible decisions that this problem is deemed to happen quite frequently.

Autonomy needs information, information, and more information.

All autonomy-oriented companies have made conscious, significant efforts to make information available and understandable to every one of their members. This is done via courses or written materials. Some even use cartoon brochures that can be often found in bathroom stalls. This way, they assure that every employee has the tools to understand where the organization is, how it's faring in the market, what its goals are, and how his or her work fits with these goals.

What about the leakage of information to competitors? Autonomy-oriented companies report that this has hardly ever happened because their workers are committed to their organization, and the benefits of having open information internally far outweigh the risks.

Immanuel Kant, the renowned philosopher, says that if we all had the same information, we would get to the same conclusions. If we have different opinions, it's only because we haven't had the opportunity to review the same information. It's the case of the elephant touched by five people with their eyes covered, who report different things (a trunk, a hose, a wall, a rope, a palm leaf). Whether you adhere to Kant's philosophy or not, it is still quite clear that to bring others to a sensible discussion, all parties need to have the necessary information. Only then will a reasonable result be obtained.

In politics, there is a considerable amount of misinformation, for which the media are partly to blame. Exaggerations and selective reporting help them increase ratings, but in consequence people become influenced by the media they've chosen to watch. This practice is so common that the biases of the different media networks can actually be objectively identified and measured.[6]

What is the problem? A little exaggeration here and there doesn't hurt anybody, some may say. But it does hurt, and we can see how divided the American political environment has become and how difficult it is to drive forward any kind of sensible legislation.

I have seen the same thing happen within organizations, between functional departments, levels, and locations. This leads to the feeling that THEY don't understand the issue or what we are trying to do. In such situations, after a little (or a lot) of digging, we realize that the lack of good quality information shared by every party is the root cause of the problem.

Sometimes parties feel they should not share problems, objectives, concerns, and fears. Group, location, function, and national pride play a role, as well as the lack of trust, the fear of being abused, and simply the desire to follow the local culture. In all these cases, we forget that we are working for the same company; that we have the same ultimate purpose; and that if we were to talk openly and honestly, our customers, our company, and ourselves would be better off.

***

So, what is Autonomy? Autonomy furnishes workers with the capacity to make decisions about their own work as much as it is sensibly possible, and allow them to act however they consider is best. We can divide it into five questions: How, When and Where, What, With whom, and How much and How fast. Let's review them.

Workers must choose HOW to do the work.

The most important aspect of Autonomy is the "how" to do the work. The principle is that the person who actually does the job must have the say on how to perform his job. For example, in an autonomous organization with customer service representatives, instead of pre-prepared scripts, the person must have the autonomy to handle the customer interaction as he thinks best. There will never be enough scripts to account for all situations. A person who understands the objective and is empowered to carry the conversation will naturally get the best result.

If the person doesn't have enough experience to do the job well, he must be given the opportunity to learn it. We aren't saying the worker won't have support or he'll be put in situations that lead to failure—quite the opposite. The best way for the worker to acquire the necessary skills is to spend some time with his mentor and learn by example and observation. If the training must be long, and the risk of failure is high, the workers should be provided with ways to practice until the skills are mastered.

Think of an airline pilot. He acquires technical instruction, but also spends several hours flying with his instructor. There's also practice in the flight simulator. Imagine there were scripts on how to react in an emergency situation. Imagine pilots weren't trusted to make the right decision and had to request some kind of permission to act. It would be ludicrous. Fortunately, pilots receive enough training and now it is up to them to keep the passengers safe.

Several organizations, such as Zappos and Semco, have eliminated scripts for their phone customers' representatives. This doesn't mean in any way that this activity isn't important for them. In fact, for Zappos, customer representatives are the flag carriers of its most important strategic advantage: customer service. But exactly because of it, Zappos believes the best customer service can be given by somebody who understands the overall objective and is free to be the best he or she can be without limiting restrictions.

Semco is probably the organization that has taken the concept of autonomy to its limit. Its CEO, Ricardo Semler, boasts publicly of not having made any managerial decision for at least 10 years. His organization even awarded him with a plaque saying so. Semler believes that letting people do what they think they need to, the way they like to do it, results in something far superior than managers dictating instructions in the usual ways in what he calls "a military structured organization."

In Semco, every stakeholder is able to ask why and what for. As a result, the company has changed several business practices that are ingrained in our modern business way of thinking. For example, Semco workers choose their own managers based on how they think the manager can advance their group. They decide whether they need to hire more people and whom to hire. They make this decision considering how much the potential employee can help them increase profits and how much he costs them. The potential employee puts his salary requirement on the table. These and other practices at Semco seem to be working. Semler's company has grown 27% per year in average for the last 25 years. This is in Brazil, which has experienced at times significant economic crises and hyperinflation.[7]

Workers must choose WHEN and WHERE to do the work.

Probably one of the easiest Autonomy elements to implement is the capacity of the worker to choose when to do his work. In principle, once an amount of work is agreed upon by the worker and the organization, the employer shouldn't really care if he is more efficient and completes the job in less time. If the worker takes a break every hour, the employer shouldn't care, either. The organization should only care about one thing: that the work is completed as required. The current system of 8 to 5 is an artificial constraint placed on the worker because he isn't trusted he'll do his part of the deal.

The belief that the amount of time used is proportional to the results is false, especially when we consider that work has become heuristic (doesn't have a set path) and more complex in modern times. The notion that the amount of time the worker spends in the company is a reflection of his interest for the work turns out to be false over the long run, too. The more time the worker spends at the company, the more it prevents him from attending to out-of-work interests, the more "costly" the work is for the employee, and the more he needs to be compensated via intrinsic or extrinsic rewards.

Every job has implicit constraints, but we should never add to them. For example, at Semco, there must be a receptionist at the office to greet visitors, but instead of creating schedules for them, the company gave this decision to the receptionists. They arrange schedules with no participation from the rest of the company.

When (to do the work) is closely related with *where* (to do it). A similar question applies here. If there's part of the work the worker can do outside the office, do we care? Do workers care? Very much so.

> A Harris Interactive poll reports that 48% of workers believe their commute impacts their job satisfaction, and 32% of workers took their commute into consideration when considering whether to accept their current job.[8]

I am a strong believer in the importance of interaction among workers in all capacities. Having autonomy means to consciously set up touch points for teams, functions, and the entire company. It's important to have social interaction, too. Thankfully, technology has made it possible to increase interaction among workers via telephone, video conferences, video chats, project or function fora (or forums), email, scheduled regular chats, and more.

> Companies have begun to realize the impact of Autonomy practices on their workers and are establishing policies that enable employees to work from home and/or work flexible hours. Sun Microsystems, a computer and computer software company (recently acquired by Oracle) have 50% of its workforce working remotely. Best Buy, Gap, and Banana Republic have implemented ROWE (Results Only Work Environment), a philosophy that supports Autonomy principles (ROWE decreased employee turnover by 45% at Best Buy).[9] KPMG, a leading accounting firm, estimates that about 70% of its workforce work flexible hours.[10] PNC, a financial services firm, reports that half of its workforce participates in some type of flexible arrangement.[11] Kraft foods implemented in 2002 a program called "Fast adapts" to assure that its manufacturing workers also benefit from flexible schedules like their office counterparts.[12]

Workers must have a saying on WHAT to do.

A bit more tricky is the concept of *what* to do. Some companies, such as Google and 3M, let the workers choose what they want to do for a percentage of their time, about 20% of it or one day per week. During this time, the worker can develop, engineer, and even launch products he conceives. What is the purpose of this? Twofold. On one hand, it's an incubator of ideas for the company. The company is tapping into its own people to see which ideas are there. On the other hand, the company is giving its workers the capacity to be free, to try out what they wish to try, and this makes the worker much more engaged with the whole business of the company.

"He's more engaged and more productive with the rest of his job," says Douglas Merril, the Google Chief Innovator Officer, when he discusses the benefits of an employee's autonomous 20% time. Think about it. How cool is it to be paid for doing what you want? But it isn't only a perk. Some of these projects, having the focused interest of the worker, may become highly profitable enterprises for the organization.

When we spend a large amount of time working on one activity, we get tired. We need a break, and often the break takes the form of a different, but still productive activity. This is why we come from the office and enjoy digging holes in the backyard to plant tomatoes or sanding the bumper of our classic automobile. Managers at Semco have realized this natural inclination and have created multifunctional roles that allow for workers to partake in a variety of activities. By limiting the size of the operation or splitting it in two every time it reaches a certain level, they create a natural tendency for people to double up functions. This way, one person may function as a lathe operator, a forklift driver, and an assembler, for example. He becomes less tired and is more productive.

Functional walls are artificial structures that often don't align with the interests of workers or the needs of the work. Semco has a very active program of job rotation in which it lets people trade jobs and move around as they please, with certain controls. Common sense must always prevail, and care needs to be exercised in order to not lose expertise. However, once the program is in place for a while, expertise resides in several people; and as people bring their own ideas, backgrounds and expertise, the overall functional expertise of the organization is increased considerably.

The process for folks to change to other jobs is as follows: Can the person do the job? What skills does he need? Can the conditions for this worker to acquire those skills, and to move to where he wants, be created? This practice of high job mobility helps organizations take down functional walls, cross-pollinate, and build expertise. If a person were to leave the organization, there are always several people ready to take up the baton.

Workers must have a say on WITH WHOM to work.

Peter has a project in mind. He knows having Tina on board would make it so much better because they've worked together before. Can they join forces without too much trouble? Every worker must take care of his responsibilities, but the more the organization lets its workers choose with whom they want to work, the more satisfied and engaged they are. We will review with further detail how others influence our satisfaction and engagement in the chapter on organizational environment.

Wouldn't workers be more engaged with a manager they respect, who helps them deliver their best performance? Some organizations allow workers to choose their managers. Every few months, they vote some out and some others in, but good managers tend to keep their job continuously.

Workers must have a say on HOW MUCH and HOW FAST.

Can workers have a say in how much money they make? We reviewed this practice in the chapter about Salary. The objective is for the employee to hold the reins, as much as possible, of this aspect of his life, too. The worker knows what steps he needs to take to increase his salary. He can decide how and when to take them. He may need to increase expertise, acquire responsibility, change to a different job within the organization, or perhaps realize his salary expectations will not be furnished in this company. His chosen path should be one the worker can reach because the organization makes the tools available for him to follow it. There is no luck, preferential treatment, or any kind of advantage over other workers.

Semco is one of the innovators in this area as well. With four questions it poses, the decision of how much an employee earns is left to the workers. Let's say Ed is a Semco worker. He proposes his salary to join a project. In Semco, workers make the decision whether their project can afford the salary that Ed has set. Is Ed bringing more than what he's costing them? They may decide that Ed is very good, but just too expensive. To come up with sensible numbers, the workers at Semco ask four questions. 1. How much can the company pay? 2. How much do other people with similar responsibilities at Semco make? 3. How much money does the worker believe he can make elsewhere? And 4. How much does he need to live comfortably?[13]

Another aspect of "How much" is related to company planning. Certain organizations like New Belgium Brewing develop their business plan with the participation of their workers. When they are asked how much they want to achieve in the next year or in the next five years, the answer is developed with a thorough understanding of the stress that the goal puts on each worker or resource. Instead of being dictated from the top, planning takes place with the participation of all workers who know the impact of the plan they are developing, both with internal and external stakeholders. It is also a commitment and a resource-planning exercise. Planning this way does much better than a group of people at the top.

How fast is closely related to *how much*. Some of us have a strong desire to advance, to learn, to have more responsibility quickly. Some of us don't; we take our time making sure we learn everything really well. If Richard, who just joined the company, wants to be a coordinator, a manager, or a senior engineer in 5 years, what are the milestones he needs to reach? What are the character traits, the experiences, and the tools Richard needs to have in order for him to be a suitable candidate for his desired position? All this information needs to be available for him. This way, he will be able to study, finesse his personal characteristics, try harder, acquire experiences, etc. In some organizations, like Semco, workers choose their managers, which would leave the final decision to Richard's peers. Richard must make sure he acquires the character traits required to be in the candidate pool.

You may have noticed that we have mentioned Semco repeatedly in these five areas of Autonomy. Semco is a great example of Autonomy and of knocking down artificial constraints. By asking "why" five times, workers realized such things as how inefficient it is to file copies of expense reports at different places (the worker's desk, his manager's desk, accounting and finance departments, etc.). Does a purchase order really need to be signed by eight people? Does an organization really need an IT department? Can the engineers spend some time working at the manufacturing shop as factory workers?[14]

This isn't a world of chaos, but a world of what makes sense.

Once they have tasted the benefit of autonomy, the organizations that practice it develop a strong dislike for rules and regulations. They know rules and regulations drive attention from a company's objectives and purpose. The organization is performing tasks that may not necessarily benefit the customer, the organization, or its workers. Rules provide a false sense of security for management that things are working the way they should, and that they, busy worker bees, are doing their part. Working hard and following the rules don't assure success.

In addition, rules and regulations create work because, one way or another, someone has to see whether the rules are being followed. It also happens that currently enforced rules attempt to fulfill a need that is no longer there.

I don't suggest you implement every one of the five aspects of autonomy in your organization (or business practice) at the same time. What to implement first should perhaps be discussed and agreed-on by workers. As a matter of fact, it may be better if THEY take the lead. The organization should start small and see how it evolves. There are many who won't like the organization to become an autonomous workplace, especially middle management that loses the little power they have fought so hard to get.

Autonomy is about respecting the very core of every human being, trusting him with information, responsibility, and a shared fate. It's one of the biggest gifts with which we can endow our coworkers, but it's also the biggest load we can give them. Autonomy may feel scary at times, but discovering the capacity for workers to reciprocate, when they know they are trusted to perform their part of the deal, is rewarding and very worthwhile.

"Money won't create success, the freedom to make it will."
Nelson Mandela.

Summary of Autonomy.

- Autonomy assumes that every organizational stakeholder is intrinsically motivated and every day strives to go home satisfied with the work he performed.

- To make it work, the employee must have access to the necessary information to make decisions and be a trusted, fully accountable, and responsible member of the organization.

- Autonomy-oriented organizations believe that not one person knows it all, and that the person who does the job knows more about his specific job than anyone else.

- Autonomy has five components:

  - How: The worker is responsible to choose the best way to complete his work. He is the expert and he brings his own characteristics and creativity to it.

  - When and Where: It attempts to eliminate unnecessary constraints such as the time workers need to spend at the office. If workers work remotely for a portion of their time, touch points must be defined to increase worker interactions.

  - What: Workers will be more engaged with the organization the more they choose what work to perform. This can take the form of pet projects, new ventures, or being able to have jobs with multiple functions.

  - With whom: Workers derive more satisfaction by working with the folks they work with best. The organization must attempt to allow workers to form their own teams whenever possible.

  - How much and how fast: Workers must have some control of how much they earn, how to increase it, and how to progress in the company. The organization must make the information available and furnish tools for the worker to advance.

1 Deci, Edward L., Nezlek, John, & Sheinman, Louise. "Characteristics of the Rewarder and Intrinsic Motivation of the Rewardee." *Journal of Personality and Social Psychology* 40(1), pp. 1—10, January 1981.

2 Muhonen, Tuija, & Torkelson, Eva. "Work Locus of Control and Its Relationship to Health and Job Satisfaction from a Gender Perspective." *Stress & Health* 20(1), 2004.

   Chen, Jui-Chen, & Silverthorne, Colin. "The Impact of Locus of Control on Job Stress, Job Performance and Job Satisfaction in Taiwan." *Leadership & Organization Development Journal* 29(7), 2008.

   Vijayashree, Lakshman, & Vishalkumar Jagdischchandra, Mali. "Locus of Control and Job Satisfaction: PSU Employees." *Serbian Journal of Management* 6(2), 2011.

3 Idem.

4 CHI Research, Inc. *Small Serial Innovators: The Small Firm Contribution To Technical Change.* Study chartered by the Small Business Association Office of Advocacy. Contract number SBAHQ-01-C-0149, 2003.

5 As reported in worldblu.com. Retrieved February 14, 2013.

6 Fowler, Nancy. *Measuring Political Bias of Network News: Study Validates New Research Method with Implications in Psychology, Political Science, Business.* Washington University, St Louis Newsroom, April 14, 2011.

7 Interview with Ricardo Semler. Aired on Australian ABC Television 7:30 Report, March 2007.

   MIT Distributed Intelligence World. *Leading by Omission*. September 22, 2005.

   Semler, Ricardo. *The Seven-Day Weekend: Changing the Way Work Works.* Portfolio Hardcover, 2004.

8 Report by Harris Interactive, commissioned by The Workforce Institute at Kronos Incorporated. *"Road Wage" Survey Shows More Than 5,000,000 Employed Adults Have Called Into Work Sick Because They Could Not Face Commute,* 2011.

9 Moen, Phyllis, Kelly, Erin L., & Hill, Rachelle. *Does Enhancing Work-Time Control and Flexibility Reduce Turnover? A Naturally Occurring Experiment.* University of Minnesota, 2011.

10 Reported by Barbara Wankoff, KPMG's national director of workplace solutions.

11 Reported by Darcel Kimble of PNC's corporate communications group.

12 Executive Office of the President. Council of Economic Advisers. *Work-Life Balance and the economics of workplace flexibility,* 2010.

13 Interview with Ricardo Semler. Aired on Australian ABC Television 7:30 Report, March 2007.

14 Semler, Ricardo. *The Seven-Day Weekend: Changing the Way Work Works.* Portfolio Hardcover, 2004.

The Driven Organization

Chapter 12:

C Is About Competence.

"Our treasure lies in the beehive of our knowledge. We are perpetually on the way thither, being by nature winged insects and honey gatherers of the mind." Friedrich Nietzsche, renowned German philosopher of the nineteenth century.

To get ahead, we need to be better; to be better, we need to learn.

When I was in engineering school, I learned something that I would often remember in my professional life. In 1995, Mexico was in the middle of a recession, and the peso had lost half of its value overnight. For Mexicans, acquiring goods from international markets became suddenly prohibitive. Manufacturing producers were incapable of acquiring manufacturing equipment internationally and badly needed supplies. I met a successful Mexican entrepreneur who owned a few manufacturing operations. Trying to sound smart, I mentioned to him that I understood the difficulties to acquire the latest equipment and the importance of having it to manufacture products with good quality and low cost. I clearly remember his reaction. He quickly disregarded my comment and said, "You know, Omar, every person in the world can go and buy the same equipment you buy. In that case, the competitive advantage becomes only about who has the cheapest labor, the most access to capital, the lowest transportation cost. And yes, right now we have trouble getting access to capital, and equipment is expensive for us, but there is something you aren't considering. It is the engineer or the team of engineers that cranks the equipment open and finds the way to make it work faster, better, or cheaper. It's the engineers who create a competitive advantage that will make their company succeed. The world is reducing all other differences, which are only temporary. To succeed, you must bring something extra to your operation."

He was talking about manufacturing processes, but the same concept applies everywhere. Only those organizations that innovate, reduce complexity, increase quality, develop innovative products, reduce costs, or produce more with the same resources will succeed. I know that this is something I don't have to tell you. You know the importance of innovation in every business field. Still, I have been constantly surprised, as I have walked my professional life, to see the pervasive belief that to become leader in a competitive market, an organization needs to acquire a new technology, new equipment, or new tools from external sources. "With this new technology," the chairman makes his case, "we'll become the most profitable player." This belief is false, and may eventually cause significant problems for the organization. Knowledge and new capabilities must be developed in-house at a minimum in regard to the strategic advantage of the organization to sustain it and succeed over the long run. This is a fact: No one can buy his way to a successful long-term business.

To crank the equipment open, the engineer or team of engineers need to know what they are doing. In effect, they need to be close to the vanguard of knowledge in their field; otherwise, they won't be able to improve the machinery in a significant way. How can the team of marketers develop successful innovative campaigns if they aren't able to create new marketing tools? How can the finance team find ways to finance operations in a cheaper way if they attempt to do things only by the book?

GM, Chrysler, and Ford have forgone important knowledge they used to have about the manufacturing of their vehicle parts. Because of their focus on reducing their workforce cost, in part because their labor unions made it too expensive, they have left the know-how to build the automotive components to their suppliers. Now, if every other vehicle manufacturer buys the same manufacturing equipment, purchases the same vehicle components, and assembles them in similar ways, what is the advantage of each of the big three? I know this isn't the entire story, and we won't explore it here, but it's a fact that the big three have allowed an important competitive advantage to leave their organizations. In contrast, Toyota has partnered with their suppliers to develop vehicle components that meet ever more stringent standards at lower costs. To do so, they need to have engineers in-house with strong knowledge who can work alongside suppliers to develop newer, better, and cheaper vehicle parts.

To understand how we can foster Competence at the organizational level, we must understand the specific ways for an individual, for a worker, to learn. It is through the learning of each individual that the organization acquires knowledge. On the other hand, learning is so important in our lives that almost every activity we enjoy doing is related to it, from hobbies and entertainment to our everyday work. We shouldn't be surprised, therefore, that Competence is part of SPACES and has become a central component of our Driven Organization.

Can we fulfill our need for knowledge at work?

I secretly admire coworkers of mine throughout my professional life who remain in their professions. While I went to other companies, functions, and industries, they stayed and became experts in their professions. I admire they mastered every aspect of their job, their constancy, and their patience. I can see how it has paid off for many of them.

We could say that my desire to learn and explore new things has been costly because I have left jobs and organizations that valued my contribution and because I have forgone valuable expertise. I know there was no option for me. I have accepted that I have had a strong desire to learn and experience new things, which took me to different places and have enriched my life in unique and great ways. But still, I wonder if it has to be like that. I wonder about an organization that allows its workers to learn, to explore other functions and jobs, to develop expertise in areas not always directly related to the business, and to experiment on new ways of working. I wonder if such a place would have furnished me with the opportunities to fulfill this desire for Competence, while protecting the experiences and expertise I was developing throughout the journey, and use them toward the advancement of the organization.

Imagine that your job provides you with daily opportunities to learn, stretching you intellectually and making you better. Imagine that you had the opportunity to go to other functions and other jobs almost seamlessly, improving your overall level of experience and helping you augment your vision. Imagine your job was actually interesting, by design. How would you feel in this job?

Learning is a key ingredient for the organization to succeed in the long run, and workers have the need to be constantly learning, too. Couldn't we find the way to meet these two requirements together: helping the worker become satisfied and making the organization better and stronger? This chapter attempts to study ways to do so. We will attempt to provide opportunities for the workers to learn, acquire knowledge, experiment, and become better while they bring knowledge, innovation, and expertise to their organization.

There are five ways we will use to describe Competence for the individual human being. We will describe each of them in detail in the following sections: mastery, novelty or natural curiosity, insight or the "aha" moment, being "in the zone" or achieving "flow," and problem solving.

Afterward, we will make sure that our organization uses, in an effective and efficient way, the knowledge developed by the individual, thus creating a learning organization. This follows the same thinking we have followed all along in this book. We are creating a Driven Organization that exists to foster the intrinsic needs of its workers, helping them and letting them be all they can be. In the process, the organization becomes a powerful business machine, capable of tackling any situation successfully.

To achieve "Mastery" is to develop expertise.

What is the main appeal of video games? The player doesn't actually win any external reward. It isn't as if the game company awards him with $5 every time he passes to the next phase of the game. Most often, these players don't get much recognition from their friends and family, either, as they would with other activities, such as perhaps building a nice coffee table or winning the summer volleyball tournament.

What about those who play the guitar? We may practice countless hours trying to become a little better and in the process probably cause a huge torment to those who don't have an easy way out of the house. I used to enjoy mountain biking a lot. My friends and I celebrated every time we reduced the time it took us to complete a mountain bike loop in Michigan; more than 9:00 minutes the first time we were curious to check, 8:00 a few weeks later, 7:30, 7:20, 7:10, 7:05, 7:03.

Being highly competent or having mastery in something makes us feel really good. Part of it is related to our esteem needs, the fourth level of Maslow's pyramid of needs. When we perceive we are better than the last time we performed the activity or when we see how far we have traveled over the last few months or years, we think quite highly of ourselves. It is perhaps a similar feeling to, when hiking, we look back from the top of the mountain and realize what we have traversed, what we have conquered. We feel proud of our accomplishment!

It probably makes us feel that we could tackle any problem to which we dedicate ourselves. We set ourselves to do something and we completed it. Esteem from others may also play a role as we enjoy another's appreciation of our accomplishment. Mastery is also related to self-actualization needs. Becoming really good at something helps us find our place in the world. This is our unique contribution to the world that might have not existed if we hadn't tried this hard to be a great musician, an amazing cook, or a brilliant engineer.

How can our organization help us with this need? By letting its workers do just that: become the very best they can be. For example, an organization can help its workers acquire mastery by providing funding or time off work to do it. The learning would take place inside the organization and it wouldn't be that costly, other than letting workers spend time on the processes. Recognition in the organization for high competence cannot but help.

An IT service company that assists customers in sorting their computer issues experienced the benefit of allowing the workers to acquire knowledge and become better at their work. In the past, when a customer called, the call was answered by the first-level, customer-care responder. A second level was always available to answer the calls that were too complex for the first level to handle. Managers asked their first-level responders to limit the time of the call to ten minutes and to pass the calls that had more complexity to the second-level responders. They had forbidden using tools like Google to find out solutions. Turnover for first level responders was high, there were frequent mistakes with the calls and reports they needed to fill out, and customer evaluations were mediocre.

Some managers realized that as workers were promoted to second level responders, their evaluations improved, fewer mistakes were made, and turnover went down. They convinced management to allow workers at the first level to grow with the work. First-level responders were allowed to work with the customers to discuss the problem without time limitations and to ask coworkers for tips and solutions. The company provided tools to find answers and allowed using Google to seek solutions. Second-level responders were still available when needed.

These changes had a positive effect: turnover was reduced, fewer mistakes were made across the board, fewer (and more expensive) second-level representatives were required, and customer evaluations improved. Allowing the workers to become "learning entities" changed the mood of the department.

The results for an organization are not always immediate, but satisfaction for the workers is. I met Dave years ago. He works in a manufacturing organization that makes a wide range of stamped vehicle parts, from small motor housings to vehicle doors and hoods. Dave studied the stamping process extensively. He convinced his management to let him and his team experiment with some of the small stamping presses because the big ones cost millions. He and his team spent countless hours perfecting their stamping, and eventually were able to tune, and achieve improved tolerances and better parts than their customers required. Throughout the years, when new, tighter dimensions were required, Dave's organization was able to meet them without major modifications to its equipment. This is a big deal because upgrading an organization's stamping equipment is a major investment.

Years ago, Dave's management understood that allowing him to keep experimenting would eventually pay off. They allowed him to play with tools, provided him with materials, and fostered his learning. Dave used scrap metal when possible for the tryouts, but this wasn't always possible. Dave's team appreciated the "investment" that the organization was doing for them, and the organization appreciated the expertise they were attaining. Allowing Dave to develop mastery on the stamping process paid off in that they had a satisfied worker, but also in that Dave developed useful expertise for the organization.

"If people knew how hard I worked to get my mastery, it wouldn't seem so wonderful at all." Michelangelo.

"Novelty" is our natural desire for new knowledge and experiences.

All human beings have innate curiosity. We need to constantly look for new things. Thanks to this need, we have many new discoveries and scientific knowledge that have made our lives what they are today. This may be one of the biggest reasons why human beings constantly experiment.

In Maslow's pyramid, we see this need for new knowledge and for new experiences reflected in the fifth level: the need to know and understand. There are many areas of our life that exploit this need, such as reality TV and soap operas. Will he lose 100 lb. in 50 days? Will she marry him? In fact, a lot of TV relates to this need, from *CSI Miami* to *Bones*.

> Our need to experiment is primal. Monkeys and other animals have the same inclination to solve problems just for the sake of the learning experience. Harry F. Harlow showed that monkeys have an innate desire to solve puzzles even when they were not rewarded for doing it. In his experiments, he had monkeys playing with a puzzle and becoming better at solving it with no reward associated with the solving of the puzzle. It was as if the monkeys enjoyed solving it.[1]

But this need goes further than TV and scientific discoveries. It may explain why some folks leave their hometown, secure life to try their luck in other places, even when that may entail a considerable amount of risk and even suffering. This need may explain why we crank open the DVD player to see how it works, why we travel to other countries, and why we enjoy meeting new people. It's why babies put everything in their mouths. Mixing Coca-Cola with Mentos, making little rockets with matches, trying to home brew beer? Yes, yes, and yes.

How can our organization help its workers? Some organizations allocate an amount of money for workers to spend to learn something new, from continuing education and specialized knowledge to community classes, workshops, and retreats. Some others pay for training that workers choose via voting. Some, like Semco, allow workers to move to other positions to get more experience and to double up with dual job responsibilities. Other organizations, such as Google and 3M, foster experimentation that allows a percentage of the worker's time to be spent on their pet projects.

When workers are truly interested and because they understand the financial concerns of the organization, they will find the way to learn and conduct experiments at a low cost. The organization may support their efforts by supplying raw materials, providing equipment for experimentation, making classrooms available, bringing experts, and helping them acquire books, DVDs, and other educational materials.

In turn, the workers may form task forces to experiment with the new knowledge, pass it on to others in the organization, and advance it beyond what was given to them. Special task forces could be formed to find knowledge that workers want and need. These teams can scan the Internet, libraries, and bookstores to find what they want, research it, share it, and use it. All this can take place on the company's time or half company time, half after-hours time.

By allowing its workers to acquire even what we could call "random, unrelated" knowledge, not only do they have a happy workforce but they also help bring other ideas into their processes.

A study by Penn State researchers concluded that "Doctors' thinking and creativity skills sharpen when they take humanities courses." Doctors took part in reading, reflection, and discussion; creative expression; technology; and ethics courses. They wrote original literary pieces, discussed and edited them with each other, and much more. "The process of literary analysis, which is both methodical and intuitive, helps to sharpen the cognitive processes inherent in medical diagnosis and treatment that are so vital in medical practice," concluded the lead researcher. The physicians reported overwhelming satisfaction with the experience, and the program has been expanded. "These courses offer

When an organization allows its workers to shift functions and try other areas, they cross-pollinate the organization and take down functional walls. The organization becomes much more connected, and there is more of a focus on the whole organization's goals (as opposed to the function's goals).

Experiments, as we saw before, are a great way to increase the knowledge base of the organization. The organization should always dedicate a percentage of resources, be it time or money, to experiment and learn. For example, if they test what happens when they lower prices in small markets, they may be able to implement more successful low-price strategies when they need to in bigger markets.

Another way to acquire new knowledge is from customers. We have heard this often before, but few organizations do it well. Some of the ones that do listen to their customers fail to act on the new information. This is often the case with big corporations. The objective isn't to ask customers to design the product for the organization, but to understand their needs and desires so that the organization is able to create highly desired products and services.

An example of an organization that learns through its customers is a small private company called BioRay that produces nutritional supplements and plays a significant role in the autistic children environment. To start, some members of this organization have autistic children themselves; they are their own customers. They participate in events related with autistic children where they provide product information, but also listen to what the customers experience with their supplements and those supplied by other companies. They have active, open lines of communication to help parents become informed and provide feedback. This way, they learn about customer's experiences with their product; keep track of successes; and document what worked and what didn't, including dosages and child reactions. In the past, they ran Internet discussion fora (or forums) as well.

Because they are so close to their customers, they know how to best price products. Workers are personally interested in learning the effects their products have in their customer's children. They want to know about new formulations or new products that have helped other children. They want to know more because the knowledge will benefit them as a company, but also as parents of a troubled child. Customers, by the way, loved BioRay and it has a significant following.

"Insights" and "aha moments" bring enjoyment and learning to us.

Try to remember when you felt an "aha" moment. It always brings deep satisfaction. "Yes! I got it," we say to ourselves after solving a difficult problem or understanding something complex. The more difficult the problem is, the better we feel. An "aha" moment is energizing, making the climb worthwhile. It is the climax of our battle with the complex problem.

I have seen that the best professors build cases and problems in such a way that the students, after battling for a while, finally get to an "aha" moment for the lesson. The students become much engaged with the subject and enjoy the process. If we had an "aha" moment every day, our lives would be wonderful because such event is closely related with wonder.

Can the organization create "aha" moments? Not really, but it can foster an environment that leads to having more of them. At Okworks, the hierarchical organization we visited in Chapter 6, the smart Harvard-educated boss tells everyone what to do, which doesn't give much space for workers to learn, other than what the boss learns himself. Soon, workers don't pay much attention to what they do, but become great command executors. In Greatworks, answers from management are fluid. Workers go search, experiment, and discuss the information they find. Meetings and reviews are embedded with a spirit of analysis and learning. This organization will tend to be one that learns, which will lead to many "aha" moments. We will discuss more about creating the right Environment in the next chapter.

Over time, having people engaged in the process of learning and solving the organization's problems will make a much stronger organization than the one led by Mr. Harvard, even if he is the most brilliant guy. The organization benefits, not only because people are engaged and satisfied but also because the organization has a much higher rate of acquisition, distribution, and use of knowledge.

Being in "flow" or in "the zone" means fun and performance.

When I was a child I used to lose myself playing with Lego pieces, building vehicles and bridges. I found it so great that I could let my imagination run wild and then attempt building the very products of my dreams. An afternoon often turned into an evening while I worked on such projects. Those who have children have probably seen it, too. The children sometimes become quite absorbed in an activity that requires all their attention and they do it for hours. It is said that Michelangelo painted the Sistine Chapel in a similar state. He used to paint for days without eating or sleeping until he passed out.

Years ago, a young researcher named Mihaly Csikszentmihalyi became fascinated by artists who got lost in time, forgetting to eat, drink, and sleep. He saw this happening clearly with certain painters, but later he observed that it happened with other professions and activities, too. Csikszentmihalyi and his team studied the phenomenon and called it "Flow."[3] The concept became widely known in the '80s and '90s and has become almost part of our colloquial vocabulary. We use a variety of names to describe it. We call it "to be in the zone," "to be present," "to be wired in," "to be in the groove," and "to keep our head in the game," among others.

Just like the children, the person in flow is completely engrossed in an activity. His eyes are on fire, completely focused. He pays no attention to his surroundings, to others, to his bodily needs, and time just passes by. According to the scientists who have studied the concept of flow, contrary to what we may think, the person's heart rate is low, and he is very relaxed. He is just "in the zone." His attention is entirely focused on the activity and he knows he can perform it. Csikszentmihalyi says that thoughts, feelings, wishes and actions are all in concert.

Although he is the one that made us aware of it in the western world, Csikszentmihalyi himself recognizes that the concept has been known for a long time in Buddhism, Taoism, Indian religion, and other old religions and philosophies. The Taoists speak of spontaneous action in complete awareness but without drive or occupation, and the Buddhists speak of Wei wu Wei, or doing without doing. Both concepts seem to describe what Csikszentmihalyi describes as flow.

I probably don't have to tell you that the person in flow performs better and with more quality.

> You have seen it often in sports. How many times have you seen the following? A forward player has been awarded a penalty score. He walks to the shooting position, and you can already see whether he is going to make it or not. Perhaps, it is the way he walks, the way he prepares for the shot, or his eyes. "He is going to do it," you say, and most often you are right; he scores as you predicted it.

Because flow entails complete focus and engagement with the activity being performed and tunes out everything else, the person in flow can perform much better.

> Researchers have confirmed that achieving a flow state is positively correlated with better performance in creative endeavors,[4] sports,[5] teaching and learning,[6] and at work.[7]

But how do we get to be in flow then? The answer isn't so simple because we cannot force ourselves into flow; actually the best way not to achieve flow is to try to force it. The good news is that we can create the conditions for us to get it and it will happen by itself. The first condition is that we must be performing an activity we find purposeful, that brings something to the world or to ourselves. Perhaps, we are attempting to be better guitar players, we are trying to perfect the caring of a bonsai tree, or we are giving a lecture on our favorite subject. It cannot be an activity we deem unimportant.

The second condition is that the activity must be something we enjoy doing, that makes us happy when we do it. The experts call this type of activities "autotelic," from *telic*, which means purposeful, and from *auto*, which means self. Autotelic means that performing the activity is its own reward. The third condition is that it must stretch, although not over utilize our skills.[8] If the activity is too easy for us, we get bored; if it is too difficult, we get stressed out. The fourth and final requirement is that the activity has clear goals and quick feedback. The person needs to see the effect of his actions in a relatively short period of time in order for him to correct and improve.

Csikszentmihalyi says that the main reason why flow doesn't happen in our workplaces as frequently as it could is because although a task may fit into a larger organizational goal, the individual worker may not see where his individual task fits with it. Another important reason is that the worker doesn't have enough feedback to realize whether his work was good or not.

One of management's most important jobs is to make sure that workers see the relationship of their work with the larger purpose of the organization. Through informal chats, formal presentations, and tours to see the effect on their customers, management can help workers see this link. In regard to the lack of feedback, there are a few ways to help with this problem. The process may be set in such a way that the worker sees the effect of his work down the line. The worker may also be rotated temporarily to a function down the production chain. There may be smart measurements that provide feedback to the worker. If the feedback loop is too long, the long task can be broken into smaller ones with quick feedback points.

We derive a lot of satisfaction from "problem solving."

You have been working on an acquisition for your company. The target is a small organization with some interesting intellectual property capital. Due diligence has been performed, and you are at the last steps of the merger and acquisition process. Suddenly, while you are having a moment of peace at your office, there is a phone call that may irrefutably change the set course. The old owners are refusing to be part of the newly formed organization, which is part of why the deal is so attractive to your company. They have sent a letter with their demands, which you know your company can't meet. You go into a meeting room and start reviewing the situation with your team.

After 90 minutes, you and your team know what to do. You understand what they really want, what is behind their words. You have found a solution that works perfectly for them and for your organization. You are excited and satisfied. Somehow this "problem" added a bit of drama to your day, but has given you and your team the opportunity to solve a big problem, which you enjoyed. You feel useful, successful, and sure that you have more than earned your salary for the day.

There is an inherent satisfaction to be gained from solving problems, for fixing things, for completing complex tasks. The more difficult to complete, the greater the satisfaction. It's about successfully solving the problems we encounter, about leaving a positive footprint in the meetings we attend and in the conversations we have. It may also be about knowing that we can do it and about exercising our capacities. This problem-solving need may be closely related with our esteem needs, the fourth level of Maslow, as we want to perceive ourselves capable or for others to perceive us the same way. It may also be related to our self-actualization needs as we are being what we can be: a great manager, a great engineer, a great wife, or a great parent.

How do we foster this happening in our organization? There are two main aspects: First, we need to have an environment of openness and inclusion, for civil discourse, objective problem solving, and continuous performance improvement. This is reinforced with every part of SPACES, but we will review it with more detail in the Environment chapter. Second is challenges: people must have opportunities throughout the day to be challenged and to face problems. This will prompt them to be interested and focused, which will help them stay active, happy, and engaged.

Learning organizations acquire it, share it, and use it.

So far, we have reviewed the need of individuals for competence in the form of mastery, novelty, insight, flow, and problem solving. We have also seen how each of these may help the organization become better and stronger, but we still need to check whether they make our organization capable of learning and improving itself, to become in effect a learning organization.

So, how does an organization become more knowledgeable? There are three things that actively-learning organizations do:

- Acquire knowledge, which entails collecting information or intelligence; benchmarking competitors; learning from experiences, processes and practices; and experimenting constantly
- Share or transfer knowledge internally throughout the organization
- Actually using knowledge to produce better or cheaper products or services.

Three simple things: get it (knowledge), share it, and use it.

Joe's vacation.

In his vacation in Guatemala, Joe learned how the descendants of the Mayans prepare their food. To cook and warm their food, they light wood fires, but manage to do it only twice a day, which saves them valuable wood. During the day, they drink a cold beverage made of corn called "pozol," which provides enough nutrients and doesn't require them to start a fire.

Joe has been concerned about the energy usage of the small factory where he works. Observing the indigenous people has given him an idea. Joe wants to propose changing the schedule for processes that require preheating to 4 days, 10 hours per day, instead of the normal schedule of 5 days, 8 hours per day.

His organization allows Joe and everyone else to spend 15% of their time on improving projects, which Joe and his friends used to study the idea. They calculated energy savings, identified concerns (such as additional inventory), and submitted their idea to the "idea system." In this phone/Internet app with the feeling of a social site, workers input ideas, potential, and expected risks. They ask for feedback, help each other, recruit team members, present status, and more. Workers own the process and they decide which teams deserve to continue ahead and receive funding.

Based on its potential, Joe and his team were given 5 minutes to present their project at the whole company monthly meeting, searching for approval to the next phase. They shared an animated screen showing what the process would look like. The result from the presentation was a "go-ahead" with further evaluation work, which entailed some real testing in a section of the factory. They also got three new volunteers: a manufacturing director and two process gals.

Eventually, the project was approved across the board, and Joe's company has saved 10% of energy expenses by carefully and smartly planning equipment usage. This tiny idea has given light to other ideas. For example, at the office floor, people stay at home on Fridays to avoid the commute, reducing building energy costs.

Four ways to acquire knowledge.

In our story, Joe began to acquire knowledge from his own personal endeavors. It came in the form of an idea. Note that he was not exerting himself or working on company problems in his free time, but because he cared about his organization, the idea came naturally to him. In general, there are four ways to acquire knowledge: Collecting information or intelligence; benchmarking; learning from your own experiences, processes and practices; and experimenting constantly. Let's briefly discuss them.

Workers can collect and gather information in a multitude of ways. These go from reading—some organizations have libraries and have active programs where folks rotate to present subjects—to sending workers to get higher degrees or specializations. Some organizations even develop programs with local community colleges tailored to their specific needs. A common program, tuition assistance, can be a great way to collect knowledge, especially when the worker is engaged with the organization.

> Classroom-style learning is always important, but it is often overrated. It is estimated that as little as 15% of learning from traditional classroom style training results in sustained behavioral change at work. Just think about all those company trainings you were forced to attend. You went, paid attention, filled out a questionnaire, and well... basically forgot about it. Fortunately, when combining it with other learning ways, we can make it much stronger.[9]

Benchmarking, be it processes, competition, or other organizations, is a great way to acquire knowledge. While it may help us catch on with competitors and partners, it may also be a source of innovation. How is company Y doing it? What other products entail similar manufacturing or development processes? How is that bank able to process that many people in so little time? Can we do the same?

The third way to acquire knowledge is by learning from an organization's own experiences, processes, and practices. This is the most important way to acquire knowledge for an organization. To do this successfully, the organization needs to have the culture of thoroughly understanding problems and experiences, and to be open to question processes and practices.

There are many tools to systematically analyze problems that could be of help such as 5 Whys, Eight Disciplines, and cause-and-effect diagrams. It is important to understand that it's the organization's problem solving and improvement culture that is the most fundamental part of this learning. Using the tools mentioned here in a non-learning organization will only add to its bureaucratic practices.

> The 5 Whys is a questions/asking method used to explore the cause/effect relationships underlying a particular problem, with the goal of determining its root cause. The process starts with the first why for the problem and digs deeper with each additional why.[10]

> Eight Disciplines Problem Solving is a method used to analyze and resolve problems, typically employed by quality engineers. Discipline Zero, D0, is planning phase. D1: Form team. D2: Define problem. D3: Develop interim containment plan. D4: Identify root causes. D5: Determine permanent corrections. D6: Implement and validate. D7: Prevent recurrences. D8: Congratulate your Team.[11]

> Cause-and-effect diagrams are causal diagrams that show the causes of a specific event. Common uses are product design and quality defect prevention. Each cause or reason for imperfection is a source of variation. Causes are usually grouped into major categories to identify these sources of variation.[12]

The fourth way to acquire knowledge is to experiment. Joe used computer simulation tools to develop a quick test for his idea, and eventually he was able to do some physical testing. Although experimenting entails failure, it's a great way to fail in a controlled manner, making knowledge acquisition cheaper than if we were to fail the regular way. We can see how these four ways of acquiring knowledge fit great with the individual needs of the worker as he pursues knowledge in his search for mastery, novelty, insight, and flow.

The best learning is achieved through performing activities that bring the same concept from different perspectives. Instead of filling workers with knowledge that will be forgotten, the knowledge that the organization needs its workers to know must be reinforced through many other activities. This could be classroom, discussion, experimenting, small-scale implementation, result analysis, and continuous improvement.

> At the Lumiar Institute in Brazil, instead of having children study subjects such as math and physics the classical way, they actually focus on working on projects that explore the subjects. For example, they may work on designing and building a bicycle. To do so, they may refer to trigonometry, physics, algebra, and perhaps more. They learn concepts, understand model solutions, experiment with ideas, and fail. In the next project, they may need to visit again the things they already learned with the bicycle.[13]

Two ways to share knowledge: formal and social.

It often happens that organizations have great knowledge, but it isn't known in the places where it's needed. This is why we must have an active capable system to share knowledge within the organization.

In our story, Joe felt comfortable enough to share his idea with his peers, and they all felt comfortable enough to work on it. Consider how important it is for workers to have the right working environment so they feel comfortable to speak up. Sometimes, workers are shy and may believe their peers may laugh at their ideas, which stifles ideation. If you think about it, every genius idea was pretty ridiculous at the ideation stage. Seriously, a computer application that lets people have audio/video chats for free? An effort to map and take pictures along every road of the world?

For most of us at work, the normal thing to do is to avoid the risk of looking ridiculous or losing our "seriousness" for work. We may get locked into the category of joker as opposed to being serious and hard-working. It is better just to do the job as it is being done. Even when people like the idea, the ideator may be perceived as the person who thinks too much of herself. In many organizations, the highest nail gets nailed down by peers or management who may think she hasn't "put her time to propose such changes." These are all possible obstacles to knowledge creation. Note that Joe's organization had a good process to share ideas with everyone in the organization with the social app and the monthly meetings. Every worker could add to it and learn from it throughout its development.

In general, there are two ways to share knowledge in the organization: formally and socially. When pieces of knowledge are created, they can be put in databases for others to access and use. This is the formal way. Within the database, it can take the form of summaries, manuals, recommendations, emails, and more.

McKinsey, the consultancy firm, has a very broad and comprehensive database of projects in which it has worked. When a consultant needs to see studies comparing local manufacturing and manufacturing in China, for example, she can get summaries, conclusions, and the names of those who participated in the studies.[14]

The second way to share knowledge is socially, which is the main way most organizations have used throughout the years, although it is rarely well done. The idea is to create an environment that allows for people to mingle socially. This way, in an organic fashion, they find the way to ask, advise, and help each other. A casual conversation at lunch, interaction in the company's social site, and even constant chatting may produce expert recommendations. At a minimum, workers may be pointed to the right person for further help.

A study published in the *Harvard Business Review* in 1996 measured the performance of different layouts. The authors concluded that having open layouts in which people can see each other's work, and having spaces in which people can interact socially lead to considerable higher performance. By having everyone close to each other in an open space, the layout allows workers to communicate and share knowledge throughout the work day.[15]

Note that these two ways to share knowledge are not mutually exclusive, but entirely complementary. Many organizations use both methods. The formal system is used as a starting point, perhaps to find the right contacts, and then the environment promotes social interaction and support among its workers.

Industry-wide, companies have also found ways to share knowledge with each other. For example, suppliers and customers help each other learn more about their processes and the fundamentals behind them with the objective of fostering a better partnership, improving their processes, and understanding their technical requirements.

"Our knowledge is only as good as our ability to share the last thing we learned." Bob Buckman, Chairman of BL Holdings.

Final step, let's use the knowledge.

After Joe's organization is on board, the project is public, and people are interested, it is difficult not to take advantage of the opportunity to use what has been learned. Joe's organization has developed a process that keeps promising projects alive. By making it organic and an integral part of their activities, the final step of the learning process, to use the knowledge, has to occur.

The role of Management.

In Joe's story, management stayed in the sidelines until later in the process, when the manufacturing director joined the team. She joined it to facilitate and help out, but not to take the lead of the project. The workers decided to pursue the idea and the workers owned the project. Management acted as a process facilitator to foster the conditions for ideas to be shared fluidly. If management were to comment on the ideas, they may signal their preference and steer the boat in the wrong direction. It is until later, when the idea has been studied and supported sufficiently when management should jump in to facilitate implementation.

Management, by the way is the most dangerous for innovation. These are the smart people with many years of experience, who may outright develop dozens of reasons why the idea couldn't work. This is one reason why breakthrough innovations frequently come from organizations with little experience in the market.

Remember William McKnight at 3M? Scott Berkun, the author of *The myths of innovation,* explains us that McKnight refused the idea of a young inexperienced technician of a paper with glue three times. The idea later became "masking tape" and surpassed profits from other lines of businesses in which 3M was involved at the time. William McKnight recognized that he was quite wrong and that he needed to protect ideas and inventions from himself and all other people in authority. He set up

"In troubled organizations, ideas flow up, and vetoes flow down." Peter Drucker, highly influential writer and management consultant.

If possible, management should leave the decision of which projects to implement to the workers. This can be done through the use of internal markets, which tap workers to assess the potential of the alternatives provided using small "bets."

Prediction markets are speculative markets created for the purpose of making predictions.[17] Several companies use prediction markets to tap into their employees to assess alternatives, which often yield better results than forecasters. Google, for example, uses prediction markets to forecast product launch dates, new office openings, and many other questions of strategic importance to Google.[18]

What is the right time to kill ideas? Douglas Merril, the Chief Innovation Officer at Google, says their intention is to postpone the evaluation and "killing" of the idea as much as possible. There is a time when they have to either kill the idea or spend serious money on it, but until then the idea can be further developed with minimum cost. Joe first used computer tools, but there was a time that when they needed to do real testing, which is expensive and presents a good opportunity for evaluation.

The environment, as we will see in the next chapter, is a key piece for workers to bring forth new proposals, new ideas, and new knowledge. An autonomous environment with soft functional boundaries and where no one pretends to have the final answer presents the right conditions for discussion, an interchange of ideas, and learning. It is the key factor to socialize ideas in an exploratory way with other workers.

The organization can post problems it wants to fix on the company intranet. Engineers, labor force, and purchasing guys read the list and sign in to voluntarily join these small "learning" task forces, based on what they find interesting. The team may be provided with a small budget and some time to study, to think, to experiment, to come up with solutions and to present them to management. Everyone can input new projects or join others.

It is important that workers are allowed to affect what kind of research, training, and experiments are performed. How do we make sure that the organization learns what needs to learn to be successful, while at the same time allowing workers to choose what they find interesting? This isn't a significant concern because when the individual goals are aligned with the organization's purpose, the worker is intrinsically inclined to do what is best for the organization.

Still, management can create the conditions for workers to find the satisfiers to their Competence needs by leading softly. They can highlight the importance of the goals, show the situation of the company, facilitate the flow of information, advise on negotiating obstacles, and suggest strategic direction to expand knowledge.

"To learn, one must be humble." James Joyce, *Ulysses.*

Summary of Competence.

- A learning organization does three things: Acquire knowledge, share it, and use it:
  - Acquiring knowledge entails collecting information or intelligence; benchmarking your competitors; learning from your own experiences, processes and practices; and experimenting constantly.
  - Sharing or distributing knowledge throughout the organization can be done in a formal way, through databases or sharing platforms; or informally, by promoting social interaction.
  - The final step is to use the knowledge to produce a better or cheaper product or service.
- An individual looks for Competence in the following five ways:
  - Mastery. Every person has a desire to master an activity, to become really good at something. If the person finds this interest related to the business, he cannot but succeed.
  - Novelty. We all have a desire to experience and learn new things. This apparently small desire takes us to new places, new experiences and constantly opens whole new worlds. The

organization may help the worker achieve this need, and in turn the worker may help bring innovation to the organization.

- Insight. This is the "aha" moment we some times enjoy. It is finally understanding something challenging. An organization can foster a learning environment in which these "aha" moments take place on a regular basis.

- Flow. This is a state of mind in which where the individual focuses entirely on the activity performed and tunes out everything around him. Performance is much higher when in flow. A worker can get into flow if he believes in the organization's purpose, if he finds work challenging and enjoyable, and if the work has clear goals and quick feedback.

- Problem solving. There are two main conditions to foster problem solving. We need first to have an environment of openness, inclusion, and civil discourse. Second, we need a challenging job. The job must bring opportunities for the worker to be challenged.

- The role of management should be of a facilitator, not the judge of projects. If possible, the organization should make decisions on which projects merit implementation and which ones do not.

1   Harlow, Harry F., Harlow, Markaret K., & Meyer, Donald R. "Learning Motivated by a Manipulation Drive." *Journal of Experimental Psychology,* 40(2), 228—234, April 1950.

2   Myers, Kimberly. Penn State Hershey Physician Writers Group, 2012.

3   Snyder C. R., & Lopez, Shane J. *Handbook of Positive Psychology,* Chapter 7. Nakamura, Jane, & Csikszentmihalyi, Mihaly. *The Concept of Flow,* 2001.

4   Perry, 1999; Sawyer, 1992.

5   Jackson, Thomas, Marsh, & Smethurst, 2002; Stein, Kimiecik, Daniels, & Jackson, 1995.

6   Jackson, Susan A., Thomas, Patrick R., Marsh, Herbert W., & Smethurst, Christopher J. "Relationships Between Flow, Self-Concept, Psychological Skills, and Performance." *Journal of Applied Sports Psychology,* 13: 129–153, 2001.

Csíkszentmihalyi. 1996.

7   Csíkszentmihalyi. 1991, 2004.

8   Engeser, Stefan, & Rheinberg, Falko. *Flow, Performance and Moderators of Challenge-Skill Balance.* Springer Science+Business Media, 2008.

9   Cromwell & Kolb. "An Examination of Work-Environment Support Factors Affecting Transfer of Supervisory Skills Training to the Work Place." *Human Resource Development Quarterly* 15(4), pp. 449—471, 2004.

10 Asian Development Bank. *Five Whys Technique.* February 2009. adb.org. Retrieved March 26, 2012.

11 Wikipedia.org. *Eight Disciplines Problem Solving.* Retrieved February 13, 2013.

12 Ishikawa, Kaoru. *Guide to Quality Control.* Tokyo: JUSE, 1968.

13 MIT SLOAN Blog. "Escola Lumiar (The Lumiar Institute)". March 14, 2011. Retrieved February 13, 2013.

14 *McKinsey Knowledge Center.* McKinsey & Company. Retrieved February 13, 2013.

15 Majchrzak, Ann, & Wang, Qianwei. "Breaking the Functional Mind-Set in Process Organizations." *Harvard Business Review.* September-October, 1996.

16 Berkun, Scott. "The Myths of Innovation." Presentation on May 14, 2007. Google Tech Talks, 2007.

17 For more information, see "Prediction Market" in Wikipedia.

18 Google official blog. "Putting Crowd Wisdom to Work," 2005.

Chapter 13:

E Is About Environment.

"What is sacred among one people may be ridiculous in another; and what is despised or rejected by one cultural group, may in a different environment become the cornerstone for a great edifice of strange grandeur and beauty." Hu Shih, Chinese philosopher recognized as a key contributor to Chinese liberalism.

The environment tells us what to do, what to expect, and how far to go.

When American drivers experience Latin American roads, they are amazed by the way Latin Americans drive. They feel the Latin American style is aggressive, and vehicles get too close to each other. There is a clear lack of traffic signals and drivers seem to regard speed limits and other traffic regulations as mere suggestions. There are potholes, speed bumps, pedestrians, and sometimes additional surprises such as tree branches or bricks on the road that make driving treacherous and adventurous. More than once, I have seen open storm drains in the middle of the road with no warning signalization whatsoever. Often, the use of seat belts, apparently understood as just another recommendation, is ignored. On highways, some people drive above 100 mph. It just seems that there are no rules in Latin America!

In contrast, U.S. roads are better designed, with stricter signalization and better maintenance. U.S. drivers follow the established traffic regulations (or much more so), which were more thoughtfully established. Vehicles are newer and safer. U.S. drivers use their seat belts, and it is extremely rare that someone drives faster than 100 mph.

I would never advocate the Latin American driving style because it is, for sure, not a better system. Still, considering these two contrasting environments, I was surprised to see that statistical numbers don't show that much difference in deaths from traffic accidents, for example. I would expect it to be five or ten times that of the United States, but it is only 1.6 times in the worst Latin American countries (Mexico's rate is 20.7 deaths per 100,000 inhabitants in a year. Argentina's is 13.7, Brazil's is 19.9, and the United States' is 12.7).[1]

It is much higher, but not 10 times higher, as we may think from the very different driving conditions. I began to wonder why. I looked carefully at the way Latin American people drive and I realized they do have rules, just not written ones. For example, Latin American drivers seem to play "chicken" with their vehicles frequently, but are quick to pull away when things get dangerous. They are aggressive, but keep a constant watch on drivers around them, avoiding possible collisions.

We can argue that these unwritten rules, along with the participants' expectations, values, and traditions, have more influence in the way people drive than probably all the written rules and existing signalization in Latin America. They tell people what to do, what to expect, and how far they can go. If a driver is too nice, he won't be efficient and effective. The trip would take much longer; other drivers wouldn't let him get in and would constantly honk at him. After a few days, this driver may find he already recognizes the cursing signage of Latin America. On the other hand, if the driver is too aggressive, he may run into trouble. He may do something that isn't "expected" by other drivers, which may cause an accident. Thankfully, what ends up happening is that most everyone conforms to each other. They drive similarly. This set of unwritten rules, expectations, values, and traditions comprise the Latin American driving environment.

An organization has its own environment too. The unwritten rules, expectations, values and traditions govern how people act, how fast things get done, and how well they are done. Those of us who have been in different organizations may have seen that they do things differently. Interestingly, just like it wasn't obvious for me to see the rules of the Latin American driving environment, but I knew how to drive there, it is also not easy for workers to spell out the organization's rules, but they are there, playing a huge role on the workers' behavior.

The organization's environment is the visible and invisible, powerful force that gently nudges people to comply with the way things are done in the organization.[2]

Environment is culture plus policies and infrastructure.

We are talking about more than culture. We can define Environment as culture plus policies and infrastructure, all of which influence organizational behavior. In the case of our traffic example, culture is the unwritten rules by which people behave; policies are the law enforcement that attempts to affect the environment in some way; and infrastructure is the roads, signs, stoplights, speed bumps, and whatever else that belongs to the physical conditions on which the culture takes place.

Each one of these three—culture, policies, and infrastructure—has a significant role in shaping drivers' behavior. The lack of law enforcement in Latin America leaves the shaping of the environment to Latin American drivers who, possibly driven by the heat of the moment (metaphorically and literally) may be acting in ways in which they would normally not approve. In the United States, law enforcement attempts to make sure that drivers don't stride too far from driving regulations, but it cannot control the environment. Even if they attempt to mandate behavior, if drivers don't believe in the regulations, they will misbehave when the police turn their backs. An example of this is throwing trash out of the window. It couldn't be stopped via law enforcement by itself; a campaign to convince people of the importance of keeping streets clean was necessary.

How does infrastructure affect us? I've done this experiment in a few cities in Latin America. As I have driven there, I have tried to avoid breaking all traffic laws, no matter how tiny or insignificant they were. I was going to be nice to people, use my turn signals, stop completely at stop signs, enter the parking lot at the entrance and leave at the exit, and respect the speed limit. You already know what happened, right? Well, I couldn't do it.

Some difficulties were with people. For example, when I used my turn signals to change lanes, folks decreased the space between them and the car ahead to prevent me from doing it. Other times, they honked because I was driving too slowly, and many used my nice attitude to get in front of me. However, other difficulties weren't related to people. Sometimes, as much as I tried to determine what the speed limit was, there were no signs. Other times, the only feasible way forward was to make an illegal turn, which everyone did and police officers ignored. I remember coming to a light that was always red. After a while, I realized that it was not just other drivers pushing me into behaving in a certain way, but that the city's infrastructure played an important role as well.

Management won't be able to change the environment of the organization if other structural changes are not performed in the organization. For example, management may have determined they want workers to increase their social interaction to reduce functional silos so that ideas and work flows better. However, the organization doesn't have a commons area, departments are divided in small floors of tall buildings, and management hierarchies are functionally organized. Unless this sets up itself in a different way, workers won't cross functions effectively.

A classic contradictory practice is when management says that every worker is the same, but executives have preferential parking and corner offices with large windows, while everyone else has a small cubicle. IDEO, a highly creative and innovative organization, fosters teamwork by having great meeting rooms, expensively decorated and with lots of tools to use in the meeting. Their cubicles, in contrast are small and a bit crummy. What is the IDEO worker left to do? Work together!

The environment governs our behavior.

We said that American drivers, who have driven in Latin America for a while, tend to adopt the Latin American style of driving. In a period ranging from a few days to a few weeks, they develop the need to defend their turf like everyone else. Soon, they are fighting for that little piece of lane disputed by another driver. And vice verse, the Latin American driver also adapts himself to the way people drive in, let's say, a small town of Tennessee. He becomes less aggressive, pays attention to speed limits and yellow lights, and lets pedestrians cross the road without making them targets to be run off when the light turns green. We can see that the environment not only governs behavior but is also learned.

"How big a driver of behavior is the environment?" you may ask. Well, a lot, really! When I entered business school, I was introduced to the concept of the honor code. This was a pledge to the school that we would be truthful, respect others and their property, and not seek an unfair advantage over our peers. This doesn't sound that unique, but because we were constantly reminded how special everyone was and because we didn't want to disappoint these special people, the honor code acquired a huge importance. We felt that being found dishonorable and not meeting the honor code was just unthinkable. This way, professors gave us tests to complete at home with a time limit with limitations on the academic material we could use to answer it, and we followed instructions precisely. We put the test away when we exhausted the time just as if we were in the classroom.

The same attitude dominated teamwork. Every member did his or her very best to do their part, to contribute, and not be a laggard to the team. I have been in several teams throughout my life, doing big and small things, interesting and uninteresting things, but I haven't seen team members that are more committed to contribute to the team than in that environment.

"Culture [or Environment] is what people do when no one is looking." Herb Kelleher, Chairman, Southwest Airlines.

We create and shape the environment, too.

Left to its own device, the environment can change to something that may not foster desired behavior. Tony Hsieh from Zappos, who is a huge proponent of the importance of environment, lived the evolution and fall of an organizational environment with a fast-growing company he co-created with his partner Sanjay Madan in 1996, called LinkExchange. At the beginning of the start-up, the folks that Hsieh and Madan hired were their friends who would come to visit for a weekend and stay to work. The environment was very enthusiastic and informal. Hsieh describes, "We never knew what time it was, we slept under our desks, and we made conscious efforts to remember to shower." They were energized, enjoyed the work, and good ideas flew by the minute.

When the company grew, they did not have any more friends to hire, so they hired people with the right skills for the jobs. Little by little, as they added tens of people, the company's environment changed. Hsieh witnessed, in a relatively short period of time, the huge change. While at the beginning of the start-up he felt energized to go to work, eventually, the company became a place where he dreaded to go. Those who were hired had different values and personalities than those at the beginning. The environment was less fun and energetic. Tony's experience highlights an important point: Participants bring their values and personalities, and by doing so, shape their environment. Therefore, it's quite important to make sure we bring the right people into the organization.

The environment is powerful because it relates to our basic needs.

Remember our Maslow's pyramid? Remember that a person will be most concerned with fulfilling the bottom needs first and then move up? At the bottom, we have physiological needs and safety needs. Researchers cannot starve people or threaten their safety significantly or with any degree of realism. This way, the first two levels pretty much cannot be tested, but the third one can. The third one is the need to belong. We can explain why social stress comes out the highest by the fact that it is the lowest need in the pyramid that can be really tested.

Scientists have conducted research to find out what stresses people the most. They have found that the type of stress that causes the highest level of physical response is social stress. They use hormonal levels, such as cortisol and alpha-amylase, to measure stress levels. They found that when people are asked to solve problems and answer questions in front of a room full of people, the physical reaction is the strongest. In fact, inducing stress socially works so well that it is becoming the standard way of increasing stress for all stress-related research, such as stress-reducing drugs and therapies.[3]

This need, the need to belong, may explain why we stress out about not disappointing others. If we don't perform as required, be it in terms of capacity or morality, we may not be desirable candidates for

The Driven Organization

their social group. If we show we aren't smart enough, we are not helping the social group get ahead or become stronger. If we aren't morally reliable, if we were to fail the "honor code," we would not be trusted and would not be welcome, either.

The high stress we feel in regard to the psychometric tests conducted in front of others could also be related to the fourth level, the esteem needs. You remember from Chapter 6, that is the image we have of ourselves and the image others have of us: the image of how good we are.

Without intending to, modern life has made us become more isolated. Perhaps because we move so easily, we depend little on our neighbors. Because we change jobs, we depend little on our coworkers. Because of modern conveniences such as credit cards and AAA towing services, we depend little on our family. This modern life has many advantages, of course, but one considerable disadvantage is that we have social interaction that is much less intimate. Some of us may increasingly find that our needs for social interaction and belonging are not met and we must actively look for ways to fulfill them. Do you wonder why Facebook and other similar social sites have become so important in our modern lives?

An organization can purposely be built to foster an environment that promotes social interaction among its workers, allowing them to fulfill the needs from the third level of the Maslow's pyramid. We will discuss throughout this chapter how to do so.

The environment teaches us what to value and what not to value.

To review another aspect of Environment, we'll continue visiting Latin America. In the north of Mexico, in the small towns plagued by drug trafficking, an interesting phenomenon has taken place. Young men with limited possibilities take different paths. Some farm their parents' land, some become workers earning a small wage, some go to the city, and some get into the drug trafficking business. Meet Maria, a young girl raised down south, whose family circumstances caused her to move north with her uncle. She describes how her own perception of the young men and their profession changed over time. When she arrived north, Maria didn't consider the boys involved in drug trafficking as suitable candidates for a boyfriend. However, as time passed, she changed her mind. She now believes that those who participate in drug trafficking are ambitious and motivated risk takers, while those who "settle" into a job are settling for a life of hard work and little means. These folks are conformists, pushovers, and insecure.

From what Maria described, I realized that she "learned" to appreciate certain values that everyone else appreciated or believed. The environment influenced her perception of what is valuable and what isn't. Maria's story, as disturbing as it may be, helps us realize the most important aspect of environment: It teaches people what to value and what not to value.

I have seen organizations in which it is perceived as "cool" to mock customers. Workers, often including management, get together to tell stories and have a good laugh. It is normally considered harmless, even a good way to let off steam. Newbies, who initially show great respect for their customers, quickly learn the ways of the organization; soon they tell vivid stories of their "stupid" customers. At some level, when workers interact with customers, do you think they don't realize it? If they have a choice of another provider, wouldn't you think they'd choose it if they felt better with it?

It is extremely important to understand what our environment values because it will affect every action we perform during our workdays.

Sharing beliefs leads to trust, and trust to friendship.

Imagine getting out of bed every day to go build great things with your dearest friends. Instead of coworkers, you'd work with great people with whom you feel well connected, who share your objectives, and who trust you and are trusted by you. How would your work day be? Sounds great, right? Friendship at work leads to great teamwork, superior results, and off-the-chart job satisfaction.

> Rackspace, a hosting and cloud computing organization, measures performance every single day. It reports that when a team has a celebration or an event, the performance of the day increases by 20 to 30%.[4] It's no surprise that many successful businesses, today's important corporations, started with a few tight friends working together.[5]

"Don't tell me that I have to be friends with my weird colleagues," someone may say. Good point. How can we be friends with those we don't like and with whom we share very little?

We said in Chapter 10 that we tend to trust those who believe what we believe, who come to the same conclusions we have after following different paths in life. With this ingredient, daily interaction, and time, great friendships can be created. In the process, we will increasingly share our personal matters and will confide in each other. Experts on friendship describe a similar process.[6]

How do we treat those who believe what we believe? One day, I needed an accountant and I asked a friend for a recommendation. As he told me about someone and explained to me how to contact him, he said, "I don't actually know him, but he belongs to my church." How can the fact that he belongs to a church be translated to how good an accountant he is? But it does somehow. My friend trusts him because they share something he considers valuable. He believes in something in which my friend strongly believes. Think of someone you trust. He is OK because he ... (finish the sentence with something that is derived from a shared belief). This is why it's fundamental to have a purpose in which all stakeholders believe.

After a person is trusted, he is considered by others, let into the circle, and stops being different; no longer an outsider.

Even when there may not be enough interaction to achieve friendship, trust is extremely valuable in organizations. Trust is believing that others will behave in the way we expect them to. We trust those who believe what we believe because we think they'll make the same decisions and act in the same way we would. Trust is knowing that while we are doing our bit, others will do theirs; that we are pulling toward the same direction, toward the same objectives, toward our purpose. Trust is not using effort to protect myself or my department.

Think about the following levels of trust. Think of someone buying illegal drugs. Neither the seller nor the buyer trusts each other much. The buyer only trusts that the seller wants money from him. The seller only trusts that the buyer wants drugs. The transaction takes place with only that little bit of common ground. It is transactional trust that allows them to make the deal, but not much more. They would betray each other if it benefited one or the other, for example. Some organizations have this transactional trust among their workers. These workers go to work carefully analyzing every move they make to be sure others in the organization won't use it against them. They document everything and archive emails and memos. They spend valuable creativity and brain power to come up with strategies to advance their objectives in spite of others "who have a personal agenda." They go through work negotiating: "I'll give you this, but you'll help me with that." What are the possibilities of success for such an organization with so little trust, feeling that others are there to get them?

Several business owners and managers have told me their workers will take advantage of them the moment they turn their heads the other way. The workers, in turn, believe that their boss is entirely focused on squeezing them as much as possible for profits or to gather personal recognition.

This situation happens with entire units that distrust others outside their group, function, location, or country. I have seen manufacturing operations hiding defects from their sales teams so they don't tell customers, customer representatives not telling their teams where the requirements can be softened as to have something in their pocket to negotiate, overseas operations hiding risky investments from their head office, and corporate offices keeping information that soon trickles down the organization as gossip.

Contrast this distrust with the trust felt by a group of experienced guides whose business is to take trekkers up the Himalayan mountains. These guides know their business, believe in the goal, and have hiked together for a while. They know their strength is greatly increased when each does what each needs to do. Working as a team, they know how to conduct their trek guiding in a way that is safe, while bringing enjoyment to their customers and to themselves. The don't feel stress because they know that their partners will, for sure, do their part. This is trust that is defined as loyalty.

In an organization, the closer we get to loyalty and away from transactional trust, the more we can concentrate on building great things. We can be energized and put forth the best ideas because they'll be analyzed on their own merit, according to how well they fit with our shared purpose. If they aren't accepted, it's only because there are other ideas that are better, and everyone is even happier. If I know that people are there for me, I can lower my level of stress and concentrate on the work, on reciprocating and gifting them with my part of the deal.

If I know others believe in the organizational objective, share my values, and are smart and capable, I know we'll find the answers together every time. We'll be much stronger with this group of coworkers than with anyone else. In a short time frame, friendship will come along.

What does research say about it? The *Journal of Business and Psychology* confirms our beliefs. It says that friendship opportunities the employee encounters at work have direct effects on job involvement and job satisfaction.[7] The Gallup organization has also studied the issue. It says that having a friend at work is more important in making a worker engaged than pay and benefits.[8] There are five times more workers who report being engaged when they have a best friend at work versus when they don't. But what about the business results? Is it noticeable at all in hard currency? The Gallup organization has also studied this question. Across companies, profitability and customer loyalty are "strongly associated with a high incidence of best friends in the workplace," says James K. Harter, a senior research director at Gallup.[9]

Researchers have concluded that the interaction of successful teams has five characteristics. First, everyone in the team participates approximately the same amount. Second, members connect with other team members, not only with the team leader. Third, members have interactions outside their team and often bring knowledge back to the team. Four, members have open and direct communication, with energetic interactions. Fifth, members continue talking about the issues at work among themselves. Do you see that all the points above will naturally take place in the environment of our Driven Organization?[10]

What would be something that hurts trust? Management saying one thing and doing another, organizational rules that aren't respected, and excessive income inequality in the organization are examples.[11] Isn't it interesting that in our current modern organizations, it seems we do the opposite of what we should be doing?

> *"We are all a little weird and life's a little weird, and when we find someone whose weirdness is compatible with ours, we join up with them and fall in mutual weirdness and call it love."* Theodor Seuss Geisel, aka Dr. Seuss.

A cohesive and tight group easily outperforms regular teams.

An organization with many brains working together will always achieve better results than the most brilliant individual with many great executors. An organization playing like a united team will always have better performance than a regular one, even when workers have marked disadvantages. Want to see one or two examples?

In the 2004 NBA Championships, the Detroit Pistons face the Los Angeles Lakers. Detroit advances to the NBA finals for the first time since 1990. Few analysts believe the Pistons can win because the Lakers won three out of the previous four NBA championships and field a star-studded lineup including Shaquille O'Neal, Kobe Bryant, Gary Payton, and Karl Malone. The Lakers also have four players who will eventually be honored at the NBA Hall of Fame. And if this weren't enough, the Lakers also have the home-court advantage. The Pistons don't have such stars on their team, but they do have team cohesiveness and determination. They play under the coach's mantra to "play the right way." They feel they are the conduit to prove the world that Detroit is still alive. The results speak for themselves. The Pistons defeat Los Angeles in five games for the team's third NBA Championship in its history. The Pistons win with double-digit wins in three of their four victories and hold the Lakers to a franchise-low of 68 points in Game 3.

Winter Olympics, 1980: the ice hockey games. A U.S. team composed of young collegiate players faces highly experienced players from the USSR. The USSR Ice Hockey team had won every Olympic tournament since 1964. Their 1980 lineup is considered the best in the world and has legendary players, three of whom would be later honored at the Hockey Hall of Fame. The game takes place amid the highest level of tension between the USSR and the United States. Later that year, President Carter will legislate the United States boycott of the 1980 summer Olympics held in Moscow because of the USSR invasion of Afghanistan in 1979. The U.S. Hockey team has a purpose for which to fight. The young men feel they represent the right values in the world. The American coach, Herb Brooks, sends them to the ice rink with these words: "You were born to be a player. You were meant to be here. This moment is yours."[12] They surprise observers with their physical and highly cohesive play, and achieve a final score of 4-3, a legendary feat that is since known as "the miracle on ice."

The same performance can be observed in business organizations. Some researchers furnish workers with smart badges that measure individual communication behavior such as tone of voice, body language, with whom they talk, and more. The smart badges allow them to have an idea of the quality of communication that takes place among members of the team. These experiments have been performed across a variety of industries, especially where performance can be easily measured, such as call centers and operations teams.

The researchers found that the pattern of communication was the main predictor of the team's success, as important as individual intelligence, personality, and skill combined. Yes, combined! According to them, face-to-face exchanges among team members account for 35% of the variation in performance. Their measurements of communication patterns are so indicative of team performance that they have been able to predict winners at business plan contests just by measuring and qualifying the interaction among the team members.

From these results, organizations have begun to do small things such as setting up coffee breaks at the same time in order for workers to interact among themselves. They have found that only this common coffee break has decreased call center average handling time by about 20% for the lower-performing teams. They have observed similar improvement measures by making lunch tables bigger so that more people can chat while having lunch.[13]

"The common wisdom is that ... managers have to learn to motivate people. Nonsense. Employees bring their own motivation." Tom Peters, management consultant and author.

The environment dangers: group-think and herd behavior.

Remember the story of Maria learning to appreciate certain things about her environment? Learning what to value and what not to value from the environment happens quite frequently, even at church. Have you ever wondered why some of the tightest religious groups create lots of activities for their members, filling up their agenda and leaving almost no free time beyond these church activities and work? "It is advised to do our best to carry our social lives only with brothers and sisters from our church," we may have heard. In fact, I've heard that it's advised not to engage in religious conversations with people from other faiths.

You know the answer. This tight environment is not leaving any space for outside environments to affect the beliefs of the churchgoers. But, what if, just by chance, we could learn one or two things from a person who has a different faith? How can we learn if we don't go away from our circle? Unfortunately, the more that we stay surrounded by our environment, the more difficult it is to understand other beliefs.

On the other hand, if a new churchgoer is too far away from the church's mentality, he won't fit at all. His values are so different that the environment won't affect him. He may, in turn, oppose every initiative, criticize every suggestion, and probably even create dissent. In effect, he may become an environment derailer.

But let's go back to this point: What if the entire group is wrong? I think of the examples in which entire groups of people have been mistaken and the cost has been enormous for many people. I think of what a French sociologist and criminologist from the nineteenth century, Gabriel Tarde, called "group-think," or what Nietzsche called "herd instinct," known today as "herd behavior." I think of all the good people of Germany who allowed the Nazis to kill millions of people, or of the partition of India and Pakistan and the people emigrating from one country to the other. They were so angry and frustrated with their situation that they started fighting with each other. About half a million people died!

There are non-violent examples of mass delirium, such as the high-tech bubble of the 1990s or the 2008 Wall Street crisis caused at least partially by the sub-prime market frenzy. And no country is immune. It happens to current and old civilizations. The Mayans exhausted all their natural resources around their magnificent cities and caused the downfall of their civilization. How could they not see it?

We tend to believe that there were certain special circumstances that took good people by surprise and didn't allow them to react in the correct way. Almost everyone is certain they would act differently if a similar situation presented itself to them. Unfortunately, research says this isn't the case.

You may have heard about the so called "Stanford Prison Experiment." In this experiment, the researchers invited students to take part in a two-week research experiment. They selected those who were deemed physically and psychologically healthy. They randomly divided them into prisoners and guards. The guards were forbidden to inflict any physical damage to the prisoners.

Soon everyone got into their role, which was somewhat expected. What wasn't expected, however, was that guards became extremely abusive. They became highly creative in coming up with ways to punish the prisoners without hurting them physically (which wasn't allowed). They interrupted their sleep constantly, had them clean toilets with their bare hands, stripped them naked, had them simulate sodomistic acts, and used lots of verbal abuse. Abuse was increased at night, when the guards knew that the "prison superintendent" Phillip Zimbardo, who was the lead researcher, went to sleep.

Abusive guards were never even told to slow down by the other "good" guards, even when their behavior became extreme. It wasn't expected, either, that prisoners didn't show solidarity with their fellow prisoners when they were abused. On the contrary, when guards used them to blackmail other prisoners as in "if he doesn't eat (a prisoner on a hunger strike), you will be punished," prisoners turned against their fellow prisoners as well. It also wasn't expected that the researchers lost sight of what was happening and didn't stop the experiment until a new researcher, who came to visit, strongly complained about it.

If you haven't already seen them, I recommend you watch the documentaries about this experiment. These and other similar experiences from real life prompt a question: How do people become so involved with the situation that they forget their moral values? Why does it feel right to act in a certain way, which later is deemed unacceptable?

The environment can take you to places you wouldn't have gone by yourself, and it's extremely difficult to get off the bus once you are on the way. Because we know that we are prone to lose ourselves in the environment, we must make sure that our organization doesn't fall into group-think or herd behavior. We will discuss ways to do so next.

"A "collective" mind doesn't exist. It is merely the sum of endless numbers of individual minds. If we have an endless number of

individual minds who are weak, meek, submissive and impotent —who renounce their creative supremacy for the sake of the "whole" and accept humbly that the "whole's" verdict—we don't get a collective super-brain. We get only the weak, meek, submissive and impotent collective mind." Ayn Rand, Russian-American novelist and philosopher.

Inoculating the environment to prevent group-think and herd behavior.

There is a number of researchers who have studied the factors leading to group-think and herd behavior. Although no one has nailed the exact causes for these negative and dangerous situations, they have identified a few factors that influence them: group cohesiveness, group homogeneity, authoritarian leadership, high-stress conditions, lack of personal accountability, and lack of questioning norms and processes.[14]

Imagine an organization called StarAmerica. This organization has a group of 55-to-65-year-old white American executives leading the company. These executives went to the same ivy league university and studied business about 30 years ago. They all live in a couple of posh neighborhoods 10 minutes away from the corporate offices in a small Midwestern town of the United States. They hang out together on weekends, and their wives do the same. Their children attend the same, albeit supposedly best, school in town. Their professional career has always been up, up, and up in the same company, whose highest leader is a respected and decisive manager.

When this group of people is faced with new market situations or with shifting U.S. market demographics, customs, and habits due to the inflow of Asians and Hispanics, will it be able to consider all possibilities and make the best decisions? Or will it suffer from group-think? I'm not saying they aren't a group of capable managers, just that they run the risk of falling into group-think because they lack diversity. Decisions aren't always black and white; how sure does a manager need to be to oppose everyone else in this group? What does he risk doing it?

How does our Driven Organization avoid group-think?

To start, the authoritative figures are non-existent. This helps everyone voice his or her opinion freely, without any concern of how it will be received by the big boss. There is considerable diversity, but this diversity exists through where group members come from, what they have seen, with whom they have met, and who they are, and not in regard to beliefs or the purpose of the organization. People who don't adhere to their purpose simply don't fit in the organization and must be let go. At our Driven Organization, while they all share a common purpose, their diversity allows them to bring different ideas on how to advance it and how to deal with possible obstacles.

In our organization, there is Autonomy, which decreases group-think. Everyone is an influencing agent and is fully accountable for what he or she does. In StarAmerica, the top leaders were the only ones "capable" of making decisions. And how could they be accountable, if they were all following the direction of the big boss?

In StarAmerica, workers are children, and the big boss is their capable, all-wise parent. In our organization, everyone is capable, everyone contributes, and everyone is responsible. The environment invites you to voice your concerns because others value that you bring something special and unique, something perhaps they have not seen before. High-level critical thinking is appreciated. Everything can and should be questioned, from norms, processes, and procedures to solutions and answers. Everyone is looking for the best decision and the best outcome, not for individual recognition. People are focused on the "what" and the "why," not on the "who." The "who" is every member of the organization.

Have you ever worked with teammates you admired and respected, but challenged you constantly and were challenged by you? If you remember, your team was far from group-think or herd behavior. Having friends at work doesn't narrow solution sets, just like having an ultimate shared objective doesn't lead to one solution path. Diversity of origin, solution process, and education are welcome and needed if, and only if, the organization's goals and purposes are shared. I would, perhaps, add a few other desired character traits, such as humility, openness, respect for each other, and a desire to make a difference.

The environment of our Driven Organization fosters humility. The organization doesn't pretend to know it all, only to be open to learning about it. The organization knows is has great people, but doesn't believe success is assured. When a path is taken, and later data suggests this path isn't correct, the organization has the humility to accept the new data and correct course. When the organization has no problem accepting new data and performing the necessary corrections at once, these changes are inexpensive and easy to do, in contrast with huge overhauls and significant power struggles. In StarAmerica, when the big boss makes a mistake, accepting it means recognizing his or her weaknesses, being wrong, and perhaps even lack of capability, all of which is an incentive not to do so. Even if he or she develops the humbleness to do it, his or hers followers will never see him/her in the same way.

And yes, our organization with its great friends, shared objective, and diverse team is still a tight, cohesive group. And this is good.

> The environment of Zappos has allowed it to become the largest online retailer for shoes and other apparel items. It credits its success to how cohesive the environment is. Managers say that instead of work/life separation, they look for work/life integration. In the early days, Zappos passed through some very difficult times, which allowed it to become even tighter. At the beginning, but for a while, it was in danger of going broke. It managed to find the way to survive but had to do many special things, which included employees living in the CEO's apartments, getting a reduced paycheck, and doing all sorts of odd but necessary work beyond job descriptions. All this created a tight community with one shared objective: the survival of Zappos.
>
> Zappos later moved its operations to Las Vegas and found that most employees didn't have any friends outside of work in their new city. Workers became even tighter among themselves. Little by little, they discovered what they were made of and how much they could trust each other. Zappos now has a tight, cohesive environment, but don't be fooled. Zappos is relentless and has managed to grow from $1.6 million in revenue sales in 2000 to surpassing $1 billion in 2008. Its environment is one of learning, working together, and becoming the best it can be.[15]

StarAmerica also had a tight, cohesive group, but it was the executive management group. Unfortunately management didn't include the lower-level workers in the group. If they wanted to develop a "we are all together" environment, what could they have done? To start, they could break organizational silos and implement programs such as "Walk a Mile," from Southwest, which allows each employee to do someone else's job for a day. The operations agents cannot fly the planes, but the pilots can, and do, work as operations agents. Because the pilots cannot let others take their role, they have come up with a way to thank their mechanics. They have held barbecues for them to thank them for keeping the planes flying. In fact, about 75% of Southwest's workers have participated in the job-swapping program, says Herb Kelleher, Southwest's founder.[16]

Good decisions don't always yield good results.

We must remember that to foster creativity, innovation, and continuous improvement, we must have a forgiving environment in which failure is part of the process. Of course, the organization must be careful when deciding what the best time in the development process of a product or service is to put the big bucks into it. There may be stringent evaluations and/or requirements it must meet.

Although failure is accepted, note that this isn't the same as not having accountability or responsibility for what has been done. The worker is an organizational agent accountable to the other workers for his or her actions. If the worker acts against the organization's purposes, values or principles, that worker shouldn't be there any longer. This is the ultimate failure. If the worker (or team) acts along the organization's principles and in good faith, but there is a bad result, then the organization must learn from this mistake. It isn't the workers' or the team's mistake. Something may have been missing (training, information, etc.) to make the proper decisions, or maybe there was just no way to anticipate what happened.

A senior investor once told me the difference between an inexperienced investor and an experienced one. He said the inexperienced one delves a lot into the consequences of his doing. He illustrated with an example: "Let's say there are two possible outcomes. Path A has a probability of becoming reality 70% of the time, and path B 30%. An investor has to make his decision based on the information he has. In this case, he should choose path A and expect the best outcome. Seven out of ten times, path A will happen, but three other times path B will happen. After the fact, he must come back to study the experience and learn, only for performance improvement. Had he chosen incorrectly path B, and had it happened, he must see he was lucky and a mistake was made. Once analysis and learning are done, he must move on."

"Newbies blame themselves or celebrate excessively depending on the actual outcome, which isn't correct. What matters is the decision process, not the outcome." This is a simple example, but think about all the complex situations there are with multiple paths and unknown probabilities. A manager, a team, an organization faces similar situations. The organizational environment must reward either explicitly or implicitly the right behaviors, respect for facts, healthy discussions, and course corrections, but not unfounded beliefs or final outcomes.

When we risk burnout.

Another factor for group-think and herd behavior is high stress. High stress goes beyond risking group-think and herd behavior; it also affects performance and it may lead to burnout.

Burnout is the experience of long-term exhaustion and diminished interest. And no, it doesn't only happen to those who have a hectic personal life or those who are weak; it happens to many of us. It's estimated that about 3.4 million people suffer from burnout in Canada.[17] This in a workforce of about 15 million. Statistics in the United States may even be worse because it is the developed country whose workers take the least amount of vacation.

Once burnout sets in, its symptoms range from cynicism and withdrawal to even suicide attempts, according to the experts on the matter. They say that burnout starts when the individual attempts to prove himself in a demanding environment, neglecting his needs and values.[18] The person may be working long hours with little downtime, often feeling that others continually survey his work.[19]

Why would burnout happen in our modern organizations? In chapter 7, we learned that after fulfilling physical, safety and security, and belongingness needs, the next most important level of the pyramid consists of the esteem needs. As we know, a great way to fulfill this need is through work. Workers frequently seek recognition and appreciation by others through their daily work.

If a worker overexerts himself, that is, if he negates his other needs, he has more probability of experiencing burnout. He may simply not have enough downtime to rest (physiological needs) or to have friends (belongingness needs), but he also may not be working on the upper levels, the growth needs. I refer to the need to know and understand, beauty and structure, self-actualization, and self-transcendence.

If this worker were able to fulfill more of the needs at work even when he was in a demanding environment, he'd have less risk of experiencing burnout. if he were working on the upper levels of the pyramid, the risk of burnout would be almost negligible. In other words, the worker who is actively performing work about which he feels passionate, purposeful, interesting, elevating, constructive, and beneficial to others has little to no risk of experiencing burnout.

Those risking burnout, the ones who work solely on the esteem needs, aren't concerned with the long-term welfare and objectives of the organization, but only with proving to themselves and others how good they are. And it doesn't always work. About 30% of executives and high-level management mention that their biggest fear in life is for everyone else to find out they are not as good as they have made everyone believe.[20]

I know folks like them. In fact, I was one of them. I can tell you that I felt better when I went home at night exhausted from work. When this happened, I felt that I did my very best; there wasn't an ounce of energy left in my body. You see, I wasn't concerned with how much the organization was contributing to the world, how much I was learning, or how much I was on my way to be all I could be. Those days, I just selfishly wanted to feel that I was a great employee.

An environment with a "sense of urgency" doesn't lead to creativity.

An engineer designs a great piece of equipment in a few hours that required many hours of observation, sketching, studying, and talking with other people. After he's done, he may have come up with a great, highly valuable design. Were he forced to work to exhaustion every day, attempting to achieve results every one of those days, he would have never developed such a brilliant design that performs the function so elegantly and effectively. When we work to exhaustion in our modern workplaces, we stop seeing creative ways to improve the quality and the quantity of the work. This is why, beyond possible health concerns and the risk of burnout, being stressed out is not conducive to highly creative results.

This seems to contradict the beliefs of our modern managers. Most organizations say they want people with a "sense of urgency." Sound familiar? Urgency is defined as a calling for immediate attention, the state of being urgent, earnest, or of pressing importance. Consider that for a second. Who can live in a state of urgency for 8, 9, or 12 hours every day? Who can treat everything as if in need of immediate attention? Can one really come up with the best decision with this state of mind? Can one really create the best path for the organization?

To contrast, there are a few things our Driven Organization does to increase performance while reducing excessive stress. We said that the organization's purpose gives passionate meaning to workers. They work intensively, but they don't feel exhausted. They also have social support, which helps people feel connected with others and not left alone. Discussions also take place only in light of how much they advance the organization, which as we said before, reduces the amount of conflict and increases understanding among workers.

In our organization, our engineer would have the focus, energy, and support to come up with great designs that would leap-frog the organization's competitors. There will be fewer mistakes and need for rework. The organization overall is stronger.

It's a fact. Creativity won't take place in a negative or stressful environment. Remember the box of tacks and the candle? Creativity can take place only in an environment that allows for mistakes, for learning, and for experimentation, in which new ideas and ideators are appreciated. Such organizations innovate processes, products, and customer interaction, and will be successful.

A good environment energizes every worker to be on the lookout to produce great ideas to improve the organization and eliminates fear from the creative process, even when there are failures. Workers self-select to join teams to advance those projects in which they believe. An environment of creativity prompts everyone to work together, eliminating hierarchies, constraints, and unnecessary obstacles. The most creative organizations have asked themselves why customary things must be done in the expected fashion, why a new technology could not be implemented, or why they cannot provide the best product or service in a certain market.

"Innovation is what you didn't know you wanted, until you got

it." Richard Branson.

We need the right environment more than ever.

Generation Y is more focused on friendship than previous generations. This is the first generation where workers often choose to stay in a job just because they like their coworkers or their bosses, which was rarely the case with previous generations. Recruiters report that nowadays college graduates often go to work for the same organization as their friends do, and some companies have begun to understand the value of friendship in organizations. For example, Gentle Giant, a privately-own moving company with numerous service and employer awards, once hired an entire athletic team.

We must have the right environment for the right organization. There are folks who thrive in an environment of fun and camaraderie, while others like a caring environment that pampers its members. Other folks enjoy the healthy discussions that lead to new learning and new discoveries. In this way, there may be variations of environments, some of which may be better for your organization, but all of them stem from the same principles.

With the right environment, the organization acts like a flock of birds flying in unison; having a common shared destiny; and using their team skills to overcome predators, to conserve energy, and to fly farther. Once everyone agrees on the destination, they all work toward the same goal without the need for authoritative leaders to direct birds to get back in line. All birds understand their agreed success is possible only with the help of each other, and team cohesiveness is at its greatest.

The environment we have today will be the brand of tomorrow.

The environment pays off in performance, innovation, and efficiency, but perhaps its biggest influence is in branding. The environment is the sure and only way to make a brand become significant. Think Apple. The same organizational environment that helped it create the original Mac is what today drives it to create iPads and iPhones. This internal environment that transpires to customers as the Apple's mojo has created a cult-like following for Apple that is far from imaginary.

> Researchers have observed in MRI scans that Apple products trigger brain reactions in some fans similar to those triggered by a deity in religious people.[21]

TV advertising, websites, banners, Internet ads: All are important, but it is the front-line employee who lets the customer breathe in the environment of the organization when he serves that customer.

Interaction after interaction, a reputation is developed. People are and always will be the best marketing tool an organization can have. How can customer representatives have an honest, sincere, emphatic, authentic relationship with customers if they don't feel they can have an honest, sincere, authentic relationship with the company?

The brand is, in fact, an external, often delayed view of the organization's environment. What the organization pays attention to, what it fosters, what it rejects, what shortcuts it takes, all of it will be eventually transpired to external stakeholders and will become the brand of the organization. Remember that people trust those who believe what they believe. The organization's values, principles and purposes become not only the reason for workers to produce a product or service but also a reason for customers to acquire it.

"The most powerful element in advertising is the truth." Bill Bernbach, legendary American advertising creative director.

Above all, be honest and mean what you say. Honesty is probably the biggest test of strength and one of the main drivers of the environment. It is those gray moments that define us, when we look into the difficult situation to find out the truth and serve others with it, making them big, accountable, and participants of the organization's decisions. This is the strength and generosity we can display each day and especially when things get difficult. People always appreciate it.

Environment is, in summary, a weird substance. It can be the glue that holds the organization together. It can be the oil that lets its members function and move the organization forward, with little friction and few problems. It can be the fuel that infuses the organization with energy to tackle the challenges it encounters. It can be the special rumbling sound the organization makes, inside and out, of what it is all about: the brand. It can also act as the testosterone, necessary to build organizational muscle and become stronger.

"A company is stronger if it is bound by love rather than by fear."
Herb Kelleher.

Summary of Environment.

- Organizational environment is the invisible but powerful force that gently pushes people to comply with the way things are done in the organization. The environment:

  - Is promptly learned, often without a conscious effort or desire to do so.

  - Governs members' behaviors and is simultaneously affected by them. It must be protected and cared for so that it becomes stronger and keeps the desired behaviors.

  - Teaches people what to appreciate and value, as happened to Maria. What our work environment values will color every action we perform during our workday.

  - Is powerful because it's related with our needs to belong, the lowest level of Maslow's pyramid that's really in danger these days.

  - Can be fostered by law enforcement (or management), but it's not the only force in play. Other workers, groups, and teams are important forces affecting it.

  - Is more than culture because it comprehends business policies and infrastructure.

- It's possible to create an organization in which workers are friends (not just coworkers), which increases performance and employee satisfaction.

  - Friendship depends on trust, and trust depends on sharing the same beliefs. Sharing a significant, meaningful purpose is a great way to develop trust and friendship.

  - A group of cohesive team members will always outperform a regular team, as happened in the "Miracle on ice."

- An environment used to healthy discussion and autonomy, diverse in its people and their experiences (not core values), and with access to information will not fall into group-think or herd behavior.

- The right environment can make the organization an innovation powerhouse.

- The organization must foster the proper decision-making process, but not prize or shame the obtained results.

- Newer generations are demanding fun, caring, learning environments, and are willing to forgo other perks to get it.

- The brand is a delayed view of today's organizational environment.

1   Compiled in Wikipedia. Data from the World Health Organization, OECD IRTAD, and others.

2   Adapted from the work of Dr. Linda Ford.

3   Birkett, Melissa A. *The Trier Social Stress Test Protocol for Inducing Psychological Stress.* Northern Arizona University Department of Psychology, 2011.

    Rohleder, Nicolas, Beulen, Silke E., Chen, Edith, Wof, Jutta M., & Kirschbaum, Clemens. *Stress on the Dance Floor: The Cortisol Stress Response to Social-Evaluative Threat in Competitive Ballroom Dancers.* Dresden University of Technology, University of British Columbia, and University of Wuppertal, 2006.

4   CNN money. "Server Smashing and Mini Golf at Work." An interview with Rackspace CEO, Lanham Napier.
    http://money.cnn.com/video/technology/2011/09/13/f_bctwf_rackspace.fortune/

5   Bill Gates and Paul Allen in Microsoft; Steve Wozniak and Steve Jobs in Apple; Sergey Brin and Larry Page in Google.

6   Fehr, Beverley Anne. *Friendship Processes.* Sage, 1996.

7   Riordan, Christine M., & Griffeth, Rodger W. "The Opportunity for Friendship in the Workplace: An Unexplored Construct." *Journal of Business and Psychology* 10(2), Winter 1995.

8   Ellingwood, Susan. "The Collective Advantage: Contrary to Popular Belief, Workplace

Friendships Boost Profits." *Gallup Management Journal,* September 15, 2001.

9   Idem.

10 Pentland, Alex "Sandy". "The New Science of Building Great Teams." *Harvard Business review.* April 2012.

11 Uslaner, Eric M. *The Moral Foundations of Trust.* Cambridge: Cambridge University Press, 2002.

12 Coffey, Wayne. *The Boys of Winter: New York City.* Crown Publishers, 2005. E-book edition.

13 More information can be found at: Pentland, Alex "Sandy". "The New Science of Building Great Teams." *Harvard Business review.* April 2012.

14 Janis, Irving. "Groupthink." *Psychology Today,* 1971.

     Flowers, M. L. "A Laboratory Test of Some Implications of Janis's Groupthink Hypothesis." *Journal of Personality and Social Psychology* 35(12), pp. 888—896, 1977.

     Cline, Rebecca J. W. "Detecting Groupthink: Methods for Observing the Illusion of Unanimity." *Communication Quarterly* 38(2), p.121, 1990.

     Park, W. A. "Review of Research on Groupthink." *Journal of Behavioral Decision Making* 3, p.230, 1990.

     Zimbardo, Phillip. *The Lucifer Effect: Understanding How Good People Turn Evil.* 1st ed. Random House, March 27, 2007.

15 Hsieh Tony. *Delivering Happiness.* 1st ed. Business Plus, June 7, 2010.

16 Kelleher Herb. "A Culture of Commitment." *Leader to Leader Magazine,* 1997.

17 As reported by The Professional Institute of the Public Service of Canada's Jean-François Simard, Research Officer.

18 Kraft, Ulrich. "Burned Out." *Scientific American* Mind, pp. 28—33, June/July, 2006.

19 Tracy, Sarah J. "Becoming a Character for Commerce: Emotion Labor, Self Subordination and Discursive Construction of Identity in a Total Institution." *Management Communication Quarterly* 14, p. 113, 2000.

20 Logan, Dave, King, John, & Fischer-Wright, Halee. *Tribal Leadership: Leveraging Natural Groups to Build a Thriving Organization.* HarperBusiness, 2008.

21 Milian, Mark. "Apple Triggers 'Religious' Reaction in Fans' Brains, Report Says." *CNNTech,* May 19, 2011.

The Driven Organization

Chapter 14:

S Is About Strategy.

"The idea that business is just a numbers affair has always struck me as preposterous. For one thing, I've never been particularly good at numbers, but I think I've done a reasonable job with feelings. And I'm convinced that it is feelings—and feelings alone —that account for the success of the Virgin brand in all of its myriad forms." Richard Branson, Founder, Virgin Group.

There are several problems with the strategy work we do today.

Today, strategy work often means to have super smart strategists working full time creating competitive scenarios, anticipating three or four moves in advance for each competitor, understanding actions by governments and the effect of new regulations, using game theory to find the competitive equilibrium,[1] developing secret projects and plans, understanding where the company wants to be in a certain number of years, and plotting its course. All of which would take place in a war room that nobody has access to other than the strategists and top management.

This is not best for several important reasons. To start, it is thinking derived from military strategy. It assumes there is a certain specific amount of land mass that must be distributed over a certain number of players. This zero-sum game is not the case in the business world in which new products, markets, and possibilities are developed every minute, and the entire market redefines itself every few years. Strategy done this way is limited to the current perception of the market and may be shortsighted to the immense possibilities that lie ahead for everyone.

Another reason is that knowing what will happen next and have the right response ready to use may be a bit more ambitious than what we would like to believe. Do you remember Deep Blue? It was the name of the first super computer to win a chess game over the then-world champion Garry Kasparov. To win, Deep Blue used brute force computing power as its main strength, evaluating several moves ahead to determine the best strategy to choose. Deep Blue could evaluate 200 million positions per second, and depending on the move, it may have evaluated 100 billion moves before actually choosing what the best move was. We humans can't do that. It would take us a long, long time to evaluate 100 billion moves. Instead, we use intuition to guide us through the options we have.

Some say intuition is a process that gives us the ability to know something directly without analytic reasoning, part from the conscious and part from the non-conscious parts of our mind; that is, part reason, part instinct. You probably can describe intuition differently, but the fact is that intuition is so good that with it we almost match the raw brute force of a super computer, at least in regards to a chess game.

> Jonah Lehrer, author of *How We Decide* describes intuition as consisting of experience embedded in the unconscious. He says that intuitive people "naturally depend on the emotions generated by their experience. Their prediction errors, all those mistakes they made in the past, have been translated into useful knowledge, which allows them to tap into a set of accurate feelings they can't begin to explain."[2]

But it is only a chess game. A chess board is composed of only 64 squares, with 16 pieces per player that have very specific rules of movement. There are only two players who alternate turns. There are specific rules within chess that make it possible for a computer to calculate every possible move. And still, the combinations of moves are so vast that the super computer's brute force is a tangible advantage. Now, how many squares are there in real life? How many players? How many possibilities and limitations on how to move?

We can't plan for new entrants coming into the market, competitors overseas producing too many units, governments changing the rules of the game, competitors finding new technological advantages, earthquakes hitting one of our major suppliers, financial crisis setting in, and the billion other possible things that can happen. Mapping the future world isn't possible and we'd better not kid ourselves we are doing it. Pretending we do may prevent us from finding the root cause of our problems.

Another significant problem related with current strategic work is related to forecasting. It's great that we human beings see things rosy for the future, but the fact is that this affects the way we forecast in the business world, too. Nobody says, for example, that in ten years he'll be dealing with this terrible disease or operating with huge business losses. Almost always, when people analyze and develop forecasts of sales or revenue for a product or business, it's optimistic. In fact, I have seen that even in those cases where the measured variable was declining, the new chart combining historical and forecast data would show a line going downward in time until today, and then after a few months, a sharp turn upward in the future. In one organization it happened so much that they began to call it the "hockey stick" graph. While it is nice to see the future, and see it with positive eyes, thinking that the business will always be better in the future may not be reality.

Researchers have proved that even professional analysts and forecasters show a significant, positive bias when they forecast future business results.[3]

Often, these forecasts are developed using complicated models. We must remember that even the most complicated models were developed based on certain assumptions. These assumptions almost always implicitly consider the modelers' expectations. Models are great tools in that they allow us to break a complex problem into pieces, but are dangerous in that they hide the assumptions used, making the forecasters believe that what they thought is in fact correct. There is a belief that if the model predicted a certain result, it must be correct because it is a model. We should keep in mind that a model is just a simplistic view of reality, seen through our own point of view and with our assumptions.

Strategy is about how to pursue our organizational purpose.

So what is the strategy work that we advocate? We will simply define *strategy* as the present knowledge and future general idea of how we plan to pursue our organizational purpose(s) successfully.

Note that it first entails knowing the reason for the existence of the organization: its purpose (as we discussed in Chapter 10). Our definition also calls for a current knowledge of how to do it; that is, of the unique ways of producing better or cheaper products or services than others, allowing the organization to have customers, stay in business, and pay the rent. We will talk about this later in this chapter. Our definition also says to have a "future idea" of how the organization will pursue its purpose in the future. We will also review this here.

Strategy involves understanding of what makes us special.

Consider an example from nature. Every living organism has something special that allows it to fight, stay alive, and flourish. For example, human beings have a great brain that allows us to create tools, develop sophisticated thinking, and much more. And it works for us; we are 7 billion strong and still counting.

Ants are not doing badly, either. There is the same amount of biomass of ants on the planet as there is of human beings.[4] Since human beings weigh a lot more than ants, ant numbers are, in fact, astounding. They have unique survival and thriving strategies, from scavengers and foragers to farmers. They gather aphids, take care of them, and milk them, as we do with cows. The Leaf-cutter ants grow food as well, cultivating a type of fungus that is fed fresh-cut plant material, which normally would be too toxic to eat.[5]

There are as many different survival strategies as you can imagine. A mosquito bites to get blood, a squirrel gathers nuts and seeds, and a pear tree produces pears so sweet that we all want a member of its species in our backyard. It's no different with organizations and their strategic or competitive advantage.

An organization does something special that allows it to be successful for a while. Henry Ford created Ford motor company to produce vehicles in a manufacturing line, achieving a low cost per vehicle. This great strategic advantage displaced hundreds of other vehicle producers of the time. Then General Motors came along. Instead of producing the same car more and more inexpensively, as Ford did with the Model T, GM changed vehicle models every few years and created products for different purchasing power and purposes of customers. Then Toyota added "with great quality," and carved market share as well. And the story continues and continues, with creative and innovative propositions. But these strategies have often lasted many years, allowing GM to be the biggest automobile manufacturer for almost 80 years.

If we think that, as a species, our competitive advantage is along the lines of the capacity for sophisticated thought and the creation of tools, it would be ludicrous for us to throw it away and began attempting to copy the chicken's competitive advantage to survive: foraging for food every minute of the day. Not only would we be forgoing our great competitive advantage but we may also actually struggle to sustain ourselves if we were to eat like chickens. I exaggerate in this example. It is, as I said, ludicrous, but it does happen that companies reshuffle themselves, throwing away their competitive advantage in pursuit of a different one that is quite difficult to make work. There are times when this is necessary, but the process is painful and risky, never to be taken lightly.

As human beings, the more we foster our competitive advantage, the more we learn and develop better and more sophisticated tools and the better off we are. It is a similar thing in business. The better understanding we have of our organization and the more we advance our competitive advantage, the better off we are.

Organizations often don't know what makes them special.

Knowing ourselves seems pretty basic, but many important organizations are confused about what their strategic advantages are, and even more on their shortcomings and how to fix them.

I found it interesting that General Motors didn't have a clear answer to what its strategic advantage was. I asked this often, and I always got different answers: scale that leads to low cost, great exciting design, worldwide market presence, history, innovation, being well managed, powertrain (engine and transmission) technology, solid all around. Each of these answers may be fine if everyone agreed on them, but they don't. The problem may stem from the fact that GM's purpose isn't known, either.

GM manufactures a variety of vehicles, from super cars to the cheapest everyday vehicles, for different functions and uses. If GM is deemed to offer a product for each customer, it must have the capacity to do it at a reasonable cost; and there must be a strong philosophy to share practices, components, and architectures. These architectures are the vehicle underpinnings on which the vehicle body is build. They have a huge influence on the vehicle form and features, and they're extremely expensive to modify, with costs that can reach hundreds of millions of dollars.

GM is good at sharing at the component level, but not so good at planning architectures to accommodate the requirements of different vehicles, which would help maximize design and quality at a low cost.

The Delta II architecture is the GM's compact vehicle architecture. It was engineered in Europe, but the first vehicle application, the Chevrolet Cruze/Daewoo Lacetti, was designed in South Korea. In doing so, the Korean team had to redesign important features of the architecture that involved significant expense. At the end, the European Opel Astra and the Korean Daewoo Lacetti don't have the same exact architecture. This problem could have been prevented if there had been more coordinated planning for the requirements of the architecture.

When I was at GM, we began seriously working on developing the process to achieve this goal—to follow a smart process and properly design architectures that have the necessary range to accommodate the needs of the vehicles at a reasonable cost. The jury is still out whether this will help GM become more competitive, while allowing it to have great designs. Today, Volkswagen seems to be a good example of architecture sharing among its regular and luxury brands, which may be part of its recent success. A few years ago, Volkswagen had only 16 architectures, from which it built products for Audi, VW, Skoda, Porsche, Bentley, and Seat.

If GM knew clearly what its purpose was and what their strategic advantage was, they'd be protecting it with every action. Producing great vehicles for different purposes and purses, at a reasonable cost for every market in the world, would be much easier if GM didn't have to often redesign architectures in different regions and markets, for example.

We must never forget who we are.

One of the strongest competitive advantages of Toyota is centered around quality. It has developed several powerful practices, such as the Kaizen philosophy of continuous improvement, Zero Defects, Just-In-Time, and Lean manufacturing, which (together with Toyota's culture of teamwork, trust, respect, and consensus bottom-up decision making) make quality an implicit, consistent characteristic of Toyota.[6]

These practices allowed Toyota to be the leader in quality and reliability for a long time. It started at the small car segment, supplying vehicles that lasted longer and were in better shape than their competition. People noticed. Every new entry was marked by better reliability and durability. Toyota began to squeeze the big three from the bottom, making stronger and stronger incursions into their segments, eventually entering the luxury car segment with Lexus, and full-size trucks with the Tundra, eventually dethroning GM as the largest automaker in the world.

Just as it occupied the top sales spot in the world, significant quality issues began to surface, including sticky pedals that caused deadly accidents. Toyota recalled millions of vehicles and the president of Toyota, Mr. Akio Toyoda, apologized repeatedly, saying that Toyota and other automakers had lost their passion for cars.

Toyota had focused in the last decade on relentless growth and had forgotten the principles that enabled it to become the largest automaker in the world. Toyota's purpose had become to be the largest company in the world, which it achieved at an enormous cost to its stakeholders. Its brand suffered a big blow that, together with the faltering economy and natural disasters, sent Toyota into the red for several quarters.

Mr. Toyoda has put more emphasis on what Toyota is. He said that Toyota strives to "enrich lives around the world with the safest and most responsible ways to move people."[7] He is committed to make that be at the core of every action of Toyota stakeholders.

Forgetting about the organization's purpose is more common than what you and I would expect. Researchers have concluded that competitive advantages wear with age, not so much because competitors replicate or undermine them, but because the organization's successful strategy brings growth and complexity, and complex organizations tend to forget what they are good at.[8]

BMW's purpose is to manufacture the ultimate driving machine. Its organization is set up toward designing, engineering, and selling vehicles that meet aggressive driving standards while fulfilling the demands of daily driving. BMW is able to hire people who are passionate about performance vehicles, to charge premium prices for its vehicle offerings, and to invest in technological innovations that further its strategic competitive advantage. The BMW brand is clear about what it promises, and BMW does quite well with its brand.

BMW gets a significant amount of customers who will never do any aggressive driving or know much about performance vehicles. They buy BMWs because others who do know about performance driving buy BMWs. The brand's prestige allows it to extend its reach beyond its core target market. However, in its pursuit of a broader range of customers, even BMW has had some strategic competitive advantage confusion. In 2006, it stopped using its tag line "the ultimate driving machine" and began a "joy" campaign that focused on the happiness people experienced when getting into their BMWs. It didn't work; in January of 2012, BMW came to its senses and changed the advertising back to its "ultimate driving machine" slogan.

From these examples, you can see that knowing who we are is actually more complex than it seems and tends to be forgotten in time, especially if it is successful. We must be brave and take a good honest look in the mirror. What is the strategic competitive advantage that brought us here? Can we still make it work? What do we have that makes us special in our organization? Above all, what is our purpose? A good strategic advantage can be there for many decades; certainly, it does not need to be reviewed with every new management that comes along.

Knowing our advantages needs to be complemented with knowing our disadvantages. If we are big and powerful, are we slow? If we are creative, are we disorganized? Perhaps, our supply costs are too high, or our distribution channels don't convey the brand message in the best way. That's fine. We are not trying to make it all perfect, but to have a crystal clear picture of who we are, what we do, how, and for whom.

Once we have a clear purpose, all these questions are much more easily answered. It guides the strategic efforts from the very top.

Everyone is responsible to advance the strategic advantage.

Long-term robust competitive advantages are built over time with the participation of every member of the organization. It is the luggage handler at a Southwest operation who comes up with new ideas on how to reduce the time to load the luggage into the plane. You see, this is important because a significant part of Southwest's strategy is to turn around planes between two geographical points as quickly as possible. This helps it squeeze a few more flights per day than other airlines, thus increasing worker productivity and aircraft utilization.

> Researchers say that successful organizations build on their fundamental strategic advantage relentlessly, improving it and adding to it every day. Such an organization lives and breathes its strategic advantage day in and day out, and has learned to sustain it over time through constant adaptation to the changes of the market. Every single worker at this organization is focused on doing his or her part to move the organization forward.[9]

Zappos knows that its competitive advantage is customer service, so it must hire people who love to talk to people and help folks choose personal items for their wardrobe. Once Zappos employees know this, a worker might ask: "What if we don't have call time limits?" Another one may say, "What if we don't focus on today's sale, but on establishing a relationship with the customer? The customer will eventually come back with the desire to purchase something." Everything that supports the Zappos competitive advantage can and should be incorporated into its operations to make it stronger.

Apple knows that its core competitive advantage is to package advanced technologies into cool, easy-to-use packages that everyone loves. Apple knows that it strives for the best user experience, so everything the customer touches must be carefully developed. Apple's in-house designers develop their own operating system, hardware, and application software, all of which support the user interface. Apple would not outsource any of these elements because they help Apple achieve the best user experience, and they know how to do it. Apple is less concerned about manufacturing or logistics[10]. Once this is understood by everyone, does it make sense for Apple engineers to be trying to outsource hardware design to India? Of course not. What about outsourcing the development of software to compress and send data through the phone network? Sure, why not?

A significant part of Walmart's strategy is to eliminate unnecessary costs at all times in every place. This can be seen when looking at its frugal mentality. Walmart keeps paychecks and benefits low; and workers, even executives, travel coach, stay in budget hotels, and sometimes share rooms with others. Store managers work hard and pinch pennies throughout their store. At the corporate level, Walmart also focuses on reducing costs. For example, it has a highly efficient high-tech distribution network and uses its purchasing power to drive down the cost of the products it sells. This same mentality, or strategic focus, has been the same since Walmart's early beginnings. It is said that Sam Walton, the founder, drove his old pickup truck and stayed at budget hotels, also sharing a room, even when he was already very wealthy. While Walmart is quite successful at eliminating costs from the system, by keeping wages too low, management may be hurting those who are responsible for its success, the workers.

Once workers know the strategy, they are to be let loose.

Once workers know their strategic advantage, the organization must empower workers to advance it. In a *SPACES*-driven organization, management doesn't need to direct efforts. Workers, from the one installing screws to the one developing advertising, do it with their own conviction and in harmony with the efforts of other organizational stakeholders. They know that their key to survival and thriving is to deepen their competitive advantage. The eyes and ears, the hands, and the brains of many workers will always be better than a few managers gathered into a room and planning for future opportunities.

Ideas for products and process improvements come from everywhere in the organization. Teams to develop these ideas are formed organically everywhere. The organization invests in the generation and distribution of information in order for every member of the organization to be able to contribute his or her best. The decisions of which projects to pursue to advance the strategic advantage should be left to workers as much as possible. Management's role is that of a facilitator and an adviser, making sure that obstacles are removed and that information is available and understood. We will talk about management in the next chapter.

We must plan for the future, strategically.

Besides "forgetting" it, the competitive strategic advantage may lose relevance as the world changes. New competitors come to the market with new strategic propositions, customers change preferences, or supplies become scarce, among others. For example, the cost of oil and its environmental concerns are now enabling new companies to compete in the very complex automotive industry. Tesla motors, which offers a 100% electric sport vehicle, is one of these new competitors that couldn't exist if previous market conditions prevailed.

Frequently, the incumbent players are so invested in their current strategy that they often fail to shift and invest in new technologies that may endanger their very own future survival. This is surprising if we consider that the incumbents have certain established advantages that often are difficult to overcome, such as customer knowledge, distribution networks, product experience, a strong brand, and customer loyalty.

> One example of an organization that had every opportunity, but still failed to shift its strategy is Kodak. In 1997, it had 80% of the U.S. camera market. In 2010, it had less than 13%. Part of Kodak's downfall was due to their failure to recognize the importance of the digital camera market, which is surprising considering that Kodak's scientists created the first megapixel sensor in 1986.[11]
>
> Another example is the GM EV1, an electric vehicle launched in 1996. GM canceled the program and didn't continue developing the technology. Rick Wagoner, the GM CEO at the time, has gone on record to say that his biggest regret was "axing the EV1 program and not putting the right resources into hybrids."[12]

We can write volumes on organizations that failed to recognize the conditions of their new world and eventually failed. This is happening as we speak; entire industries are being replaced: Skype-type services are leapfrogging regular cable phones, e-books are replacing regular books, and camera phones are replacing digital cameras.

The incumbents' easiest action is to cash in on their current technology. They have little incentive to spend money on unproven technologies and to open the Pandora's Box of new ones, endangering the profits they would surely otherwise enjoy. (Remember the unfocused manager who was replaced by the more focused one in chapter 3.) This is why, quite frequently, innovations come from small organizations that develop entirely new ways of solving customers' problems. To complicate matters, managers in the incumbent organizations tend to pursue what they have seen works, not realizing that it may not do so anymore.

For the human species, population growth is a good example from which we can learn. As you know, excessive population growth may endanger earth's natural resources to the point of extinction. In no way is this danger unique to human beings. It is a well-known effect known as the Malthusian or Irruptive growth, in which a species suffers an explosion in population numbers, leading to an exhaustion of resources, and then suffering a population crash. We human beings are supposed to be smarter and able to prevent that disaster from happening to us. But we aren't preventing it, not yet at least. According to most leading thinkers, the rate of usage of resources is much, much higher than the replenishment rate. How could we establish a process to realize such important things?[13]

Our democratic political system does a fair job in addressing the concerns of the day, but drops the ball with regard to planning far into the future. A forward-thinking politician who dares to sacrifice the present to plan for future concerns puts himself in a tough political situation and risks his reelection. Consider, for example a tax on gasoline, which may be a good action to reduce gas consumption and foster renewable propulsion technologies. It would also generate tax income that otherwise ends up as oil company profits, considering that the equilibrium between supply and demand would not change. Even addressing the concerns of lower-income folks, no politician would dare to propose something along those lines.

We said we cannot plan the future with specificity, but how could we avoid falling prey to our own human or organizational shortsightedness, making sure that we implement the necessary changes on time? Doing well as a species or having a great technology that works, how do we avoid becoming a victim of our own success?

"The urgent tends to drive away the important." Anonymous.

A group of "wise elders" may help sense changes that will affect us.

Suppose we grab elders who don't occupy any political position from each country of the world and put them in a room for a month every year, asking them to discuss, agree, and tell us what the biggest concerns in our world are, and what to do about them. They would come up with sensible information and targets to achieve. They would perhaps tell us that the weather is changing too fast, the population is growing too much, and water is poised to be a major concern in the future. This is perhaps not too far from Nelson Mandela's Elders.

Nelson Mandela's Elders is an international group of public figures who work together on solutions for seemingly insurmountable problems such as climate change, HIV/AIDS, and poverty; and to "use their political independence to help resolve some of the world's most intractable conflicts." The group was brought together in 2007 by Nelson Mandela and is chaired today by Archbishop Desmond Tutu.

The Elders represent an independent voice, not bound by the interests of any nation, government, or institution. They are committed to promoting the shared interests of humanity and the universal human rights we all share. They aim to act boldly, speaking difficult truths and tackling taboos. They don't claim to have all the answers, and stress that every individual can make a difference and create positive change in their society.[14]

I know there are many tactical problems to achieve such an enterprise, but if done well (and if we listened to the Elders), we would be better off as a species, for sure. Perhaps we could do something similar in our Driven Organization.

Because what makes an organization special may lose relevance as the world changes, the company needs the keen eyes of the "elders" to sense the changing tide and advise how to adjust course. These elders can study the market and its long-term trends, and provide sensible recommendations while upholding the integrity of the organization's purpose and values. They would not only help us remember and strengthen our strategic competitive advantage but also help us make the necessary investments in order for our organization to succeed in the far-away future. We know that building strong competitive advantages takes a long time, which determines the need to promptly make the right investments.

The ideas, the process improvements, the opportunities, and the projects the organization faces on a daily basis must, as we said before, come from workers. Our group of elders detects opportunities, risks, and dangers far into the future. It is a matter of focus. While the focus of managers and workers is placed on daily concerns and challenges, the elders' is on future concerns. This way, the organization would never experience a situation such as the one Kodak experienced with digital cameras.

The group of elders can be composed of workers from each department or function, without titles, without power. They can be chosen by the rest of the organization. They have been around for a while and are visionaries who are trusted by the rest of the organization to propose what will result in significant advancement.

Note that when I say elders, I refer to the seniority, knowledge, vision, and experience, not to their age. A 20-year-old may not be the best elder, but our focus is on their wisdom, not age. A group of elders may be composed of retired, not-compensated folks, experienced managers, knowledgeable workers, and trusted stakeholders such as suppliers and customers.

Our group of elders is different from the current board of directors in that they are emotionally linked to the organization, perhaps through many years of work in the organization or through their commitment to the organization's purpose. They hold no significant power or economic interest in the organization and will not do so when they act as elders. The group, comprising several experienced and visionary senior managers, will develop strong recommendations on which the organization may act, but not force any course of action.

As a species, humans shouldn't anticipate the moves of other species, develop game theory scenarios, or consider that their success will endanger us. We know there are so many variables that it doesn't make sense. But we know we must open our eyes to the future and understand threats and opportunities. The more successfully we do it, the better off we will be. This is no different with organizations. Let's scratch the competitive map and develop a sound process to identify trends and develop the right investments. Our elders are our eyes on the future.

"Think small and act small, and we'll get bigger. Think big and act big, and we'll get smaller." Herb Kelleher, Southwest Airlines.

Summary of Strategy.

- Current ways of performing strategic work is often flawed because:
  - It is seen as a military conflict in which people must divide a given set of land.
  - It pretends to anticipate competitive moves as a chess player would, not realizing that the number of "moves" is significantly larger.
  - It doesn't account for a natural positive bias forecasters have.
- Strategy is the present knowledge and future general idea of how we plan to pursue our organizational purpose(s) successfully. We must know:
  - The organization's reason for existence, its purpose.
  - How to do it (unique ways of producing better or cheaper products or services than others), allowing the organization to stay in business. This is the strategic competitive advantage.
  - A general "future idea" of how the organization will pursue its purpose in the future.
- As successful strategies make organizations grow and become complex, it is easy to "forget" the strategic competitive advantage.
- A group of "elders" may serve as advisers who help the organization maintain a reasonable position toward the future. It can advise the organization:
  - Whether the organization is following the strategic advantage.

- Whether the world is changing and the development of a new strategic advantage is required.

- To make the necessary investments in order for the organization to be successful.

1   Oberholzer-Gee, Felix, & Yao, Dennis. "Game Theory and Business Strategy." *Harvard Business Review*, January 4, 2005.

2   Lehrer, Jonah. "Chess Intuition." *Scienceblogs.com,* January 18, 2010.

3   Lim, Terence. "Rationality and Analysts' Forecast Bias." *The Journal of Finance* LVI(1), February 2001.

4   Schultz, T. R. "In Search of Ant Ancestors." *Proceedings of the National Academy of Sciences* 97(26), pp. 14028–14029, 2000.

5   Schultz T. R. "Ants, Plants and Antibiotics." *Nature* 398(6730), pp. 747–748, 1999.

6   Basu, Shankar. *Corporate Purpose: Why It Matters More Than Strategy.* Routledge, 1999.

7   "Toyota Global Vision." Mission Statement Announced on March 9, 2011 by Mr. Akio Toyoda.

8   Zook, Chris, & Allen, James. "The Great Repeatable Business Model: Leveraging a Simple Formula Allows Corporations to Create New and More-Lasting Differentiation." *Harvard Business Review,* p. 107, November 2011.

9   Idem.

10   Stewart, Thomas A. "Apple's Secret Sauce: The Real Ingredients." *CBS Money Watch,* March 2011.

11   Bellis, Mary. "History of the Digital Camera." About.com: Inventors. Retrieved January 2013.

12   Rick Wagoner Interview. *Motor Trend,* p. 94, June 2006.

13   Roughgarden, Jonathan. *Theory of Population Genetics and Evolutionary Ecology: An Introduction.* Prentice-Hall, 1995.

14   As described at www.theelders.org. Retrieved February 13, 2013.

Let's explain SPACES by using a car as an example.

At the heart of our car is a strong engine that drives us forward. This is the purpose, the reason why we push ahead.

A good steering system helps us make proper decisions and react to obstacles promptly. We'll call it Autonomy.

Our car constantly updates itself with the latest technology, from infotainment, to engine technology, to safety intelligent systems. This is Competence.

The refined interior, the amazing sound system, the ergonomic controls, and the many other things that make passengers enjoy the trip is the Environment. We don't want to be in any other car!

Our car can't work without fuel. This is the Salary that every one of us needs in our daily lives. It must be enough so that we are not constantly concerned with where the next refueling opportunity is.

How do we get to our destination safely and quickly in this ever changing world? We need a smart navigation system. This is our Strategy.

With SPACES, let's have a safe, long, and fun journey!

The Driven Organization

Part IV: Other Important Considerations.

How does good management look like in the Driven Organization? What is different from what we normally see in a regular company? How can we become good managers? We will contrast management styles and discuss these concerns in detail in Chapter 15, "What about management?

The room is set. The music is arranged. Beverages are served. We know that bringing the right people to the party will make it a success or a huge failure. How do we make sure we bring the right people to our Driven Organization? We will talk about it thoroughly in Chapter 16, "What about hiring?"

Chapter 15:

What About Management?

"A good director creates an environment, which gives the actor the encouragement to fly." Kevin Bacon, actor.

Mr. Marin, the owner of an IT company, was eager to implement SPACES in his organization. He felt he had all the components to make his organization a powerful market player with satisfied associates, but he wasn't sure what his role was.

He asked me, "Isn't management the entity in the organization with the most power and the most responsibility to affect the organization and move it forward?"

"It is," I answered.

He said, "But so far, it seems we need to take away most of the capacity of management to lead the organization. We push most of the responsibility and power to the workers. How can management lead without limiting the capacity of workers to be autonomous or discouraging workers to bring forward their innovations?"

"I mean," he continued, "What is good management in a Driven Organization?"

These are excellent questions that we will discuss in this chapter.

A leader is a strong figure who sets paths and energizes others.

When we think of a true leader, we picture a strong individual who exudes energy and knows where to go and what to do. Her highly contagious enthusiasm infuses others to participate with her thinking, with her objectives, with her ideas, and with her work. She inspires others to give their best. Because of her certainty and convictions, she pushes hard to convince others of her proposals until they are on board with her as well. She is tenacious, relentless and doesn't back up. As a charismatic and likable leader, she has many ways to get others on board. In fact, she is so sure of her convictions, her capacity, and her achievements that she is borderline cocky. She enjoys working in teams, helping and leading them to accomplish objectives.

She has acquired experience, knowledge, and status. She has grown in the organization's ranks and is responsible for others below her. Workers come to her for help and direction every day. She worked hard to be able to direct them, acquiring knowledge, getting herself in a good reputable position within the company, and showing time and time again she wants things to be done the right way.

Leaders such as the one described here have rescued declining enterprises, turned around companies, and moved impossible mountains. They have attended the best universities in the world and have had great experiences. I heard one of these leaders say once when pounding on the table, "It may take ten years, but we will show them!" referring to the competition. Everybody at the meeting was impressed with his energy. It sounded great. They enjoyed being in the hands of this great leader. And great he was! What else could we ask for?

In our Driven Organization, we don't want this leader.

The classic leader is no good for the Driven Organization.

This is why. Although she may be a leader who accomplishes objectives and energizes the company, ultimately the results, the organization's motivation and energy, and the specific, chosen ways are all coming from her and from her alone. In contrast, in our Driven Organization, workers are self-motivated. They believe in the organization's purpose and they are given opportunities to learn and to affect the company in a positive way. They exert their entire capacity as intelligent individual members of the organization. They love working together and really don't need someone inspiring them.

A strong character leader, such as the one described previously, believes he is right, and his task is to convince other less gifted individuals to open their eyes and listen to him. His charisma, good looks, and energy only helps him do so more effectively. Although he likes working in teams, the teams are only enablers for him to achieve what he thinks must be achieved in the way he wants to achieve it.

This is the type of leader that believes he is helping others by providing direction, by telling workers how things must be done, and by solving their problems. Secretly, he enjoys being the person whom everyone seeks, the problem solver without whom the organization or department would become paralyzed, the only visionary who can see far enough to identify problems and opportunities in the future. He enjoys being responsible for the lives of others, believing he is as important as the number of people he manages.

By controlling so much, by being responsible for so much, he feels his life is purposeful and important. He needs to feel this way and his job takes a whole different meaning in his life. This is the reason why he goes home late, why the day doesn't have enough hours for him to finish his job, and why he enjoys more being at work than at home. He wants to be there when others need him, when things get stuck, when the answer isn't clear. If he wasn't there, God forbid, they may think and come up with a solution on their own! Or perhaps somebody may fill up the position of authoritative problem solver and decision maker.

At night, sharing a drink with friends, he talks with pleasure about how his company messed up that day and how he helped out. He describes how some people were doing the completely wrong thing. They all share similar stories. They may believe that by talking about them, they are simply letting their frustrations go away, but this is only partially true. About 90% of this type of talk has another objective. Complaining about people is pleasurable. It exalts us above our coworkers, making us better, smarter than them. They are stupid, they don't understand, and we do.

To be fair, this type of feeling is not only experienced at the management levels, but at all levels. This feeling of "they are stupid" is often even described on TV, in shows such as "The Office," "Parks and

Recreation," "30 Rock," and "Scrubs." It is a way in which we all have to feel smarter or better than others, but it is experienced more frequently at the top because there is more ego to fuel it.

This leader wants to grow the company and to create the biggest organization it can be because being larger is better and because achieving growth implies a well-done job. He wants to take out the competition for the sake of winning the game. This is a huge chess game that must be won, both within the company, in regard to other managers and workers, and toward the company's competition.

And what is the problem with him enjoying the game? What is the problem with him growing the organization? Doesn't everybody win this way? The problem is that in becoming bigger and better than the competition, just for its sake, we run over many other considerations. We run over the worker's welfare and satisfaction. We run over resources that could be better used. We use strategies that may not be the best in the long run, but provide a short-term advantage. We actually make the organization weaker over time. Perhaps we enter markets not core to our objectives, and we force other organizations to fall into distress mode, fighting for their survival, and forcing them to retaliate.

This could be why sometimes great turnarounds led by these type of leaders eventually come back crashing down after a few years, or why large organizations overreach beyond what is sensible. Think of Stan O'Neal, the ex-CEO of Merril Lynch, who guided the firm from its familiar turf—fee businesses such as asset management—into the lucrative game of creating collateralized debt obligations (CDOs), which were largely made of subprime mortgage bonds. He has been named one of the "25 People to Blame for the Financial Crisis."[1] This may also be the reason why certain leaders become so focused on getting the results they want, that they are willing to perform illegal actions. Think Kenneth Lay, the Enron CEO, who used creative accounting fraud to prop up business results.[2]

But not every leader like the one we just described is bad for business. Great accomplishments have been completed by leaders in this category throughout much of history. This is especially true in military campaigns. It is just that in our dream organization we have special workers and a special way of conducting business that allows all workers to give their best, instead of only a few "smart ones." Rather than a soldier and executor, we have an individual thinker and a doer in each worker. It's obvious, then, that we must have special leaders as well.

Most leaders described here won't realize they are egocentric. They may see one or two traits that fit, but in general, they believe they are constantly helping others in the organization. Remember that, by definition, they are egocentric because they are focused on themselves, but by the same dynamic, they don't know it. They believe they are helping, but secretly enjoy when they are the heroes of the situation. They go home satisfied and happy for having solved the organization's problems. Would they feel as happy if they somehow enabled others to be the heroes of the situation?

This doesn't mean they are bad people. Quite the contrary, they are great people. It is through lots of self-reflection, years of experience, and/or life events that a few of these leaders may become what we will call here, "sensible leaders." I believe that egocentric leadership is a step that often is necessarily experienced to eventually become a sensible leader.

"A man wrapped up in himself makes a very small bundle."
Benjamin Franklin.

As technology forces us to change, leaders must adapt, too.

Before we talk about the leader we do want in our organization, let us briefly talk about how an increased flow of information in our modern business lives forces certain changes in our organizations. Nobody doubts that the flow of information of today exceeds many, many times that of past years. Previously, a manager could act as the brain of a unit, making all decisions in it. Today, because the information flow is much higher, one person cannot handle it all by himself, forcing him to delegate to his employees, not only the processing, but also the decision making.

In order for the base-level workers to be trusted to perform as required, they must be coached and advised by those with experience. The function of the manager changes, therefore, from a decision maker to an adviser, and the function of the base-level worker, from an executor to a decision maker.

The same cheap and easy flow of information helps the adviser get close to those who need help in his unit, notwithstanding distance. Thanks to this accessibility, an adviser can help several folks in the unit, reducing in effect the number of advisers required in an organization. This pressures our hierarchical structures to become flatter and less hierarchical. This is why we find democratic organizations able to function nowadays effectively in a more massive scale and better than in the past. Workers in these organizations need little management, some coaching, and lots of trust and independence.

The fact that information acquisition, processing, and transfer are so cheap today allows us to be less rigid toward our business planning. Think of a missile as an example. If in years past, a missile was able to send its position to the control tower every three minutes, the tower could make path corrections every three minutes. If today's missile technology allows it to send data every ten milliseconds, the missile could get a path correction every ten milliseconds. We can derive three consequences from this faster, more frequent feedback. First, the missile has a much better overall path, closer to the ideal path. Second, the missile can react faster to big changes, such as if a new better target has been identified, and not have to wait until a certain point in time to change course. Third, there is more need for information processing. All of which prompts the need for independent, accountable individuals, who are guided by certain values, principles, and purposes.

We don't need stodgy, rigid, and expensive business plans. While our purpose and values never change, and our strategy varies so rarely and by small increments, our organization must be fast and nimble to react to everyday changing concerns. When new information comes up, which happens at a much more frequent rate, it should have empowered, capable personnel ready to act.

Our "sensible" leader.

So, who is the leader we want in our Driven Organization?

This "sensible" leader has great expertise in the job. Even so, instead of providing solutions, his role is to ask questions that prompt others to think. He facilitates, connects people, and helps everyone generate new concepts and thoughts. He provides experience to the team, but works as hard as anybody else, often doing common tasks, as well.

He doesn't think his job is any more important than that of the rest of his team. If this were in a sports team, he'd be the front man who passes the ball to his teammates in order for them to score or helps assemble a play that leads someone to score. He doesn't need to be the star of the game. Our leader's capacity resides in fostering the strength of each player and using it in a cohesive and coordinated fashion to improve the capability of the entire team.

> One example of such a leader is Magic Johnson. He played in the NBA for the Los Angeles Lakers as a point guard, which is the position that organizes the offensive play. He has a range of achievements including three MVP (Most Valued Player) honors; a spot on the 50 greatest players in NBA history; a membership in the basketball Hall of Fame; and honored as the greatest NBA point guard of all time by ESPN, among others. It was, however, his focus on making everyone else on his team play the best they could that made him one of the most beloved players of all time. Magic Johnson has the highest assist record per game of all time, at 11.2. To assist is to pass the ball in such a way that it leads to score. There were countless times when Magic Johnson could have scored, but passed the ball to someone else to make a great and exciting score.[3]

I have repeatedly seen that this type of leader, the one we want in the Driven Organization, has no trouble connecting with the principles of SPACES. In contrast, the egocentric, command and control leader immediately finds dozens of reasons why SPACES wouldn't work.

"I view my role more as trying to set up an environment where the personalities, creativity and individuality of all the different employees come out and can shine." Tony Hsieh, CEO of Zappos.com.

True leaders lead from the trenches.

Often, the leader doesn't even have the actual title. Dunga, a Brazilian soccer player who led the Brazilian team to win the 1994 soccer world cup explains it to us. He says that having the captain armband is only a symbol that doesn't matter much. In reality, several players, when they believe in their objectives, become captains throughout the game. A leader, he says, is not the one who makes others follow his opinion. A leader is led by his teammates. Discussing the situation, making agreements and decisions on what to do and how to do it must happen first. Once this is done, everyone in the team can act as a leader, only reinforcing the agreements and reminding everyone of the path they chose to take.

How much agreement needs to take place in a soccer game, somebody may ask? Those who are sport fans may answer that question easily; agreements such as who will mark whom; how will the ball travel forward, by air or ground; how fast will the game be, how far will the players go; how to control the other team's offensive, and many more. In a business, don't you think there are many more decisions that need to be agreed by the team members in order for everyone to pull toward the same direction? The leader that Dunga describes is not one who imposes his opinions, but one who facilitates others making agreements and helps them achieve them.

Our leader doesn't need to have the solutions, but he must be sure that with his team, they will find the best ones. Instead of being necessarily handsome, tall, or even charismatic, his strength resides in creating special working environments in which every teammate can act his best. The leader helps others achieve a superior level of performance.

"The best leader is the best server. And if you're a servant, by definition you're not controlling." Herb Kelleher, CEO, Southwest Airlines.

The best leaders drive from purpose.

Like any other worker at the Driven Organization, our leader is an adept believer in the organization's purpose. This way, instead of worrying about advancing herself, she is preoccupied with moving the organization and its purpose forward. This contrasts with the regular modern leader, who must divide her energy into worrying about advancing the organization and looking good in the eyes of bosses and coworkers.

Because the purpose matters to her, our leader doesn't need to be paid an exorbitant high salary, make all decisions, or sit in a huge corner office to feel successful. She derives her success by how much the organization advances its objectives. She needs money to live, but doesn't need to receive additional "prestige perks." The office of Tony Hsieh, the Zappos CEO, is exactly the same as any other worker's cubicle at Zappos, providing us with a good example.

As a matter of fact, two of the most important parts of the job of our leader are to help workers connect with the purpose. First, our leader helps workers visualize the impact the organization can have when they work toward their purpose. She leads them to imagine a world in which the thing they strive to achieve is a reality. Second, the leader makes sure that workers understand how their daily, individual work activities advance the organization toward this purpose. Doing so eliminates functional barriers, increases motivation, reduces friction, builds an environment, and much more.

The Driven Organization leader establishes relationships with others.

Our leader doesn't think everyone else in the organization is less capable, stupid, or plain evil. He doesn't go to have a drink after work to complain about his organization. Instead, his nights out frequently take place with people from his organization, friends whom he respects and about whom he feels fortunate to have met.

He knows that each of them is working as hard as he or she can to fix the organization's problems. He knows this is the best caliber of people with whom he will ever work, and if there is even a remote possibility to make the organization work, they will do so together.

As a matter of fact, our leader uses every opportunity available to spend time with workers and establish an affective relationship with them. But why is that important?

We now agree that those who actually do the work and are at the forefront of the organization are ultimately in charge of advancing the organization and generating outstanding solutions and ideas. This, in itself, should be the reason to establish close communication with them. But it is not the main reason.

We all seek to be in places where we are liked, where our presence is valued, and our input is appreciated. We know the importance of this from our chapter on environment. Our leader knows that he has the largest capacity of anyone to make people feel satisfied, at ease, and to help them feel that their contribution is valuable. This is his job.

> Researchers have found that the simple action of greeting students at the door when they come into the classroom causes them to improve in performance. The student measurement of out-of-seat and on-task behavior was found to be strongly correlated with the teacher's greeting.[4]

Everything we do in life is about relationships. Work is not an exception. No manager will succeed and become a good leader if he is not interested in developing personal bonds with others. This is fundamental for our leader to do his job: to provide assistance and help to other workers and to make them see how their work is related with the objectives of the organization.

There are many ways for our leader to foster relationships. An open door, work meetings, social gatherings, and a friendly smile work fine, but he should also actively and overtly create opportunities to sit down and chat with as many workers as possible.

> Affection is so important for all living creatures that its effects can be seen in the most unexpected places. For example, cows that are named by their farmers produce more milk, says a study of the Newcastle University in England. They claim that affectionate treatment increases milk production per cow for about 68 gallons per year. "A cow that is happy and calm is going to produce more milk," a farmer involved with the study commented.[5]

"Managers are appointed, leaders are elected." Unknown.

Our leader may take the reins in emergency situations.

On rare occasions, there are emergency situations. Note that this situation is not normal, nor is it frequent in our Driven Organization. In those situations, our sensible leaders, who are trusted by the organization, must and will act decisively, and with straightforward clarity and direction. This is the only time that the opinion of others may not be taken into account. I talk about a situation such as an earthquake or a problem that in a short time may ruin the month supply of flour for a baker. After the fact, the leaders must discuss these events with everyone: have everyone involved in planning how to prepare for future events and discuss how to recover from emergency situations.

Becoming a "sensible" leader is not easy, but it's possible.

The ideal leaders for our Driven Organization are special. Their commitment to the cause, combined with their common sense and reflection capacity, allow them to generate the best behaviors from everyone around them. It is my empirical observation that they have had life experiences that have helped them open their eyes and acquire a special level of wisdom. In most cases, they experienced a strong hardship situation, which crystallized their values and character. But what is there to do for all of us who did not have such experiences, or that if we did, we just didn't get it?

Today, you are reading this book. This tells me you are concerned with improving your place of work. You know you want to be part of new "sensible" ways of conducting businesses that yield the best results. This already sets you apart. You are on your way!

You may feel you can influence your organizations in a better way, or perhaps that there is room for you to do more as a leader. If you feel you have not reached the leadership capacity you can achieve, I would suggest the following: Put yourself in situations that help you crystallize who you are, what you think, and what you need to do.

For some, this means to travel places; for others, to change jobs or to launch a new business; for some others, to take risks, perhaps to propose a new way in our workplaces, to modify how it has always been done and to fail. Yes, try it out and fail. Fail a lot and you will learn. Fail a lot and you will realize who you are. Somebody once told me, if you never push your boundaries, you will never know what you are capable of doing, how strong you are, what you must change, and what is worth fighting for.

"Good decisions come from wisdom. Wisdom comes from

experience. Experience comes from bad decisions." Anonymous.

Great leadership, explained by an orchestra conductor.

Itay Talgam, a renowned Israeli orchestra conductor, explains in a much better way how leadership is still able to foster great results for the organization while giving workers the space to do their side of the bargain. Itay gives a great presentation on different leadership styles and brings to light the effect these leadership styles have on those being led and the results they generate together. He uses classic orchestra conductors to help us understand. He gave this talk at one of the TED events.[6] If you haven't seen it, look for it on the Internet, as my description will never make justice to his presentation.

In order for an orchestra to play, there needs to be a conductor, several players, and other unseen folks like the ones that built the instruments or the theater hall. Each one of them brings something to the ensemble that gets combined to produce great music. What is the role of the conductor in bringing these individual stories together in such a way they produce the very best?

Itay shows us Riccardo Muti in action. He is what we would probably expect in a conductor. He deploys much energy. He is clear, commanding, even forceful. He is a great leader, we can readily see. This is the typical leader we would expect to have in any modern organization. This is, until Itay explains that Riccardo Muti was asked to resign by his very own musicians because they felt left out of the process of creating music. They felt he was controlling them excessively and not allowing them to add anything or to grow. They felt Riccardo was the only one in control.

Itay then shows us Richard Strauss, who through paying close attention to the music score, suggests that orchestra members do so. It isn't about their story or his story, but about the score's story. For Strauss, things have to be done by the book with no input from him or from the players. Have you met a manager like this?

Another conductor is shown, Herbert Von Karajan, who provides fuzzy direction and makes soft gestures. Because timing of the sounds have to be precise, players under Von Karajan have to watch each other in order for them to find unison. His eyes are closed, as if he's trying not to suggest anything else. He lets folks do what they think they need to do. Players are very aware of each other and find unison and harmony. So we ask, what is the role of the conductor, of management? Is it to let their workers loose?

Itay answers this question by showing us Carlos Kleiber, who leads by bringing the expression of the music without tight control so that the players can add their own interpretation of what the music calls for. As a former amateur piano player, I can tell you that there are many ways to play that C sharp half note, and even though there is a score to follow, no score can precisely indicate the emotional sensitivity that the piece needs. It is the interpreter who adds that part.

Carlos Kleiber allows his players to do this by giving them little control. But because in an orchestra there are several interpreters, they have to agree on what the music calls for. Through his gestures, Carlos Kleiber brings the content of the piece for everyone to follow. If it is a sad song, he is sad as well, but in a way that helps the player play the note only in a sad way. Both Carlos and another conductor that Itay shows us, Leonard Bernstein, bring the meaning of the music for every player to feel and understand.

All players are in effect participating in the creation of what Itay calls a rollercoaster, which will take them all on a ride from which they cannot get off. The conductor has become an emotional or spiritual guide who helps them understand what the weather should be and how the music must feel. Carlos and Lenny create a special process in which everyone can add their own bit, but they also create the conditions for this process to exist, and exist well in accordance to the feel of the music. Their role is to give the players trust, responsibility, accountability, and recognition.

Most often, they act only as facilitators among the players, but when somebody gets out of tune, they provide direction, as an adviser would: when necessary and with clarity. Carlos and Lenny demonstrate their enjoyment of a player's performance by rolling their eyes in a special way, which is the kind of recognition that really goes deep in the player's chest. This is motivation. Carlos and Lenny bring meaning to the music, the feeling that what the players are doing really matters, that it is something that must exist, something great. This is the role of management. To make sure everyone realizes that what the organization does is extremely important, that their individual contribution is significant to achieve the organizational goals.

I paraphrase Benjamin Zander, another famous classical music conductor who says that at work he doesn't make a sound or play a key. He says his job and his power is to make others powerful. His job is to awaken the possibility of greatness for everyone to fill it in, to inspire them. Only with the contribution of the greatness of each player, an ensemble can truly produce magic.

"The growth and development of people is the highest calling of leadership." Harvey S. Firestone.

Summary of Management.

- The usual great, strong, modern leader doesn't fit well with our dream organization. This leader:
  - Does not foster every worker in the organization to contribute the best he can.
  - Is secretly and often unknowingly focused on his own benefit: being the hero in difficult situations.
- The modern world has a much increased flow of information.
  - Because there are too many decisions to make for one man, managers must delegate and make every team member a decision maker.
  - Because managers need to be able to trust their teams, they must become coaches, and prepare workers to act and respond properly when they are not around.
  - The objective is to have independent, accountable individuals who are guided by certain values, principles, and purposes shared by everyone in the organization.
- The right leader for our dream organization, a "sensible" leader, is not looking for recognition, which allows him to focus on helping others become the best they can be, and achieve the organization's purposes. This leader:
  - Does not believe he is superior than others at his organization.

- Passes the ball for others to score. Think Magic Johnson and Dunga.
- Does not need extra perks to do the job because he believes in its purpose.
- It is possible to learn to become a "sensible" leader, but it isn't easy. It entails doing and failing. It may even entail putting ourselves in situations that help us crystallize who we are, what we think, and what we need to do in this life.
- One of the main jobs of management is to make sure that workers understand the importance of the purpose and how their daily activities advance it.

1   TIME Lists. "25 People to Blame for the Financial Crisis: The Good Intentions, Bad Managers and Greed Behind the Meltdown." Retrieved January 26, 2013.

2   TIME Lists. "Top 10 CEO Scandals." 2010. Retrieved January 26, 2013.

3   Wikipedia. *Magic Johnson.* Retrieved January 26, 2013.

4   Allday, A., & Pakurar, K. "Effects of Teacher Greetings on Student On-Task Behavior." *Journal of Applied Behavior Analysis* 40(2), pp. 317–320, Summer, 2007.

    Patterson, S. "The Effects of Teacher-Student Small Talk on Out-of-Seat Behavior." *Education and Treatment of Children* 32(1), 2009.

5   Douglas, Catherine, & Rowlinson, Peter. "Exploring Stock Managers' Perceptions of the Human-Animal Relationship on Dairy Farms and an Association With Milk Production." *Anthrozoös,* January 28, 2009.

6   Talgam, Itay. *Lead like the great conductors.* Ted.com, 2009.

Chapter 16:

What About Hiring?

"Train for skill, hire for attitude." Herb Kelleher, Southwest
airlines.

The organization we are creating is like a party with its own specific
characteristics. It can be noisy or quiet. It can have dancing or invite a
relaxing experience. Perhaps there is beer, or maybe tea with small
sandwiches. We have set up a great place that will have great following.
The only remaining question is who needs to be invited and who doesn't.
We must make sure that we bring in those who will let loose, have a
great time, benefit from it, and help others do the same. We will talk
about how to do it in this chapter.

Our attitudes make work easier or much more difficult.

When I was in college, my family was building a house. Instead of
hiring a construction company to do it, we decided to do it ourselves. We
hired workers, we bought building materials, we chartered drawings and
layouts, and we went ahead with our project. Since I had more free time,
it became my project. I hired the workers, I set objectives and
expectations, I paid them, and I thanked them and let them go when
needed. I won't say that I did it all in a proper way; actually between you
and me, I did few things in the proper way, but this opportunity helped

me learn something hugely important. I learned the importance of attitude.

Throughout this time, I got to know many workers. There was one with whom I enjoyed working the most. It wasn't that he was particularly skilled or had special knowledge. In fact, it was obvious he had almost no formal education, but Mark had something that made him special. He had a great attitude. When we needed to do something with which he didn't have experience, he would say, "Let me think about it." He would go away for a while, try a couple of things, and come back with a couple of proposals. In every case, when faced with difficulties, he'd always say, "We'll figure it out. We have to."

And we did. Mark and I carried on projects with which each of us had none or little experience. Mark participated in installing marble countertops for bathrooms and kitchen, tiling, window construction, electricity wiring and fixture installation, plaster, and plumbing. We didn't always get it right, but we experimented constantly and were willing to start all over again if the result wasn't as desired. There were mistakes, too, but Mark helped me with complicated projects, which I would have found difficult to complete considering my lack of experience. I, in turn, tried to help Mark feel appreciated with letting him know the impact of his work, with continuous work even when other workers had to go, and with a small amount of additional money.

Mark's attitude was displayed in regard to the project and his customers. He had the sense that each person had a role to fulfill, and there were no conflicting emotions about it. He didn't think that the contractor job, my job, was any more important than his, nor was he resentful because I had such job. Each of us had responsibilities and difficulties. Once this was established, it was easy to see that it was a win-win relationship in which none of us was trying to take advantage of the other. Contrast that with other workers who resented the fact that I was younger than them, that I knew less than them, or that neither the market nor my family could afford what they wanted to earn. These workers were often resentful, cut corners, used materials in a wasteful manner, tried to take advantage of me, and (most importantly) were often unhappy.

Even when he had less experience, Mark's attitude made it easier to complete difficult projects. Skill, knowledge, and even brain power were not as important as the attitude toward the work, toward teammates, and toward me. Mark's attitude made him a capable individual who devised brilliant solutions that saved money and increased the quality of results.

It was a powerful lesson that I have corroborated over and over in my professional life. With the right attitude, anything is possible. With the wrong attitude, even having skill, resources, and luck, everything is impossible or extremely difficult, at best. With the right attitude, problems are something to work through and nothing more.

The attitude, apparently, is more important than what it seems at first sight. It actually determines how lucky people feel and in turn how lucky they are. Researchers have studied the behaviors, attitudes, and test results of people who feel lucky and who feel unlucky with an interesting experiment. Once they know how people rate themselves, researchers ask them, one by one, to count the pictures in a newspaper. Those who feel unlucky take about two minutes to complete the task. "Forty-three pictures," they say. Those who feel lucky need only seconds to complete the task. On the second page, there is a sign that reads "Stop counting. There are 43 photographs in this newspaper." While the message is right there, the "lucky" people can see it, but the "unlucky" people don't. Even when researchers add the message "Stop counting. Tell the experimenter you have seen this and win 250 pounds," the results are exactly the same. They explain: those who feel lucky and fortunate are less tense and more able to consider alternative solutions. Anxiety, he says, disrupts people's ability to notice the unexpected. The researchers believe that a person can become luckier by changing his attitude.[1]

To build the right environment, we must have the right people.

In our little house project, workers came and went, and the environment changed accordingly. At times, Mark and I could foster a working environment in which everyone was satisfied and happy. Workers cared for the work and felt appreciated. The workers had fun among themselves and with me, and felt good building this house. At other times, with other workers, the environment was different. A few of them were negative and frequently complained to each other. I could feel that even the workers who had enjoyed the work before didn't feel they had it so good any more. Resentment toward the project and me took place. Even for our small temporary organization, we needed to have the right people to function properly, both for the project's sake and for their own.

We know that the attitude of the people that we bring into our organization influences our environment. A helpful person fits easily into an environment geared toward customer service. An introverted person may fit well in an environment of independent work. A controlling person may cause friction in an Autonomous environment, even if he "converts" into the way of the others. Instead of stretching the capacity of the environment to shape behaviors, we must bring people that naturally reinforce it.

In the strategy chapter, we discussed how important it is to know ourselves. In this case, knowing ourselves means knowing which characteristics we should foster in our organization, knowing which type of people would foster those characteristics, and knowing how to let them do what they do naturally.

> Most organizations don't do a good job selecting the right candidates. One of the main reasons why is that they don't have a clear understanding of what environment they must promote and what kind of people would protect and enjoy this environment. Everything seems the same when one doesn't know what one wants.

In getting the right people in, the first question is about skills.

Once we know who we are, the first question to start the hiring process is to ask whether the candidate has the necessary skills to do the job. There are many ways to check this, from psychometric tests that measure the abilities of the candidates to exercises such as performing a financial analysis, making an essay, developing a presentation, or solving a hard problem.

Some organizations put the candidates into real or mock situations such as taking care of customers, answering phone calls, and so on. I believe that these tests, especially the psychometric tests, should be a pass/no pass requirement, as opposed to a measurement of how smart a candidate is or how badly the candidate is wanted by the organization.

Let me tell you why. Psychometric tests describe very few of the many skills a person can display. They don't describe negotiating, speaking, motivating, handcrafting, sensing, listening, observing, or being dexterous, to name a few. Psychometric tests wouldn't explain why yesterday, for example, after watering two plants, I left the faucet open for the entire night. But bear with me. Psychometric test results are often taken out of proportion. After college, many of my friends and I were tested by several companies using psychometric tests. One of these companies was an industrial conglomerate that made glass products. I knew I had done the tests well because I was able to complete problems that my friends had not, as we obviously discussed afterward.

I get the impression that the hiring managers at the company thought that my results would be translated into a big impact to the organization. You see, I was planning to go to another company, but my way to say no to them was telling them that my salary objectives were 70% higher than what they had offered me. While most companies would have laughed at my request at a time when the country was only coming out from a serious financial crisis, they came back with a much unexpected counteroffer of about 50% higher. At this point, recently graduated from college and with student loans to pay, I accepted. I was basically bought. Two months later, I resigned, accepted the other offer for where I wanted to go in the first place with a much deserved pay cut.

The problem, you see, is that I wasn't in love with the offered job. Years later, I ran into the human resources coordinator, and I asked him why they had come back with that offer. He only said, "Your test results came back really high."

The folks at this company decided to weigh that factor much higher than other important considerations such as … yes, my appreciation for the job. I, in turn, weighed money much higher than … yes, my own appreciation for the job. At the end, this experience provided me with a great opportunity to learn a valuable lesson. We have already discussed the importance of money (or lack thereof) in previous chapters.

The second question is about the job itself.

The second question for an organization to ask is whether the candidate connects with the job. It may be that the candidate can do the job, but the job doesn't represent the life he wants to lead, doesn't bring enough challenge for him to find it interesting, or simply entails certain obstacles the candidate will find difficult to withstand. When I graduated from college, I visited a company called Delphi, a Fortune-500 automotive supplier, for a second round of interviews. I was interviewing for a job in the Design department. I clearly remember at the end of the interview what the hiring manager said to me.

"I just don't believe you will be happy sitting down with a drafting computer in front of you for hours on end every day."

I felt rejected. Not much later, I realized he was quite right. He was able to see that I wouldn't be happy doing it for a long time or have the patience to do it. The job wasn't rocket science, but the desire to do it wasn't going to be there in the long run.

Our dream organization is special. With competence, it allows workers to learn, become better, and discover new improved ways; with autonomy, it gives them the control of their schedule; it doesn't use salary as a coercive tool to drive behaviors; it expects every worker to participate in improving the organization's strategic advantage. Does the candidate fit well with these ways? For example, will the candidate's work life be improved by the freedom provided by Autonomy or will he be stressed by the lack of structure? Will the candidate take advantage of the opportunity to become better at his job provided by Competence, or will he feel overstressed by learning new things or by the fact that everyone else is doing so? Does he enjoy having the opportunity to figure out how to deepen the strategic advantage or does he believe it only increases the load of his job?

One way of thinking about this question is with another question. What will the job bring to the candidate? One answer may be related to the interest in learning the technical aspects for the job, as in steel manufacturing or computer design. Another answer is related to what the job entails. Some people need to be talking with people at all times or they'll feel lonely, which makes them great candidates for customer service or sales. I have a friend, a brilliant engineer, who doesn't like to be working in a closed space. His work at oil exploration sites provides him with great opportunities to be outdoors. The answer to the question must be clear for both the candidate and the hiring group.

The third question is about the organizational environment.

The third question we can ask is whether the candidate fits well with the environment of the organization. Many organizations give the last decision about whether to accept the candidate or not to those who will be working directly with him. They must answer a question along the lines of "Do you want this person on your team?" To evaluate candidates, they often take them to lunch or to social gatherings, perform group interviews, and have them perform group exercises. Often, the groups have to be unanimously in agreement in order for the candidate to be hired.

It is important to ponder the balance between fitting into the environment and diversity. While these two concepts seem to be opposed, they don't necessarily have to be. Diversity brings different perspectives and ideas, prevents us from falling into group-think and herd behavior, and helps the organization become stronger. These are characteristics that we must seek with each and every candidate.

There are areas where we don't want diversity. For example, we may need every team member to be honest, respectful, responsible, and accepting of others; to challenge others to work better, and to attempt to lead a happy harmonious life. We need every team member to support all characteristics we need to protect in our particular environment. Potential workers with these characteristics come from all walks of life, human races, countries, education levels, and social groups. Differences in these latter characteristics are the ones that provide diversity and enrich the organization.

The fourth question is about Purpose, principles, and values.

The fourth question is whether the candidate believes in the organization's purpose. If he doesn't have any particular inclination toward the organization's Purpose, it will eventually feel as if the folks in the organization aren't serious enough. He won't respect and advance the efforts toward it. But if he finds the Purpose worthwhile, he will feel energized every morning coming to work because he knows that his work matters way more beyond getting a paycheck for him and profits for the business owners. The organization matters to the world!

Workers are the best to determine the right hiring process.

These are four simple questions that when correctly answered will make a huge difference for the people that join our organization. Each one of them may entail activities, exercises, and maybe even more questions. I don't believe that there is a specific process to answer them. What matters is that the organization takes the time to conduct a carefully designed and thoroughly executed hiring process. Having an empty position is always better than having the wrong individual in the organization.

At the end of the process, the objective is that both the organization and the candidate know each other very well. As candidates, we can all get clean and smile for a couple of hours, but if we must interact in more than one occasion, with more than one person, in more than one activity, it becomes more difficult to keep up an artificial facade. The same is true for the organization. By exposing the candidate to several workers, he will get a great idea of the specific ways of the organization.

How to get to know the candidates better is a question for the workers to answer. The workers may come up with their own unique process that allows them to more effectively evaluate what they feel is most important. In doing so, they will infuse the process with the specific characteristics of the organization. They also become participants and are accountable for the people they bring. By learning from the experience and outcome, soon the organization will have a great hiring process.

An example of a hiring process comes from Semco, the Brazilian conglomerate and one of the leader organizations applying Autonomy concepts. Its objective is to make sure that both parties, the candidate and the hiring organization, discover and communicate who they are, how they are, and what they want and need from each other. The hiring process, they say, is the courting process to decide to get married or to decide not to get married. At Semco, whoever wants to participate in the hiring process can do so. It starts by conducting a similar process to most companies with the usual resume elimination, the initial rounds of interviews, and so on. At this time, the technical skills, fit with the job, and obvious character traits are evaluated, and candidates are filtered in or out. The questions to answer are whether the person can do the job, whether his technical preparation is enough, and whether he is a good candidate.

Once the company has, let's say, ten finalists, they are put in a room together and are interviewed by Semco employees. Semco interviewers vote on the candidates, and the two who get the most votes are invited to spend some time at Semco. During this time, the two selected candidates will attend lunches, visit the company, and talk with whomever they please. After a while, the candidate and a representative from Semco sit down to discuss whether they do want to get married or not.[2]

As with a partner, we are better off being honest and transparent.

It is in our organization's main interest to make sure the candidate will be happy and fulfilled as a worker because only this way will he support the organization's environment and results. We must show him who we are and what we do. We must open the closet for him to see the clothes we sometimes wear when no one is looking. We must make sure that he really grasps what it means to work in our organization. An unhappy, cheated worker will never deliver the expected results. Worse, he may damage the environment we have fought so hard to build. Avoiding the smallest feeling that he was cheated is important. Having the usual "dress well and be nice for hiring day" isn't desirable.

When we are young and we meet potential partners, we try to protect and hide those sides of ourselves we find dark and scary. On first dates, we don't say we pick our nose or that we stink at the 20 hour mark without a shower. We show only the good side of ourselves. Often we do it so well, that sometimes people carry on having a relationship for a long time only to later discover new things that should have been probably learned on the first or second date. After doing this for a while, we learn better and we decide to speak openly about who and how we are, and about what we like to do. We lower our walls of fear and we let the other person see it all. It may be that in the process, we realize this isn't the right person for us. We keep looking, until eventually, the surprising thing happens. We find that by letting the other person know us better, we develop closeness, trust, and love. The relationship becomes stronger, and we both become happier.

It is the same with our organization. We can be open and let the candidate see. Through games and other activities, we take time to get to know each other. We may find we are not right for each other and we must keep looking, but when we find the right person or the right organization, we know it's just great. It is only by a good courting (or hiring) process that our relationships will be stronger and our lives better with each other in it.

"I found that there were these incredibly great people at doing certain things, and you couldn't replace one of these people with 50 average people. They could just do stuff that no number of average people could do." Steve Jobs.

Summary of Hiring.

- Bringing the right people to the organization is fundamental to foster the right environment and achieve the right results.
- As with two people deciding to get married, hiring is the courting process for the organization and the potential worker to decide to get into a relationship or not. Four questions must be answered during this process:
  1. Does the candidate have the necessary skills to do the job?
  2. Does the candidate fit with the job and with what it entails?
  3. Does the candidate fit well with the environment of the organization?
  4. Does the candidate believe in the organization's purpose?
- Letting the candidate know about as much of the organization as possible is hugely important in order for the candidate to evaluate whether this is a good marriage or not. An unhappy employee is neither good for the environment, nor good for the organization's business results.

"Everybody is a genius. But if you judge a fish by its ability to climb a tree, it will spend its whole life believing that it is stupid." Albert Einstein.

---

1   Wiseman, Richard. *THE LUCK FACTOR: Changing Your Luck, Changing Your Life.* Miramax, 2003.

2   Semler, Ricardo. *The Seven-Day Weekend: Changing the Way Work Works.* Portfolio, 2004.

The Driven Organization

Chapter 17:

Final Thoughts.

"For the past 33 years, I have looked in the mirror every morning and asked myself: 'If today were the last day of my life, would I want to do what I am about to do today?' And whenever the answer has been 'No' for too many days in a row, I know I need to change something." Steve Jobs.

It may seem overwhelming to think about all the components necessary to build the Driven Organization we have described. However, they all point toward the same direction and stem from the same principles. You will see that as soon as your organization begins implementing one or two concepts of SPACES, others will be naturally brought in, and soon you and your coworkers will be making great strides toward creating the Driven Organization.

You and your coworkers can take your organization as far as you feel comfortable doing it. Any step toward this direction will yield positive results. The only thing I advise against is to use the principles of this book with the sole objective of squeezing more profits from workers. Workers will see through management's words and actions. Cynicism, negativity, and lower productivity, which are difficult to get rid of, would result.

I suggest you be authentic at all times. Be true to yourself and to your coworkers. Find the purpose that suits all of you, not the one that sounds good or your priest wants. Develop the autonomy measures that go with the business and adapt them to your specific settings with creativity. Foster the environment that promotes what the organization is at its core, even if that is not the standard or expected way. Help coworkers learn about what they find interesting, whatever that is. Talk with management to arrange fair pay for all workers. And keep working on that which makes your organization special.

Although part of my background is as a strategy management consultant advising corporations, I suggest being careful when working with "the experts." The best answers and the proper ways for your specific organization are already lurking in your company; they only need to be extracted. A good consultant will be able to get these answers from your organization and work with your coworkers to develop sensible initiatives based on your organization's desires, needs, and objectives. A bad consultant (of which there are many) may not only be a waste of money but may also derail the good efforts your organization is already implementing. You may be able to name your own consultant task force internally.

No effort in the direction of the Driven Organization will go to waste. There is a tale of the boy and the starfish. Do you know the story? There is a boy who is returning starfishes to the sea so that they don't die on the beach. A man tries to show the boy how puny his efforts are, considering the miles and miles of beach and the thousands and thousands of starfishes lying on the beach. "You can't make a difference," he says. The boy considers what the man is saying and, while throwing one starfish to the sea, simply replies: "I made a difference to that one." Well, my friends, throw the first starfish into the sea.

You already know that your organization is capable of much better performance than what it currently achieves. Let it flourish. Let it become all it can be. You will be improving the lives of every coworker, of every stakeholder. Most importantly, you will be improving your life and having the opportunity to be a much happier worker, owner, employee, and human being. This has an impact on how many heart attacks will take place (or not) and how many children won't grow up in happier households (or will).

Along the pages of this book, we have talked of the many ways for workers to be happy, engaged, and satisfied. There is, however, one more thing to say; the most important one. At the core, the reason why we find ourselves dissatisfied with our job is that it doesn't let us do what we came to do in this life. Some of us believe that we came to try to be happy. Others think that we came to try to be all we can be. More say that we came to prove our worthiness to a higher being. Others are sure that we came to serve our fellow human beings. Which one is it for you? Whichever one you feel is the right one, the Driven Organization will help you get closer to it. Isn't that just wonderful?

> *"The problems of the world cannot possibly be solved by skeptics or cynics whose horizons are limited by the obvious realities. We need men who can dream of things that never were."* John F. Kennedy.

Where to go now? At DrivenOrganization.com, there is an increasing collection of articles, podcasts, and a forum in which you can interact and ask questions of others who are working on their own Driven Organization, creating powerful workplaces with happy and satisfied coworkers. DrivenOrganization.com is a place to share and to learn.

Part V: Organizations in Search of a Better Way.

"If I tell my Facebook friends about your brand, it's not because I like your brand, but rather because I like my friends." Mike Arauz, *Undercurrents*.

So far, we have seen several examples of superb and interesting practices sprinkled throughout the book, but here is a deeper look at some of the organizations that incorporated many of these practices in their everyday performance. I believe that studying them as holistic entities provides a more comprehensive and realistic perspective. This is why we have created this section of the book.

Although these organizations may call it differently, the practices and fundamentals behind them stem from the same roots: our desires and needs as human beings. They all seek to fulfill these needs in a way that leads to a better, happier worker; and they all lead to superior results for every stakeholders.

For each organization, we have a brief description of what it is and what it does. Then, we add the statements of purpose, values, principles, or organizational objectives that the organization has chosen to pursue, written in the exact words it uses. We then take a look at what each does relating to the components of SPACES.

In these organizations, in each of the SPACES components, you will see weaknesses and strengths, opportunities and red flags. See what works well for them and what doesn't. I am sure that, by now, you will have something to suggest to them.

The Driven Organization

New Belgium Brewing

What it is.

New Belgium Brewing Company[1] was born in 1991 after Kim Jordan and Jeff Lebesch toured several European villages and became inspired to take their home-brewing passion commercial. With a bunch of ingredients and many new ideas and recipes, New Belgium Brewing started as a small craft brewery in Fort Collins, Colorado.

Today, New Belgium Brewing produces 712,000 barrels of its various labels (2011 data), and it was the third-largest craft brewery and seventh-largest overall brewery in the United States, with 412 employees and sales of more than US$ 100 million.

Company Core Values and Beliefs

- Remembering that we are incredibly lucky to create something fine that enhances people's lives while surpassing our consumers' expectations.
- Producing world-class beers.
- Promoting beer culture and the responsible enjoyment of beer.
- Kindling social, environmental, and cultural change as a business role model.
- Environmental stewardship: Honoring nature at every turn of the business.
- Cultivating potential through learning, high involvement culture, and the pursuit of opportunities.
- Balancing the myriad needs of the company, our coworkers, and their families.
- Trusting each other and committing to authentic relationships and communications.
- Continuous, innovative quality and efficiency improvements.
- Having fun.

- "To operate a profitable brewery which makes our love and talent manifest."

SPACES and New Belgium Brewing.

New Belgium Brewing doesn't have access to strategic resources that provide competitive advantage, such as a pristine water source with a rare mineral combination or a 1,000-year-old secret beer recipe. This makes New Belgium Brewing a great example of the use of SPACES to build a robust brand and a high-performing organization. Such a brand can be possible only with the autonomous and sensible participation of all stakeholders, who join together to build a cohesive environment. The creative customer beer tastes, bicycle tours, and other customer events only serve to transfer this internal environment to external stakeholders. Advertising without the environment would be empty and eventually seen as such.

This environment would not be possible if the other SPACES components were not in place. New Belgium Brewing and its workers have a shared set of values that are important in their everyday work and it resonates with customers. Through their voting and joint decision making, they put their money where their mouth is. They invest in clean environmental processes, customer events, worker satisfaction, use of bicycles, and more. SPACES helps them do everything right. New Belgium Brewing has a driven workforce that watches over expenses, develops new products, and works harmoniously and productively.

This is how New Belgium Brewing does it:

Salary

- Sharing upside: 43% of New Belgium Brewing is owned by the workers through an "Employee Stock Ownership Plan."

Purpose

- Social responsibility through:

- Giving $1 dollar for every barrel of beer produced to nonprofits.
- Researching, reviewing and granting funding to worthy organizations through a Philanthropy Committee, a cross-departmental group open to all interested co-workers.
- Giving workers one hour of paid time off for every two hours they volunteer with philanthropic organizations.
- Promoting beer education and the responsible drinking of beer.
- Using events to contribute to the efforts to certain nonprofits (e.g., Tour de Fat).
- Environmental stewardship through:
  - Donating 1% of its revenue for the planet (www.onepercentfortheplanet.org).
  - Giving small and large grants to organizations with green objectives.
  - Including "mother earth" in strategic planning, for example:
    - Producing 17% of its electrical needs on site and offsetting the remaining through renewable energy credits.
    - Leading its industry in lowest CO_2 footprint.
    - Achieving one of lowest water-used-per-beer-produced ratios.

Autonomy

- Involving all workers in business planning and fostering their participation in business decisions. Everyone can see the books, and there are no secrets.
- Instead of using command and control, coaching workers and giving them all information in order for them to become autonomous, responsible, and accountable agents.
- Limiting structure to four levels: Board of Directors, Senior management (by function), departmental Managers, and individual contributors.

Competence

- Fostering worker's learning from their teams, peers, and cultural events.
- Sending workers with five-year seniority to Belgium to learn about beer culture.

- Educating its workers, customers and other stakeholders about the environment.

Environment

- In the hiring process, assessing not only the skills, knowledge, and competencies of applicants but also their attitudes and values.
- Making every worker responsible to model social norms (to speak and to hear, to teach and to learn).
- Bringing all workers to Colorado once per year to jointly develop the company plan (the retreat), fostering high worker involvement.
- Fostering communication with the use of a comprehensive menu of technology (including video and web apps) to promote worker involvement, information sharing, and social interaction.
- Holding events to foster social learning and integration, such as:
  - Ownership Ceremony (in which a worker becomes an owner)
  - Relationship-building events (Ranger Shadowing, Volleyball, Holiday parties, Mothership events, team fun days, and so on)
- Building an environment of compassion, kindness, respect, love, fun, and trust.
- Developing fun and interesting activities with customers that energize workers, builds their brand, and helps workers learn about them (e.g., the Tour de Fat, a "ballyhoo that encourages people to get out of their cars and on to their bicycles").

Strategy

- New Belgium Brewing's carefully crafted brand communicates hard-working attitude, respect for the environment and their communities, and fun. These three messages resonate with educated, conscious customers, who after a day of hard work want to have fun and relax. A Fat Tire beer works as the cherry on top of a good hard workday. These customers feel happy drinking New Belgium Brewing's beer because it makes them feel good, morally and physically.
- New Belgium Brewing uses the natural inclination of workers to innovate, experiment, and acquire expertise to develop new products and find ways to make their product offerings achieve a superior market position. This can be seen in every department, from marketing, which excels developing highly creative campaigns, to purchasing, which constantly finds creative ways to source raw materials with lower CO_2 impact.

Zappos.com

Zappos.com[2] was established in 1999 to sell apparel and footwear online by Nick Swinmurn, who became inspired when he couldn't find a pair of brown Airwalks at his local mall. In his search for investors, he approached Tony Hsieh and Alfred Lin. Hsieh was initially skeptical and almost deleted Swinmurn's voicemail, but after hearing that "footwear in the United States is a 40 billion dollar market and 5% of that is already being sold by paper mail order catalogs," Hsieh and Lin decided to invest $2 million.

After a bumpy ride with frequent visits to the verge of bankruptcy, Zappos has today become the largest online shoe retailer. The Zappos family generates gross merchandise sales exceeding $1 billion annually. Zappos.com currently showcases millions of products from more than 1,000 shoes, clothing, handbags, accessories, and housewares brands. It has 3,866 employees and its headquarters is in Henderson, NV. In 2009, Zappos became part of Amazon.com.

Zappos Family Core Values

- Deliver WOW Through Service
- Embrace and Drive Change
- Create Fun and A Little Weirdness
- Be Adventurous, Creative, and Open-Minded
- Pursue Growth and Learning
- Build Open and Honest Relationships With Communication
- Build a Positive Team and Family Spirit
- Do More With Less
- Be Passionate and Determined
- Be Humble

Zappos and SPACES.

Zappos could be a strong business competitor even if it did not have such strong customer service capabilities. Its centrally located warehouse in Kentucky, minutes away from the most important UPS hub, allows Zappos to reach most U.S. customers in a short time. Its size enables it to get preferable purchasing conditions and its knowledge of apparel makes it an important customer option.

It is, however, through the use of the practices advocated by SPACES that Zappos exercises impressive customer service capabilities and achieves a whole new business-performance level. Because of it, Zappos doesn't need to incur advertising expenses; it has a culture of continuous self-improvement and creativity; and it can hire the best workers, those with a natural helping attitude, which helps to make customers feel at ease when acquiring apparel online.

And it shows. The Zappos legendary script-less customer service goes well beyond the expected service. Some customer calls have lasted longer than eight hours; others have received unexpected, thoughtful gifts because of something going on in their lives; and many have received unexpected perks that has make them enjoy their shopping experience.

Zappos is a market player that not only overcomes most online stores solely focused on logistics, price, and delivery conditions but also competes successfully with brick-and-mortar establishments. Zappos has helped expand the apparel online sales market. Everything it does in SPACES helps, beyond achieving some of the best customer service capabilities ever known, to have a well lubricated Zappos machinery that makes it an excellent business competitor.

A final thought is that its strategic advantages, such as knowledge of apparel, the efficient Kentucky warehouse, and even its size, belong to Zappos because it followed many of the practices of SPACES since it was a small organization.

This is how Zappos does it:

Salary

- Giving its workers saying about their salary. When customer service representatives become certified on certain core competencies, they automatically get salary increases. Zappos also helps workers see continuous progression by splitting job promotions into smaller, more frequent ones.

Purpose

- "Delivering happiness." Workers are convinced they are working toward something meaningful and they have extended this philosophy beyond selling shoes and apparel. For example, some of the workers have self-imposed goals of becoming 1% better every day, or of going through their working and personal lives "WOWing" everyone around them (doing something above and beyond what is expected).
- Attempting to make work be the shared activity that helps them traverse the road toward happiness and self-fulfillment.

Autonomy

- Letting customer service representatives have no script, sales quota, or time limits; and giving them complete discretion on customer service.
- Giving customer service reps freedom to promote customer orders to priority shipping or to add extra gifts.
- Allowing workers to try whatever new thing they feel will improve their jobs.

Competence

- Having a Zappos book library with titles from personal development, marketing, happiness, employee engagement, and business strategy.
- Requiring every worker to have five weeks of training answering phones at the beginning of his journey with Zappos.

Environment

- Actively promoting the environment with such things as the "Culture book" and frequent events.
- Using culture fit in hiring; performance reviews are based on culture fit.
- During and after training, offering $4,000 to help those who feel Zappos is not their place to move on.

Strategy

- Focusing on best customer service.

- Giving customers a superior service so that they come back for every apparel need, even if it means losing the current sale. (more than 75% of businesses come from repeat customers).

- Treating customer service as an investment, not an expense. Everything they do to foster a suitable, positive, fun environment will yield positive results down the line.

- Reducing customer fear of not being able to try out the outfit by offering hassle free returns to minimize this disadvantage.

- Having the undivided attention of a customer for a few minutes, is worth more than a bunch of advertising. Zappos uses customer's calls as a way to position itself as a special outfit.

- Keeping inventory of all products at their centrally located warehouse open 24/7 allows Zappos to deliver to customers in short order. Often, the customer orders at 8 pm and receives the product at 6 am the following morning.

Note: On June, 2012, Zappos announced that they will be shedding their Kentucky warehouse. It is understood that Zappos' customers will get their orders fulfilled through the Amazon fulfillment processes. Whether that diminishes the Zappos customer experience is yet to be determined.

Whole Foods Market

What it is

In 1978, John and his girlfriend Rene opened a small food retailer with a $45,000 loan from family. John was only 25 and Rene 21, and both had little business experience, but they had a strong belief. Natural and organic foods are fundamental for health and well-being, which America needs. They lost half of their money in the first year and barely survived the second. However, their beliefs on natural foods kept them alive and helped them secure investors and community allies. In 1981, the worst flood in 70 years devastated the city of Austin. The store's inventory was destroyed and its equipment damaged. Customers and neighbors voluntarily joined the staff to repair and clean up the damage. Creditors, vendors, and investors provided breathing room for the store to get back on its feet and it re-opened only 28 days after the flood.

Throughout the years, the company strictly followed its values and implemented programs that support natural foods, such as sustainable agriculture and animal welfare. Its purpose, beliefs and values attract workers who desire to contribute to the health of humankind. These commitments propelled Whole Foods Market to be the global leader in natural and organic food, with more than 310 stores and sales in excess of US$10 billion.

Whole Foods Market[3] is a food supermarket chain based in Austin, Texas that emphasizes "natural and organic products." The company is the world's largest retailer of natural and organic foods, with stores throughout North America and the United Kingdom. WF has more than 320 stores as of March 2012 and generated more than US$ 10 billion in revenue in fiscal year 2011.

- "Whole Foods, Whole People, Whole Planet."

Whole Foods Market Values

- Selling the highest quality natural and organic products available
- Satisfying and delighting our customers
- Supporting team member happiness and excellence
- Creating wealth through profits & growth
- Caring about our communities & our environment
- Creating ongoing win-win partnerships with our suppliers
- Promoting the health of our stakeholders through healthy eating education

Whole Foods Market and SPACES

In a premium grocery store, customer service and a pleasurable grocery shopping experience are fundamental. The best way to achieve these is through employee engagement. Whole Foods Market is a great example of cohesive, congruent practices in every area of SPACES.

For example, starting at the top with Purpose, workers believe that they are "healing America" through food, nutrition, and education. They are not just restocking shelves but also providing a life-saving service to every customer who comes their way.

Customers who are interested in organic food tend to have environmental and social concerns, too. WF is also focused on sustainable and social programs and protection of the environment, which resonates well with customers and workers, and enhances their "healing" power.

Workers actively learn about health foods and health products for their own and the organization's purpose, which helps them fulfill their Competence needs. Every piece of information that comes their way benefits them personally and makes them more effective and valuable customer representatives.

In Autonomy, workers are responsible to find ways to improve customer interaction, reduce environmental impact, increase store income, find learning opportunities, and much more.

The employee satisfaction that WF achieves gets channeled to its customers, who then find it easy to pay WF's premium prices, which more than covers higher-than-average WF expenses and leaves a substantial return for shareholders.

This is how Whole Foods Market does it:

Salary

- Following a "shared fate philosophy with a salary cap that limits the compensation (wages plus profit incentive bonuses) of any Team Member to nineteen times the average total compensation of all full-time Team Members in the company."

Purpose

- Healing America through the use of better nutrition and lifestyle.
- Creating a more sustainable agricultural system that also has a high degree of productivity.
  - Sustainable Agriculture; supporting organic farmers, growers, and the environment.
  - Wise Environmental Practices such as a philosophy to recycle, reuse, and reduce waste; 100% wind-powered facilities, Seafood Sustainable programs, bio-diesel usage, water conservation, ecological packaging materials, conscious animal welfare, and organic food.
- Helping end poverty across the planet.
  - Whole Planet Foundation; working with Grameen Trust and other organizations gives micro-credits to people.
  - Community Citizenship: WF gives a minimum of 5% of its profits every year to a wide variety of community and nonprofit organizations.
- Spreading of conscious capitalism, which is divided into four principles:
  - Have an organizational purpose.
  - All stakeholder mentality. In every action, WF attempts to consider all stakeholders: shareholders, workers, suppliers, customers, WF communities, and the environment.
  - Conscious leadership, focused on helping the organization work toward the purpose.
  - Conscious culture that reinforces everything else.

Autonomy

- Letting self-directed teams discuss and solve problems themselves.
- Helping every worker make the right decisions by emphasizing an open book policy with education materials.
- Sharing success with Gain share: The higher the performance of the team, the higher its compensation.

Competence

- Promoting a mindset of educating workers, customers, and other stakeholders about natural and organic foods, health, nutrition, and the environment.
- Welcoming knowledge that workers bring regarding food, supplements, and new environmental practices.

Environment

- Focusing, across the board, on a superior customer service.
- Making sure that two-thirds of team members have to be in agreement when hiring a new employee. The financial rewards of the team will be affected by the performance of the new worker.
- Fostering an environment in which employees use their highest potential.

Strategy

- Focusing on being the biggest and most reliable supplier of organic and natural grocery items and of those sought by educated and demanding customers. Constantly raising the bar for its organic and natural standards.
- Maintaining a large variety of organic and natural products on shelves to make customers believe that WF is the reliable grocery store option for their specific needs.
- Keeping a pleasant and premium store environment.

Southwest Airlines

What it is

In 1967, a small airline files for incorporation, marking the beginning of a complicated legal battle for permission to fly. With only $500,000, a unique business plan, and a different idea of how to treat workers, the small airline repeatedly fights off court challenges and blockages from major, established airlines. It takes three years of legal battles and a ruling by the state supreme court to get permission to operate.

The "love" airline is born in 1971, making employees the core focus of its business, instead of its customers or shareholders, as the business mantra of the time suggests. The unique Southwest culture embraces its employees, making them part of a unique, caring family. Its business and operation processes, it seems, are designed to improve the life of its workers. In return, Southwest workers are much more productive than those at their competitors. The small airline begins to grow at giant steps.

Other airlines notice and attempt to copy what Southwest does. They believe it is the Southwest business model that flies point to point or uses only one type of aircraft. This way, dozens of airlines are formed with these characteristics and later fold. Almost every major airline creates an airline-within-an-airline that follows the so-called "low-cost carrier" model. Southwest, in the meantime, keeps doing what it always does.

On 9/11/2011, when a huge part of the airline market stops flying, several airlines go into bankruptcy and every one lays off employees. Not so Southwest. Although the airline is also caught off guard and struggles to stay afloat, it doesn't lay off a single employee. Southwest decides to make shared income sacrifices but stick it out together. This way, even with multiple attempts by other airlines to block it and copy its business model, culture, and processes, it takes them less than 30 years to become the largest airline in the United States.

Southwest Airlines Corporation[4] is an American low-cost airline based in Dallas, Texas, established in 1967. On June 5, 2011, it became the largest airline in the United States based upon domestic passengers carried. Southwest has 37,000 employees as of December 2011 and operates more than 3,300 flights a day. As of January 2012, Southwest Airlines operates scheduled service to 97 destinations in 42 states.

Mission

- "The mission of Southwest Airlines is dedication to the highest quality of Customer Service delivered with a sense of warmth, friendliness, individual pride, and Company Spirit."

To SW employees

- "We are committed to provide our Employees a stable work environment with equal opportunity for learning and personal growth. Creativity and innovation are encouraged for improving the effectiveness of Southwest Airlines. Above all, Employees will be provided the same concern, respect, and caring attitude within the organization that they are expected to share externally with every Southwest Customer."

To SW Communities

- "Our goal is to be the hometown airline of every community we serve, and because those communities sustain and nurture us with their support and loyalty, it is vital that we, as individuals and in groups, embrace each community with the SOUTHWEST SPIRIT of involvement, service, and caring to make those communities better places to live and work."

To the Planet

- "We strive to be a good environmental steward across our system in all of our hometowns, and one component of our stewardship is efficiency, which by its very nature, translates to eliminating waste and conserving resources. Using cost-effective and environmentally beneficial operating procedures (including facilities and equipment) allows us to reduce the amount of materials we use and, when combined with our ability to reuse and recycle material, preserves these environmental resources."

To SW stakeholders

- "Southwest's vision for a sustainable future is one where there will be a balance in our business model between Employees and Community, the Environment, and our Financial Viability. In order to protect our world for future generations, while meeting our commitments to our Employees, Customers, and Stakeholders, we

Mission

will strive to lead our industry in innovative efficiency that conserves natural resources, maintains a creative and innovative workforce, and gives back to the Communities in which we live and work."

Southwest and SPACES

SW is one of the first organizations that understood that investing in its workers' welfare and engaging them leads to superior performance and happy employees. By most measures, SW employees work harder than their counterparts at other airlines, yet they are happier and enjoy what they do. Workers have the autonomy to find the best way to do their work. This way, a flight attendant may sing a song or recite a poem to give passengers instructions, or a pilot may help the baggage handler to ready the plane in the specified amount of time.

SW has found a hiring formula where workers are naturally inclined to do their very best for the benefit of the SW family. There are no free riders at SW. Its environment, in which hard-working employees are appreciated and loved, strongly reinforces this mentality, helping everyone deliver high performance. Southwest hires people who want to be appreciated for their hard work, and SW makes sure it makes workers know they are appreciated and are important for SW.

For example, when all airlines began to charge luggage fees, SW knew that customers would pack as much as possible in their carry-ons, which would make flight attendants work harder packing them in the overhead bins. So SW decided not to modify its luggage policy. Flight attendants appreciated the important gesture, and customers loved it.

This is a great example of coherent actions that are aligned and yield superior results. Turning the plane around with more bags in the overhead bins takes more time, which forces airplanes to stay on the ground longer, decreasing aircraft utilization, one of SW's core strategic advantages. Carrying more luggage on the plane makes flight attendants' work more difficult, risking their job satisfaction and their capacity to provide superior customer service. It is also a great brand differentiator.

Another example. While every airline charges between $100 and $250 to change a ticket, SW doesn't charge anything beyond the ticket price difference. The customer understands that there is little cost in making the change and it buys them considerable customer loyalty.

These examples are not unique. We can easily observe that SW performs coherent and consistent practices throughout its operations, which speaks to its principles and values.

SW touches every single component of SPACES, but as more organizations learn to take care of its employees, SW is attempting to do more to strengthen other components of SPACES to keep its huge competitive advantage. Their recent focus on the environment and on their communities makes me believe that SW understands the importance of these components. SW is focused on finding new ways to make its workers even more autonomous and competent. I believe there is more that can be done, but fortunately for SW, it has an open mentality for which good ideas, reasonable projects, and new proposals, notwithstanding their origin, can be put in place.

This is how Southwest Airlines does it:

Salary

- Southwest workers are generally the highest paid in the industry. Still, SW has the lowest labor costs in the industry because it has about 30% fewer workers for comparable work performed.
- Management are also better compensated than at other airlines, but SW has fewer management staff.
- Through employee stock options, employees own a considerable portion of the airline.

Purpose

- Southwest is committed to a triple bottom line: performance, workers, and the planet. Its motto of "Do what's right," is applied throughout the organization.
- Performance:
  - With every worker focused on the well-being of SW, it is the only airline that has 39 years of consecutive profitability. SW has a "do more with less" mentality that permeates every single aspect of its operation. SW workers are significantly more productive than employees of competitors.
- People:
  - With mottoes such as "Luv 'em in tough times," and "People give as good as they get," SW has put employees in the

forefront of its objectives. This attitude is easily transferred to customers, who report the fewest complaints of any airline. SW is also concerned with the well-being of its communities, with several volunteer programs at work, from donating tickets, money, to organizing employees to volunteer with several NGO organizations. SW workers see their communities as part of their responsibilities. For example, SW employees painted park benches in NYC when they began to fly from La Guardia Airport, as a way to thank the city.

- Planet:
  - Through initiatives such as the "green team," which is composed of SW volunteer employees, SW gathers idea, gets energy to support projects, and communicates throughout the workforce. This way, it has come up with a greenhouse inventory, recycling programs, emission-reduction research, electrification of equipment (from gas powered), new airplane interior materials, fuel conservation practices, and so on.

Autonomy

- Workers often perform activities that normally do not belong in their job descriptions. For example, pilots help clean up cabins and ramp workers sell tickets.

- An environment of ownership and distributed leadership places responsibility on each worker to improve performance, to come up with new ideas, to lead new initiatives and projects, and to protect the [corporate] family. This is not only fostered by SW but it is expected and highly rewarded.

- A culture of transparency, of open information, and accountability is at the core of SW. Goals, roles, responsibilities, and metrics are trusted to each worker throughout the organization.

- Workers can trade shifts as they please. Instead of a formal flexible program, SW believes that a shift-trading system allows for further culture integration.

Competence

- Southwest's motto, "Keep 'em learning," highlights company's policy to keep learning. For example, employees who attend seminars or read good management books are encouraged to buy copies for other workers at Southwest's expense. Southwest has "Rocking Chair Sessions" in which soon-to-be retired employees are invited to sit in rocking chairs at department meetings and share the history and the culture of the company from their perspective. With the University for People, SW uses experienced members to distribute knowledge throughout the organization.

Environment

- SW has an environment in which every worker is a member of a family that likes to hug and have fun with each other. It believes it must "find the kid in everyone."

- The environment fosters high performance in two ways. First, the high performers are much celebrated. Employees are, in fact, constantly finding new ways to recognize exemplary performance, which causes every worker to want to belong to the high-performing group. Second, there is a strong component of peer pressure, where low performance is not well seen.

- Southwest takes very seriously the protection of its fun-loving, positive attitude environment. It looks in its hires for extroverted, passionate, fun, loving, caring, people-oriented folks. Its hiring motto is "Hire for attitude, train for skill." SW receives hundreds of resumes for every position it intends to fill.

- New hires are connected to a "co-heart," who welcomes them and takes them under their wing for six months or longer. This is not someone who is training them on how to do their job, but rather is a "friend" who socializes with them, spends time with them, and helps them acclimate to their role regardless of what it is.

- Workers' wives, husbands, and/or children become part of and take an active participation in the SW corporate family. Every worker is expected to nurture and protect it.

- A "culture committee" is in operation to make sure that the environment of SW stays as strong as always, and that as the company grows, there are no barriers between functions. This committee is formed by front and management workers throughout the southwest system. It organizes social and community oriented events.

- The Southwest employee-loving environment can be seen throughout its operations. Often, flight attendants get their three-minute opportunity to shine by singing instructions; pilots get theirs by telling jokes; flight attendants put "misbehaving" passengers to work passing out snacks; and employees are often surprised by an unexpected hokey flight, which relieves them from their tasks while they relax enjoying drinks and other treats.

- Herb Kelleher, the founder, continually cultivated such a fun-loving attitude at the company. He arm-wrestled the CEO of another airline for the rights to use a slogan, and posed as Elvis for an advertising campaign. When he was made aware that workers on the night shift could not attend company celebrations due to their schedules, he turned up at an airport at 2:00 am to throw a special barbeque.

- At SW, employees are considered part of its family, which must be cared for and protected. This way, SW has never had layoffs.

Strategy

- Southwest's operation is different from long-haul and hub-and-spoke airlines. It has frequent flights between two points, where the objective is to maximize the number of flights per day. By minimizing the time the plane is on the ground, it does so and achieves high aircraft and crew utilization. This high-efficiency model can successfully compete with other transportation options such as cars, buses, and trains.

- Supporting this business model, SW flies only one type of airplane, making sure that everyone is familiar with it, so maintenance costs are low. There are also no assigned seats, no meals, one service class, and no extra fees. All of which help SW be efficient and support its "keep it simple" mentality.

- SW's workforce, carefully chosen, yields more productivity per employee than any other airline. Its focus on having fun allows them to work harder than at other airlines. At the same time, workers enjoy significantly more when performing their work. SW has happier employees than other airlines.

The Driven Organization

JetBlue Airlines

What it is.

JetBlue[5] Airways Corporation is an American low-cost airline. It was founded in 1999 by David Neeleman, who was a Southwest Airlines employee. Several other executives also came from SW. JetBlue started by following Southwest's approach of offering low-cost travel, but sought to distinguish itself by its amenities, such as in-flight entertainment, TV in every seat, and Satellite radio. The company is headquartered in Long Island City, NY. Its main base is John F. Kennedy International Airport.

As of December 7, 2011, JetBlue serves 71 destinations in 21 states and 12 countries in the Caribbean, South America, and Latin America. Its 2011 revenues were US$ 4.5 billion; as of December 31, 2011, it had 10,243 full-time and 3,779 part-time employees.

Marketing slogan

- "You above all."

Mission

- "Bringing Humanity Back to Air Travel."

Principles of Leadership

- Inspire Greatness in Others
- Communicate With Your Team
- Do the Right Thing
- Encourage Initiative and Innovation
- Treat Your People Right

JetBlue and SPACES.

JetBlue does a very good job with SPACES. Its main objective, to get everyone to travel and have a pleasant experience, is shared and believed by its workers. Several activities throughout JB's operations support this objective, starting with a focus on customer service.

The customer service starts with the right environment, which begins in turn with its hiring practices. JB is one of the few organizations that has a consistent hiring process to only hire workers who like people. This environment, full of energetic and fun people, lets workers have a great time, allowing them to do their job naturally without much coercion required. Workers have fun, do what makes sense (based on accurate information), and grow with JetBlue.

The JetBlue customer focus can be observed throughout its operations, which allows it to streamline processes at all levels and improve customer experience. JB is one of the organizations that asks itself, "Why not? Why couldn't we offer free WiFi at the terminal? Why couldn't we have a TV on every seat at the plane? Why couldn't we have WiFi on the plane? Do people care for airplane food?" Its autonomous environment helps it answer these questions and act on them.

This focus on customer service makes customers participant stakeholders of the success of JetBlue. For example, when a crew member asks customers to help clean the plane at the end of the flight to keep costs down, almost everyone helps, which is not the case at other airlines.

Still, even JB makes mistakes. For example, JB increased its ticket change fee from $40 to $100 in 2009. What was a major differentiation factor for JB has gone away. It also charges for the second bag. These and other similar actions risk the positive perception that customers have about JB: customers are the reason for JB's existence.

This is how JetBlue Airlines does it:

Salary

- Paying fair salaries. JetBlue workers are paid in the top third of all airlines. In addition, 20% of workers' pay depends on the results of the business, which promotes a shared fate mentality.
- Discouraging unions. JetBlue believes well-paid, non-unionized workers are more engaged, driven, and productive.
- Keeping David Neeleman's (ex-CEO) and David Barger's (CEO) salaries at a reasonable level.

Purpose

- From JB's website: "JetBlue Airways is dedicated to bringing humanity back to air travel. We strive to make every part of your experience as simple and as pleasant as possible."

Autonomy

- Serving leadership: When flying, the JetBlue CEO goes around the plane talking with crew members and passengers to try understand their concerns, to answer questions, and to gauge customer satisfaction.
- Fostering performance by having a focused, driven, and engaged workforce; technology to make it easy; and openness to flexibility. JB has many flexible-hour arrangements, and most reservation agents work from their homes.
- Encouraging JetBlue crew members to see all business information, make decisions, and take action.

Competence

- Offering JetBlue University, in which crew members learn safety, efficiency, and customer service practices.

Environment

- Hiring people suitable for customer service. JetBlue says, "We believe we know how to hire people who like people."

- Keeping the environment deliberately "feeling small" as JetBlue grows and expands to new markets, with the objective of keeping workers connected and accountable.

- "Taking care of your coworkers and they will take care of the customers," says the JetBlue CEO.

- David Neeleman, who owned a considerable chunk of JetBlue, decided not to take stock options in order to make the available pie [of stock options] better for the rest of the workers. Actions such as this one are meant to reduce the differences of compensation among JetBlue stakeholders.

Strategy

- The strategy of JetBlue involves high aircraft utilization. The objective is to keep planes flying as much as possible, thus reducing capital expenditures, maintenance, and additional workforce.

  - JB flies its planes, on average, 11.6 hours/day, which is one of the highest averages among major U.S. airlines.

  - JB has arranged that airport operations allow them to schedule aircraft with minimum ground time.

- A mentality of keeping things simple through the use of smart technology increases customer satisfaction and reduces cost. For example, JetBlue has chosen to use only e-tickets and has been a leader of e-booking, which has reduced costs and a simplified booking operation. Most people today book their flight through the JetBlue website. It also offers only one class service.

- Technology is extensively used to automate tasks and free workers for more productive and engaging activities.

- To reduce maintenance costs and improve aircraft transfers, JetBlue uses only two new and efficient airplanes: the Airbus A320 and the EMBRAER 190, which, with an average age of only 5.4 years as of 2011, is the youngest fleet of any major U.S. airline.

- JetBlue has low advertising expenses. Most new customers come to JB through word of mouth.
- JetBlue is focused on incurring the expenses that matter for customers. For example, most people who fly prefer TV in their seats versus "airline" food.

The Driven Organization

Semco

Semco[6] was created in the 1950s as a company that manufactured centrifuges for the vegetable oil industry. Over the years, the company has expanded its range to other businesses, moving extensively into the services area in partnership with other companies. Some of these businesses include environmental consultancy, facilities management, real estate consultancy, inventory services, mobile maintenance services, industrial equipment, and postal and document management.

Principles and Values

- To be a dependable and reliable company.
- Value honesty and transparency over and above all temporary interests.
- Seek a balance between short-term and long-term profit.
- Offer products and services at fair prices which are recognized by customers as the best on the market.
- Provide the customer with differentiated services, placing our responsibility before profits.
- Encourage creativity, giving support to the bold.
- Encourage everyone's participation and question decisions that are imposed from the top down.
- Maintain an informal and pleasant environment, with a professional attitude and free of preconceptions.
- Maintain safe working conditions and control industrial processes to protect our personnel and the environment.
- Have the humility to recognize our errors and understanding that we can always improve.

Semco and SPACES.

Semco is, by far, the organization that has taken autonomy to its limits. It has really asked "why" to all business practices we find today in our modern workplaces. Semco has also asked "why not" to the ideas it has developed over the years. Kudos for Semco. Relinquishing control to the extent Semco has done it would be extremely difficult for most of our organizations. Even the other highly progressive organizations are behind Semco in this area.

Semco uses the self-driven human inclination to learn, to explore, and to become the best they can be to thrive in the businesses they work for. It uses the intrinsic desire of each worker to do his best to get the best work from that worker. It uses small- and medium-sized teams to foster an environment of hard work, of doing what makes sense, of achieving business results, and of life balance.

In one interview, Ricardo Semler reported that workers are not yet as happy as he believes they should be. I believe the reason is clear. Although I understand that Semco exists in part to provide an area for workers to explore their entire professional capacity, I believe that what is missing is a strong shared purpose directed toward improving something beyond themselves, such as their communities and the world. This purpose would grab Semco workers from the inside and connect them emotionally much more with their everyday work.

This is how Semco does it:

Salary

- Semco lets the candidate and his hiring unit decide how much he should earn. The profitability of the unit, which determines the compensation of its members, will be affected by the new candidate. Does he bring more than what he costs? If the hiring unit and the candidate agree on a number, the applicant will be hired. Semco workers use four questions to set salaries: How much can the company pay? How much do other people with similar responsibilities at Semco make? How much money does the worker believe he can make elsewhere? And how much does he need to live comfortably?

- Workers have an incentive to accept only those workers who will improve profitability for their team. Profits are distributed between Semco and the small unit.

Purpose

- Semco doesn't have an official goal, mission statement, or purpose. Semco does provide the space for workers to be what they can be and to be treated respectfully with the objective of fostering business results and happiness.

- Semco has a foundation, the Ralston Semler Foundation, to mentor educational, cultural, and environmental projects.

Autonomy

- Every worker is welcome to ask why and what for; in doing so, Semco has changed several customary business practices that do not yield positive results. Semco also has the practice of asking themselves "why" five times to arrive to a suitable root cause that justifies the requirement. This way, Semco has changed several practices it felt did not contribute to its performance.

- Workers choose their own managers, based on what they think the manager can do to help advance their group. Every six months, Semco employees fill out a questionnaire and say what they think about their immediate superior. If the manager doesn't get a high enough grade, he will not continue being a manager.

- Semco workers decide whether they need more people on their team. A new team member will contribute to their efforts, but will also get a share of their profit bucket.

- There are no standards or practices. Semco doesn't have scripts for customer service workers. It believes that the Semco employee will do what is best by their own accord.

- Semco has a very active job rotation program, in which people constantly take other jobs.

- There is no space in the Semco Group for formalities. The doors are always open, and people say what they really think, without worries or inhibitions.

- For Semco, it makes no difference whether someone has a high ranking or a humble position. The most important thing is to follow the most reasonable course of action.

- The Semco Group has flexible working hours where possible; each person controls their own working hours. The company is only concerned about results. The unit teammates will exert pressure on the worker to deliver because their profitability is being affected.

- Semco makes important efforts to keep everyone abreast of financial concerns for the company and the business unit. It develops cartoon-like booklets "teaching" workers how to read financial statements. Semco believes that when people have all the information, they all arrive at the same conclusions.

- Semco doesn't have a business plan because it feels that it is based on unfounded assumptions for the future and because it constrains its capacity to act.

- At Semco, no one approves reports or expense accounts.

- Workers can veto a deal or close a factory with a show of hands.

Competence

- People are given room to explore so they can find out where their talents and interests lie.

- All Semco businesses are in the "highly engineered" category, and Semco comes in as a premium player. Semco fosters people learning and trying out new things, developing expertise, and becoming the best they can be in whatever their interests are.

Environment

- Whenever there is recruitment or a promotion, people in the department have the chance to interview and take part in the discussions and decisions to choose the right candidate.

- From high-ranking executives to the lowest-ranked employees, everyone is treated with a lot of respect and equality.

- Semco has an environment of assigning value to data, learning, work, open doors, freedom, and honesty; not to hierarchies, appearances, and formalities.

- Semco has a dynamic environment in which major changes take place from time to time.

- The hiring process is very carefully done at Semco. It believes it is a courting process to decide to get married or not. It tests for technical skills first. Once candidates pass those requirements, they are interviewed by many people who vote on the ones they like best. The two who get the most votes are invited to spend some time at Semco. They will attend lunches, hang out with other workers, and attend social gatherings. Eventually, a representative from Semco and the candidate will discuss what they have learned from each other and if they want to get married or not.

Strategy

- Semco enters businesses with the following characteristics:

  - The businesses must require high-engineering.

  - Semco can be a premium player in that market.

  - Semco can occupy a unique niche in that market.

- Most of Semco's businesses have a partnership with a global leader producer or service provider.

1 Compiled from:
- NewBelgium.com and http://www.newbelgium.com/culture/faq.aspx
- http://en.wikipedia.org/wiki/New_Belgium_Brewery
- New Belgium Brewery. *Strategy Summary: Building Community at New Belgium. Our Strategy and Efforts to Continue to Reach our Vision with a Strong Community.*

- New Belgium Brewery. *2007 Sustainability Report.*
- Ferrell, O. C., & Fraedrich, John. *Business Ethics: Ethical Decision Making & Cases.* 9th ed. South-Western College Publications, January 1, 2012.
- Ferrel, O. C., & Drever, Melanie. *Brewing Up Fun in the Workplace.* University of Wyoming, 2006.
- http://www.newbelgium.com/files/nbb_employee_perks.pdf. Retrieved April 2012.
- The Climate CO_2nservancy. *The Carbon Footprint of Fat Tire® Amber Ale.*
- http://www.newbelgium.com/Files/NBB_student-info-packet.pdf. Retrieved April 2013.
- Interviews with New Belgium personnel.

2   Compiled from:
- Zappos Culture Book, 2010.
- Hsieh, Tony. *Delivering Happiness: A Path to Profits, Passion, and Purpose.* Business Plus, June 7, 2010.
- http://about.zappos.com
- http://www.zapposinsights.com

3   Compiled from:
- http://en.wikipedia.org/wiki/Whole_Foods_Market
- http://www.wholefoodsmarket.com/
- "Conscious Capitalism: Whole Foods' Way." *CNN Money.*
- "Whole Foods' Hiring Recipe." *CNN Money.*
- Bailey, Ronald. *Whole Foods Founder John Mackey's Free Market Plan For Creating Jobs.* Reason.com. November 17, 2011.
- "Whole Foods: A Retail Phenomenon." *BBC News.*
- Hamel, Gary, & Breen, Bill. *Creating a Community of Purpose: Whole Foods Market: Management Innovation in Action.* Harvard Business Press, March 3, 2009.
- Mackey, John. "Defending the Morality of Capitalism." John Mackey's blog, June 24, 2011.

4   Compiled from:
- *2009 One Report*. Southwest Airlines, 2010.
- Grubbs-West, Lorraine. *Lessons in Loyalty: How Southwest Airlines Does It—An Insider's View.* CornerStone Leadership Institute, August 1, 2005.
- Hoffer Gittel, Jody. *The Southwest Airlines Way: Using the Power of Relationship to Achieve Higher Performance,* 1st ed. The McGraw-Hill, 2005.
- "About Southwest." www.southwest.com
- Hoffer Gittel, Jody. *The Southwest Airlines Way: Using the Power of Relationship to Achieve Higher Performance,* 1st ed. The McGraw-Hill, 2005.

5   Compiled from:
- http://en.wikipedia.org/wiki/JetBlue_Airways
- http://www.jetblue.com/
- JetBlue *2010 Annual Report.*
- McCartney, Scott. "Your Bad Luck Is a Windfall For Airlines: Ticket-Change Penalties Yield Billions in Revenue For Industry, Data Show." *The Wall Street Journal,* July 30, 2009.

- Mount, Ian. "David Neeleman, JetBlue: For Creating an Airline Fit for Humans." *Inc.*, 2004.

- Gunther, Marc. "Nothing Blue About JetBlue. In a Chronically Troubled Industry, JetBlue Focuses on a Culture of Low Costs, Great Service, and a Certain Fun Factor." *CNN Money,* September 3, 2009.

- Neeleman, David. "JetBlue: Establishing Organizational Structure and Culture." *Ecorner, Stanford University's Entrepreneurship corner,* April 30, 2003.

- Brodski, Norm. "Learning From JetBlue: One Day Flying JetBlue, I Found Myself Being Served by David Neeleman, the Airline's Founder. When Was the Last Time You Met Your Customers and Asked How You Could Better Serve Them?" *Inc.*, March 1, 2004.

- "JetBlue Airways Customer Bill of Rights." JetBlue.com

6   Compiled from:

- http://www.semco.com.br
- http://en.wikipedia.org/wiki/Ricardo_Semler
- Semler, Ricardo. *The Seven-Day Weekend: Changing the Way Work Works.* Portfolio Hardcover, 2004.
- Semler, Ricardo. *Maverick: The Success Story Behind the World's Most Unusual Workplace.* Warner Books, 1993.
- Ricardo Semler talk at MIT. http://video.mit.edu/watch/leading-by-omission-9965/ Retrieved May 2013.

The Driven Organization